ADVANCE PRAISE

"A lively, amusing, galvanizing charting of ‹ ... register our pervasive ambivalence about work: our dependence on it, our complicated ways of being shaped and plagued by it, and our desires to escape it. Rooted in our antiwork moment, but historicizing comedic forms from the sitcom to the stand-up routine to the COVID-19 comedy special, Lane-McKinley sees comedy as revolutionary laughter, bulwark against despair, collective complaint, and utopian longing because the world of work we've known—abuse, compulsion, mortal danger to self and planet—isn't the only possibility."—**Sarah Brouillette**, Professor of English, Carleton University

"Comedy can be a weapon, Madeline Lane-McKinley reminds us, in any hands, for good or for fascist purposes. In her hands, it is a scalpel for taking apart the world of work, for teaching us how it got so damn bad. But it is also, she brilliantly reminds us, a tool for dismantling capitalist common sense. Join her as she encourages us to embrace laughter as a refusal of work and to claim the rich pleasures of being a killjoy."
—**Sarah Jaffe,** author of *Work Won't Love You Back*

"From working-class sitcoms to podcasts about making podcasts, this whirlwind tour of American comedy brings labor to the front, where Madeline Lane-McKinley reveals it has been all along. You'll never laugh the same!" —**Malcolm Harris,** author of *Kids These Days: Human Capital and the Making of Millennials*

"What a deeply creative exploration of humor and its discontents Madeline Lane-McKinley has given us, one which takes readers on a tour of sitcoms, standup, late night and comedy strikes. What is so funny about late capitalism, anyway? This is a book about the wages of laughter and it's for anyone who has wondered whether the joke is on capitalism or them."
—**Leigh Claire La Berge**, Fellow at Free University of Berlin and author of *Wages Against Work*

"Moving deftly between mordant critique and radical hope, *Comedy Against Work* illuminates both the comedy of work and the work of comedy. Attuned to comedy's history and politics as well as to its form, Lane-McKinley offers a compelling and original narrative that gets us from Lucille Ball frantically trying to keep pace with an assembly line to contemporary feminist stand-up and its antiwork 'dream of rest.' *Comedy Against Work* also provocatively breaks the form of the traditional scholarly 'work' by interweaving personal narratives—from Lane-McKinley's memories of watching her grandmother watch TV while doing housework to her own experiences as an academic 'gigworker.' Smart, moving, and politically fierce, this book will change the way we think about comedy and illuminate the way to a world beyond work." —**Annie McClanahan**, author of *Dead Pledges: Debt, Crisis, and Twenty-First-Century Culture*

"When work sucks and society appears on the verge of collapse, the laugh-makers are there to numb us back into passivity. But sometimes, Madeline Lane-McKinley reminds us, there are class clowns who help us envision a more egalitarian alternative and future. In this radically insightful and critical analysis of the relationship between labor, comedy, and political economy, Lane-McKinley looks closely and clearly at the anti-utopian and utopian potential of comedy alongside the social and political divides that pervade our everyday lives." —**Raúl Pérez**, author of *The Souls of White Jokes: How Racist Humor Fuels White Supremacy*

"Madeline Lane-McKinley is among the brightest fruits in the anglophone critical ecology of utopian thinkers, and this hotly anticipated book does not disappoint. Here, the labors of laughter—in and against capitalism's work society—become a way of understanding structural violence, a gauge for shifting economic logics, and also a possible weapon for liberation. In these pages, Lane-McKinley showcases the full potential of the unique tendency of antiwork cultural criticism for which Blind Field, the journal she co-founded, is known. *Comedy Against Work* not only educates our desire for a world utterly transformed, it provides us with tools that can help us actualize it." —**Sophie Lewis**, author of *Abolish the Family: A Manifesto for Care and Liberation*

"*Comedy Against Work* is the most pleasurable, wide-ranging, and deeply knowledgeable guide to the contradictions of contemporary capitalist culture that I have read in a very long time. It offers a framework for thought to an audience longing to understand why things are the way they are and what we can do to change our conditions for the better. A great addition to the growing corpus of popular manifestos coming from leading thinkers of the Left." —**Jordy Rosenberg**, author of *Confessions of the Fox*

Comedy Against Work: Utopian Longing in Dystopian Times
Madeline Lane-McKinley

ISBN: 978-1-94217-370-0 | eBook ISBN: 978-1-942173-80-9

Library of Congress Number: 2022944937

10 9 8 7 6 5 4 3 2 1

Common Notions
c/o Interference Archive
314 7th St.
Brooklyn, NY 11215

Common Notions
c/o Making Worlds Bookstore
210 S. 45th St.
Philadelphia, PA 19104

www.commonnotions.org
info@commonnotions.org

Discounted bulk quantities of our books are available for organizing, educational, or fundraising purposes. Please contact Common Notions at the address above for more information.

Cover design by Josh MacPhee / Antumbra Design
Page Design and typesetting by Graciela "Chela" Vasquez / chelitadesigns

Printed by union labor in Canada on acid-free, recycled paper.

Comedy Against Work

Comedy Against Work

Utopian Longing in Dystopian Times

Madeline Lane-McKinley

Brooklyn, NY
Philadelphia, PA

Dedicated to Tuli

"And I dream of our coming together
encircled   driven
not only by love
but by lust for a working tomorrow
the flights of this journey
mapless   uncertain
and necessary as water."

—Audre Lorde, "On My Way Out I Passed Over You and
the Verrazano Bridge"

". . . remember
you can have what you ask for, ask for
everything"

—Diane di Prima, "Revolutionary Letter #19, for The Poor
People's Campaign"

CONTENTS

ACKNOWLEDGMENTS

At every step of writing this book, I have been supported by some of my closest friends and co-thinkers. Johanna Isaacson, my writing partner and coeditor of many years, was always there to swap drafts, commiserate, and everything else. I want to thank Max Fox and Kenan Bezhat Sharpe for our epistolary relationships, which have kept me so often afloat. I am forever grateful to Sarah Brouillette, Sophie Lewis, and Annie McClanahan for their support, intellectual engagement, and comradeship. And it's hard to imagine where I'd be without Jasmine Bridges, my best friend since 1999.

Many more friends have showed up for me as I worked on this project. Thank you Ann Altstatt, Josh Muir, Neti!, and Penske!, for co-parenting and caring for kids together and being committed to the pod. And thank you to Amanda Armstrong-Price, Wren Awry, Barms!, Hunter Bivens, Josh Brahinsky, J. Dakota Brown, Kelly Brown, Marija Cetinic, E Conner, my neighbor Danny, Amy De'Ath, Ian Dolton-Thorton, Angel Dominguez, Kendra Dority, Keegan Finberg, Jo Giardini, Michelle Glowa, Malcolm Harris, Justin Hogg, Jane Hu, Jesse James, Jen Jones, Joshua Jones, Caroline Kao, Alirio Karina, Dominick Knowles, Anna Kornbluh, Natasha Lennard, Zachary Levenson, Brooke Lober, Phil Longo, Nadia Lucia Peralta, Geo Maher, Bob Majzler, Margot!, Liz Mason-Deese, Sarah Miller, Chloe Minervini, Maga Miranda, Michelle O'Brien, Sean O'Brien, Andrew Osborne, Vicky Osterweil, Jason Read, Margaret Ronda, Gabriela Salvidea, Andrés Sandoval, Clarice Sargenti, Lisa Schilz, Abigail Schott-Rosenfield, Louis-Georges Schwartz, Zach Schwartz-Weinstein, Wilson Sherwin, Eric Sneathen, Oki Sogumi, Juliana Spahr, Rei Terada, Wendy Trevino, Nicole Trigg, Amy Vidali, Hunter Villa Gawboy, Olivia Warner, Aaron Wistar, Hannah Zeavin, and Viktoria Zerda—you've each been there in your own way, and it means a lot.

I want to also express my gratitude to my mom and my stepdad for their support and their dedication as grandparents, and to my siblings.

I feel a profound appreciation for the teachers, nurses, single moms and activists in my family, who have shaped so much of my thinking and politics about work, care (and comedy) over the years: my partner's mom Cheryl, a retired schoolteacher / union leader / feminist single mom and badass; my grandma, one of the funniest people I've ever met, who raised my mom as a single parent and worked as a nurse in Chicago for 28 years; and my dad, who brought me up with his own stories of university occupations and war protests, and who worked tirelessly for his union as a community college instructor when I was a kid and explained to me what it means to strike, and who let me stay up late on Friday and Saturday nights to watch comedies.

And of course, much thanks to my editor, Andy Battle, whose insights into my writing and research have been absolutely crucial; and to Alya Ansari, Aparajita Basu, Nicki Kattoura, Malav Kanuga, Josh MacPhee, and the whole team at Common Notions.

Lastly, the irony is not lost on me in describing this book as a labor of love. Much of what follows was written from a desk in my kitchen, where I would sneak away during insomniac hours. Many of the ideas were refined during hikes with my dogs, Stella and Mona. My cat Mega has also been very supportive. Thank you, most of all, to my partner, Kyle, and to our kid, Tuli, for your patience, encouragement, and care. I love you both so much. Thank you for believing in me, and for sometimes telling me to just relax.

—M
November 2022

INTRODUCTION

Work Is a Joke

> "'Labour' by its very nature is unfree, unhuman, unsocial activity[.]"
> —Karl Marx

> "Humor is reason gone mad."
> —Groucho Marx

Nothing quite captures the dystopianism of our everyday lives as precisely, and exhaustively, as the idea of work. In its most capacious sense, work is waged, unwaged, valued, exploited, secure, precarious; work exceeds the boundaries of jobs and careers, sometimes called love and care; work is what it takes to "not work," whether in the fantasy of leisure, the work of others, or the day-to-day work of surviving unhoused, unemployed, and uninsured. Work is our social totality, comprising all the activities we cannot know without compulsion under capitalism; it is what we struggle to see beyond, think outside of, or imagine alternatives to. Work, in short, is what robs us of life while being simultaneously indistinguishable from whatever life might be.

Work is also killing us, and not just metaphorically. In 2016, the World Health Organization (WHO) conducted a global study which determined that roughly 745,000 people died from overwork that year alone, while an estimated 488 million more were exposed to over-work-related health risks.[1] Between 2000 and 2016, the study found that work-related disease burden had risen substantially, with the number

---

1   "Long Working Hours Increasing Deaths from Heart Disease and Stroke: WHO, ILO," accessed December 31, 2021, https://www.who.int/news/item/17-05-2021-long-working-hours-increasing-deaths-from-heart-disease-and-stroke-who-ilo.

of deaths from heart disease associated with overwork increasing by 42 percent. Four years later, work was made even more dangerous with the spread of COVID-19. Across workforces, so many people continue to die unnecessary deaths, sacrificed for the sake of capitalism's survival in a regime of "going back to normal." Meanwhile, the pressure placed on households has intensified housework and caretaking, along with rates of domestic violence. And workers who were lucky enough to have remote jobs in this time, lessening their chances of exposure and transmission, have faced their own set of risks including increased rates of substance abuse, self-harm, and suicide.[2]

Definitions of work have long been debated, precisely because to define something as work has such tremendous political stakes. In Marxism, whether certain kinds of work are *value-producing*, and how, will remain a point of contention for the foreseeable future. The crucial Marxist-feminist interventions of the twentieth century focused on the integral role of reproductive labor under capitalism—labor primarily based in the household, naturalized as labors of love—including cooking and cleaning but likewise, childcare, eldercare, nursing, sex, and much more. The last decade in Marxist-feminism has seen a trend toward social reproduction as a framework through which, as Tithi Bhattacharya suggests, "we begin to see emerge myriad capillaries of social relations extending between workplace, home, schools, hospitals—a wider social whole, sustained and co-produced by human labor in contradictory yet constitutive ways."[3] To the extent that 'work' describes the dystopia of capitalist life, in this sense, it also illuminates a utopianism through these capillaries of social relations, orienting us towards the possibilities of a wider social whole. "Because reproduction is inherently an affirmative process," Amy De'Ath explains, there has been a strong tendency in Marxist-feminism to conceive reproduction through "its potentiality as a site of resistance."[4] What happens, De'Ath asks, "when we conceive of reproductive labor not as an outside or excess to the sphere of value-production . . . but as a negative dialectic internal to capital and labor?" While drawing from

---

2 Nora D. Volkow, "Collision of the COVID-19 and Addiction Epidemics," *Annals of Internal Medicine* (2020) 173(1): 61–2, doi: 10.7326/M20-1212; "Mental health and psychosocial considerations during COVID-19 outbreak: WHO, ILO" (2020), accessed May 24, 2020, https://www.who.int/docs/default-source/coronaviruse/mental-health-considerations.pdf.
3 Tithi Bhattacharya, "How Not to Skip Class," in *Social Reproduction Theory: Remapping Class, Recentering Oppression*, ed. Tithi Bhattacharya (London: Pluto Press, 2017).
4 Amy De'Ath, "Reproduction," in *Bloomsbury Companion to Marx*, ed. Andrew Pendakis, Jeff Diamanti, and Imre Szeman (London: Bloomsbury Academic, 2021), 401.

different Marxist-feminist conceptions of reproductive labor and social reproduction, this book approaches work as both expansionary and profoundly conflicted—by no means just a matter of jobs and employment, and very often a matter of what is unseen or even disacknowledged. Rather than approach work as a category, however, I want to think about work as a *problem*. To the extent that a category seeks to contain, distill, and organize, a problem generates an opening for critique, disruption, and transformation. In *The Problem with Work*, Kathi Weeks describes work's problem as "not just that it monopolizes so much time and energy, but that it also dominates the social and political imaginaries." Work exhausts our capacities to imagine a life against it, dominating our dreams, and even our attempts at refusal. To this problem, Weeks asks, "What might we name the variety of times and spaces outside waged work, and what might we wish to do with and in them?"[5]

At the heart of 'work'—like any dystopia—there are utopian questions. In *Lost in Work*, Amelia Horgan beautifully formulates this contradiction: work, she argues, must be understood for its world-transforming capacities, yet as it stands, these capacities "are channeled into activity that causes harm on a massive scale . . . [toward] the destruction of human life."[6] While epitomizing so much of our shared misery, the various activities that comprise 'work' in our life under capitalism also reflect back to us the ways that human effort, as Horgan writes, "has the power to change the world."[7] Work, on the one hand, typifies our life under capitalism—the conditions of living in a world that creates so much harm, on so many scales—and on the other hand, work gives us insight into the desires and longings over which capitalism continually exerts its control.

In recent years, this contradiction has threatened to burst the world of work. "Work itself is no longer working," Sarah Jaffe argues in *Work Won't Love You Back*.[8] Today's ideal workers "love their work but hop from job to job like serial monogamists; their hours stretch long and the line between the home and the workplace blurs," she explains, exploring the ways in which this idea that we should love our work has been "cracking under its own weight" since the 2008 financial crisis. The "world that constructed

5 Kathi Weeks, *The Problem with Work: Feminism, Marxism, Antiwork Politics, and Postwork Imaginaries* (Durham: Duke University Press, 2011), 36.
6 Amelia Horgan, *Lost in Work: Escaping Capitalism*, Outspoken by Pluto (London: Pluto Press, 2021), 113.
7 Horgan, 113.
8 Sarah Jaffe, *Work Won't Love You Back: How Devotion to Our Jobs Keeps Us Exploited, Exhausted, and Alone* (New York: Bold Type, 2021), 322.

that desire is falling apart around us," she writes, "the exposure to capitalism's cruelty makes the demand to love our jobs a brutal joke."[9]

This book is about that brutal joke and how we inhabit it, while dreaming of ways out. It's a story that begins with the post-crisis era, during which, as Jaffe suggests, the illusions and false promises of work steadily eroded—just as, paradoxically, the world of work became ever more suffocating. I trace these dynamics in the comedy boom of this period, looking to comedy as a complex terrain of capitalist work ethics and antiwork longings. I consider the ways the comedy industry has thrived in capitalist crisis, and how comedy has been produced and experienced through different media ranging from live performance to stand-up specials, serialized shows and podcasts, films, as well as popular histories and memoirs, all while teasing out how and why these uneasy feelings about the world of work become legible and collectively thinkable through comedy. The attempt, throughout this book, will be to examine and question antiwork comedy as a utopian impulse of contemporary culture, with the potential to disarticulate and challenge dominant conceptions of work. In thinking through this critical potential, I'll focus on comedy in the context of three historical turning points: capitalism's ideological and economic post-crisis recovery, the workplace critiques of #MeToo, and the transformations of work in the COVID-19 pandemic. During each of these junctures, in distinctive ways, comedy not only flourished, but brought the world of work into question—never taking one step without the other. Through these important historical transformations, this book follows antiwork critique and post-work longing as key aspects of contemporary comedy, and as sources of insight into collective, political vacillations in this time between revolutionary eruptions of energy and descents into melancholia, nihilism, and dystopian dread.

Comedy drains these competing impulses from our political imagination against capitalism, during a period in many ways defined by the ideological parameters of "capitalist realism"—what Mark Fisher described as the "anti-mythical myth" of Margaret Thatcher's doctrine that "there is no alternative."[10] Coined in 2009, Fisher's concept enunciated the anti-utopianism of this doctrine, but also a prospective break from the historical and revolutionary (and utopian) foreclosures of the last several decades. At the outset of the post-crisis years, "capitalist realism" was a strong diagnostic, expanding from Fredric Jameson's infamous version of the brutal

---

9   Jaffe, *Work Won't Love You Back*, 323.
10   Mark Fisher, *Capitalist Realism: Is There No Alternative?* (Winchester: Zero Books, 2009), 14.

joke, that "it's easier to imagine the end of the world than it is to imagine the end of capitalism."[11] Between 2007 and 2008, so much broke loose. But what that was is still not entirely clear.

Just as hatred of work has grown more and more palpable, the idea of work has never seemed so totalizing. However much some may know, at a visceral level, that work is an instrument of violence under capitalism—to ourselves, each other, our planet—there is still a prevailing sense that this is just how it is, that it's not going to change, and we just have to get used to it. Here, comedy can help to numb the pain of a world that seems impossible to change. But comedy can also pose questions, and push ideological boundaries, moving us toward political horizons otherwise occluded by nihilism, at the core of "capitalist realism." Like any utopian demand, the abolition of work sounds to many like a crazy proposition, stupid or even unsafe. Perhaps the best place to start is the simple recognition of work's brutal joke.

To articulate work as a joke is a potentially radical gesture. Jokes can be brutal, silly, caring. At their best, jokes denaturalize everyday life, breaking apart the logic of capitalist realism. Adding to Fisher's account, Alison Shonkweiler and Leigh Claire La Berge insist that "recognizing capitalism with capitalism," as opposed to a natural social order, "is the only way to account for the enclosures of capital, the scenes of indebtedness it produces, and its ability to form the most real of our horizons."[12] This act of recognition—simply acknowledging that capitalism has constructed a world in which life outside it is so thoroughly inconceivable—can generate revolutionary and anticapitalist critique and struggle. It involves a making-strange, a stepping outside of, both psychologically and politically. And yet, it can also bring us to the brink of ideological defeat, as Shonkweiler and La Berge suggest of a counter-revolutionary "realism of lowered expectations," echoing Lauren Berlant's notion of "cruel

---

11 For the key iterations of this citation see Fredric Jameson, *The Seeds of Time* (New York: Columbia University Press, 1994), xii; and Jameson, "Future City," New Left Review 21 (May/June 2003), 76. Of this quote's strange and prolific history, Sean Austin Grattan remarks that "it circulates as a ghost citation," noting Jameson's coyness when he later refers to the line's author as "someone." Mark Fisher himself attributed the quote to both Jameson and Slavoj Žižek, but I prefer not to. (See Sean Austin Grattan, *Hope Isn't Stupid: Utopian Affects in Contemporary American Literature*, University of Iowa Press, 2017, 8.)

12 Alison Shonkwiler and Leigh Claire La Berge, "A Theory of Capitalist Realism," in *Reading Capitalist Realism*, ed. Alison Shonkwiler and Leigh Claire La Berge (Iowa City: University of Iowa Press, 2014), 23.

optimism."[13] The point can't just be to understand the brutality; part of this is about learning to understand the joke of capitalist realism *as joke*, and moving from there.

Jokes have long been theorized as a site of release (Freud) or domination (Plato, Hobbes), but also incongruity (Aristotle, Cicero, Kant, Beattie). At times, each of these schools of thought in humor (Relief Theory, Superiority Theory, and Incongruity Theory) provides useful analytic tools, though I have little interest in defining the joke—much like work—in anything but slippery and inquisitive terms. Jokes can certainly provide catharsis, and they can also be weaponized. However, the joke is at its most powerful as a collective thought-experiment. Jokes brush up against what's thinkable. The capacity of a joke to surprise us must be understood as a political capacity. The politics of joking is not formal, but practical.

Much like jokes, utopias are rarely evergreen. They often fall short, out of style, or out of memory. As endeavors to represent "the good place," utopias come to reveal, instead, the historical situations from which they were imagined, and the political and cultural conditions by which they were imaginable. And like comedy, utopias are hardly ever taken seriously. "If political realism tends to be associated with a mode of hard-nosed, hard-ball politics," Kathi Weeks explains, "utopianism can be understood—building on this traditional gender logic—as both softhearted and softheaded, or, more precisely, softheaded because softhearted."[14] Weeks maps these genre distinctions onto a gendered logic, specifically between political theory and feminism, which could easily be extended to the historic dynamic in literature and theater between the hard-nosed, hard-ball world of tragedy and the softheaded because softhearted world of comedy. What would it mean to be as much hard-nosed as softhearted in looking at the politics of comedy, and utopian thought? What is at stake in taking comedy seriously, but also with care?

Comedy mirrors and distorts the world of work, our shared predicament of capitalist life, re-interpreting it both critically and recuperatively, in both utopian and dystopian terms. On the one hand, comedy is a mode of estranging and interrogating the very idea of work and its brutality; and on the other hand, comedy has interpenetrated the imaginary of work, as part of what Lauren Berlant and Sianne Ngai observe

---

13 Shonkwiler and La Berge, 8–9, 13.
14 Weeks, *The Problem with Work*, 182.

as the "commedification" of modern social life, described by sociologist Arpad Szakolczai.[15] Under these conditions, comedy has "morphed into an overarching tone of late capitalist sociability, affecting how people self-consciously play as well as work together and the spaces where they do so (including Twitter, Facebook, Snapchat, Instagram, and YouTube)," Berlant and Ngai argue, theorizing comedy in relation to broader shifts in the temporalities and social conditions of work, including the rise of affective labor. "This does not mean that all affective labor is comedic," they write, but that "affective labor is caring labor, and caring labor absorbs a range of moods. But the demand for play and fun as good and necessary for social membership is everywhere inflecting what was once called alienation."[16] Comedy is this while it is also something bigger, something that always threatens to burst these logics, and which emerges instead as a way of locating the incongruities, fissures, and thresholds of imaginability in this world of work.

Paradoxically, critics of utopia, at the same time that they scorn utopianism for womanly softheadedness and softheartedness, seem to fear it, never ceasing to point out that utopian thinking is *dangerous*. At perhaps their most convincing, anti-utopians have historically pointed to the formal similarities between utopia and dystopia, as in Karl Popper's denunciation of utopia as "the Platonic belief in one absolute and unchanging ideal," asserting that dystopia is the "shadow of utopia."[17] Of this Cold War regime of anti-utopianism, for which totalitarianism is the dominant threat, anti-utopianism is entirely indistinguishable from anticommunism. Deep fears are made legible by anti-utopianism, including "the fear that utopia will lead to the end of history, politics and change," writes Lucy Sargisson, uprooting the association between utopianism and perfection: "This is complicated. And it is important. Exponents of this view believe that utopianism is, at some essential and definitional level, perfection-seeking, authoritarian and intolerant of dissent."[18] The fixation among anti-utopians on utopian impossibility conflates the supposed goal of a *perfect society* with the "good place" (eu-topos) evoked by Thomas More's 1516 text, often without engaging the complexities of More's

---

15   See Arpad Szakolczai, *Comedy and the Public Sphere: The Rebirth of Theatre as Comedy and the Genealogy of the Modern Public Arena* (London: Routledge, 2013).

16   Lauren Berlant and Sianne Ngai, "Comedy Has Issues," *Critical Inquiry* 43, no. 2 (Winter 2017): 237.

17   Karl R. Popper, *The Open Society and Its Enemies*, vol. 1 (London: Routledge, 2011), 161.

18   Lucy Sargisson, *Fool's Gold?: Utopianism in the 21st Century* (New York: Palgrave Macmillan, 2012), 21.

satirical play with ou-topos, Greek for "no-place." Anti-utopianism instead reduces utopia to this singular meaning, as a blueprint or map, doomed to failure—that is, to imperfection.

But there are many ways to think of utopia. Feminist utopians have been among the critics of this utopianism of maps, plans, and programs. With its "emphasis on stasis and control to its logical conclusion," this version of utopianism is fundamentally masculinist, Elaine Baruch argues.[19] Ursula K. Le Guin described this as Euclidean utopianism, colonial and patriarchal at the level of form. In the attempt to conceptualize a non-Euclidean utopianism, Le Guin writes "in an evasive, distrustful, untrustworthy fashion, and as obscurely as [possible]," suggesting that "our final loss of faith in that radiant sandcastle" of the supposedly perfect society "may enable our eyes to adjust to a dimmer light and in it perceive another kind of utopia."[20] Along with her feminist and queer contemporaries in science fiction like Octavia Butler, Joanna Russ, Marge Piercy, and Samuel Delany, Le Guin's writing is part of a critical utopian wave in the sixties-seventies, devoted to interrogating and re-imagining "utopia" from the elsewhere of More's island—bound to Robinson Crusoe's fantasy, of inventing capitalism anew. Le Guin's *Hainish* series, and especially her 1974 novel *The Dispossessed* (subtitled "An Ambiguous Utopia"), actively grapples with utopia not as a genre, but as a problem of the imagination. Similarly, Butler's *Patternist* series begins to explore utopian themes in the dystopian genre, a strategy Butler retained throughout her prolific career. Marking a shift from structure to process in utopian thought, Raffaella Baccolini and Tom Moylan trace the proliferation of critical utopias and critical dystopias in the cultural imagination of the post-sixties, during which utopia "becomes more fragmentary, provisional, contested, ambiguous": "Utopia is not dead," they write, but regenerates as a utopianism "that is holistic, social, future-located, committed, and linked to the present."[21]

Like science fiction, comedy can give us glimpses into other worlds, partially and problematically, never perfectly but sometimes profoundly. Comedy can take what appears most inescapable and unchanging about

---

19 Elaine Baruch, *Women, Love, and Power: Literary and Psychoanalytic Perspectives* (New York: NYU Press, 1991), 222.
20 Ursula K. Le Guin, *Dancing at the Edge of the World: Thoughts on Words, Women, Places* (New York: Grove Press, 1989), 86.
21 Raffaella Baccolini and Tom Moylan, "Introduction: Dystopia and Histories," in *Dark Horizons: Science Fiction and the Dystopian Imagination*, ed. Raffaella Baccolini and Tom Moylan (New York: Routledge, 2003), 15.

the world and help us to see it, instead, for the joke that it is—however brutal.

Inasmuch as comedy can redirect and defamiliarize the capitalist realist logic of work, it can also expose and disrupt the false utopian dimensions of contemporary work ethics. False utopianism, "[sells] the future short . . . imprisoning the present within it," as Terry Eagleton ascribes to postmodern capitalism.[22] The false utopia of work promises what it can never deliver: not only a means of survival, but fulfillment, self-actualization, and spiritual enlightenment. But we are beginning to awaken from these false utopian dreams, in times of accelerated crisis and pervasive dystopia. Throughout this book, I'll discuss this change in our everyday thinking about work through undercurrents of utopian longing in contemporary comedy, looking to comedy not for a map of the "good life," but as a site of conflict and confrontation. In showing us our dystopia, and helping us to see the brutalities and banalities of work alike, antiwork comedy demands utopian interpretive methods. The utopian impulse calls for "a hermeneutic, for the detective work of a decipherment and a reading of utopian clues and traces in the landscape of the real," what Fredric Jameson conceives as a process of theorizing "unconscious utopian investments in realities large or small, which may be far from utopian."[23] This ambivalent, ambiguous quality attaches to each of the comedies I discuss in this book. None are unproblematic, and none are purely utopian without dystopian dimensions. In tracing this utopian / dystopian dialectic in contemporary comedy, feeling through this dialectic as a source of revolutionary possibility, I want to also draw out the poison of false utopianism.

In many ways, comedies about work are portraits of our hell and how we make that hell livable. Any episode of *The Office*, for instance—more popular today, through multiple streaming platforms, than during its nine-season run on NBC—is driven by this conflict, between a persistent critique of the meaninglessness of work (as in the obsolete premise of Dunder Mifflin, a paper company in a paperless economy), and an unrelenting desire to love work and love being at work. This desire is managed through pranks, inside jokes, and other forms of casual everyday humor, but it also becomes the false utopian kernel of the show, rendering the office workplace as a place of romantic courtship and family. More than

---

22 Terry Eagleton, *The Illusions of Postmodernism* (Oxford: Blackwell, 1997).
23 Fredric Jameson, "Utopia as Method, or the Uses of the Future," in *Utopia/Dystopia: Conditions of Historical Possibility*, ed. Michael D. Gordin, Gyan Prakash, and Helen Tilley (Princeton: Princeton University Press, 2010) 26.

a simply pro- or antiwork vision of office jobs, the show bares these frictions between utopian desire, dystopian dread, and anti-utopian denial in the world of work. Likewise, *The Good Place*, possibly the most obvious example of a recent and popular comedy about utopianism, is an utterly dystopian exploration of various false utopias. Set in the afterlife, the series charts the uncertainty of its central characters, who move between believing they're in heaven to wondering if they're in hell or somewhere else entirely, all while grappling with ethical questions about the meaning of life. The absent center of the show is the question of whether it is possible to be "good" under capitalism, while the virtues of protagonists all become measured through some version of a capitalist work ethic.

I look to comedy as symptomatizing a set of problems, more than presenting us with any direct solutions. At the same time, many of the comedies and comedians I explore in this book make what I understand to be inspiring attempts to critically negate the world of work, in some cases daring to envision a world against it. At stake in antiwork comedy is a practice of refusal, a mode of critique, and a place to begin imagining and enacting a life against work. Comedy, in its most utopian sense, can be a way of challenging, but also transforming everyday life. The critical utopian possibility of antiwork comedy is to question, re-think, and experiment, precisely in the gap between capitalist realism and our everyday experience.

Early into the post-financial crisis era, the critique of capitalist realism applied pressure to certain cracks forming in the political imaginary of "No Alternative." Countless uprisings made it clear to a growing number of people that while alternatives to capitalism were perhaps not (yet) fully imaginable in the present, a post-capitalist world was worth fighting for anyway. Even while occluding all other possibilities, and however gradually, capitalism has been losing its sense of inevitability. Too many of us know that it shouldn't be this way—that this is not, in fact, how it's always been and always has to be. In a 2016 study conducted by Harvard, the majority of 18–34 year-olds in the U.S. rejected capitalism.[24] A study of British youth in 2021 found that nearly 80 percent blame capitalism for the housing crisis, and 75 percent believe the climate crisis is "specifically a

---

24 "Harvard IOP Spring 2016 Poll," The Institute of Politics at Harvard University, accessed December 31, 2021, https://iop.harvard.edu/youth-poll/past/harvard-iop-spring-2016-poll.

capitalist problem."[25] Across generations and different countries, a global study in 2019 found 56 percent in agreement that "capitalism as it exists today does more harm than good in the world."[26] A growing majority find themselves in this shared recognition—but what will we do about it?

Since the global uprisings of 1968, "Be Realistic—Demand the Impossible!" has been the revolutionary cry of generations and a utopian refutation of capitalism's monopoly over our collective sense of political possibilities. What does it mean to demand the impossible today, I keep wondering, when by now the impossible has become more and more imaginable as a distinct feature of capitalist crisis? A recent heat wave in the Pacific Northwest, where I live in a state of constant worry about the ever-growing threat of wildfires, was declared "statistically impossible" by environmental scientists studying the region's weather patterns.[27] In the summer of 2021, as I completed a draft of this book, the ocean was literally on fire, the result of a burst pipeline in the Gulf of Mexico. I grew up as a child of the "end of history," and now I am the parent of a child living in a global pandemic, who watched the Capitol building get taken over in Donald Trump's attempted coup on TV and lived through the largest series of protests ever in the United States, following the murder of George Floyd on May 25, 2020. As hundreds of racist monuments were destroyed, vandalized, and removed that year, the experience of history—as in ongoing, active, and potentially revolutionary social transformations—has never in my lifetime seemed more vital.

The initial weeks of shutdown during the pandemic furnished many of us with an image, however partial and incomplete, of various post-capitalist worlds. Things slowed down. Coyotes roamed empty city streets. Mutual aid efforts proliferated. By early April, daily global CO_2 emissions decreased by 17% compared to 2019 levels. A study of global energy patterns during lockdown periods in 2020 found that emissions plummeted

25 Owen Jones, "Eat the Rich! Why Millennials and Generation Z Have Turned Their Backs on Capitalism," *The Guardian*, September 20, 2021, https://www.theguardian.com/politics/2021/sep/20/eat-the-rich-why-millennials-and-generation-z-have-turned-their-backs-on-capitalism.

26 "Capitalism Seen Doing 'More Harm than Good' in Global Survey," *Reuters*, January 20, 2020, https://www.reuters.com/article/us-davos-meeting-trust-idUSKBN1ZJ0CW.

27 Ronald Brownstein, "The Unbearable Summer," *The Atlantic*, August 26, 2021, https://www.theatlantic.com/politics/archive/2021/08/summer-2021-climate-change-records/619887/.

in individual countries by an average of 26 percent.[28] And as the disease continued to spread, its correspondence with work became all the more apparent, as jobs went remote, disappeared, or became increasingly dangerous. The absurdity of so many workers being called "essential" while being paid shit wages to risk their lives seemed abundantly clear. With the disease came a growing sense of the false choices of work, still leaving little else to even dream as the terms of our collective survival. Whatever utopian elements were distinguishable could only be seen through a lens of ongoing apocalypse. The pandemic merely clarified many of the ways that we were already living in a sick world.

Of laughter, Henri Bergson describes a "momentary anesthesia of the heart"—an effect which Theodor Adorno and Max Horkheimer take up as a point of caution. In their searing critique of the culture industry, Adorno and Horkheimer declare that "there is laughter because there is nothing to laugh about," claiming that laughter "whether reconciled or terrible . . . echoes the inescapability of power." Fun is merely a medicinal bath, they quip, "which the entertainment industry never ceases to prescribe." [29] Plato condemned comedy, and claimed that "taken generally, the ridiculous is a certain kind of evil, specifically a vice."[30] While countless philosophers have claimed that humor is a distinctly human attribute, others have claimed the opposite—for Simon Critchley, it is what "return[s] us to physicality and animality."[31] Some theorists emphasize the distinctions between comedy, laughter, and humor—Schopenhauer belabored this point. Others deemphasize stylistic and generic distinctions, avoiding taxonomies but also various schools of comedy. And some discourage any theorizing at all. "Humor can be dissected, as a frog can," E.B. White famously warns, "but the thing dies in the process[.]"[32] Cutting to the chase, Berlant and Ngai explain *comedy has issues.*[33]

Swimming in these tensions, this book investigates comedy—and comedy's relationship to work—as a constellation of utopian problems, calling for a utopian epistemology. Like utopia, comedy expresses

28 Corinne Le Quéré et al., "Temporary Reduction in Daily Global CO2 Emissions during the COVID-19 Forced Confinement," *Nature Climate Change* 10, no. 7 (July 2020): 647–53, https://doi.org/10.1038/s41558-020-0797-x.

29 Max Horkheimer and Theodor W. Adorno, *Dialectic of Enlightenment: Philosophical Fragments*, trans. Edmund Jephcott (Stanford: Stanford University Press, 2002), 112.

30 Donald Davidson, *Plato's Philebus* (London: Routledge, 2013), 47d–50e.

31 Simon Critchley, *On Humour* (New York: Routledge, 2002), 68.

32 Robert Mankoff, "Killing a Frog," *The New Yorker*, March 21, 2012, https://www.newyorker.com/cartoons/bob-mankoff/killing-a-frog.

33 Berlant and Ngai, "Comedy Has Issues," 233.

a friction with the unknowable. In his philosophy of laughter, Georges Bataille argued that it is the unknown which makes us laugh.[34] In laughter we "pass very abruptly, all of a sudden, from a world in which each thing is qualified, in which each thing is given in its stability, generally in a stable order," Bataille writes, and we move into "a world in which our assurance is suddenly overthrown, in which we perceive that this assurance is deceptive, and where we believed that everything was strictly anticipated[.]"[35] What might we do with this world, which seems as much ours as any other?

In laughter there is the possibility of a literary communism, as Anca Parvulescu suggests. Drawing from Maurice Blanchot, she conceives of "a certain practice of reading and listening," which demands much of us: "We need new ears to listen to the communal voice of the sea," she writes, continuing, "What literature makes audible is the nonmusicalized sound of a voice. If one reads / listens carefully, one slowly begins to hear its distant laughter."[36] With this, I turn to the possibilities of comedy—not for models of being, but for methods of listening. To listen for utopia in anti-work comedy involves disentangling ourselves from work, but also from anti-utopianism. It is not enough to show us what's wrong with work, or to let ourselves feel free enough from work to see our own hatred of it.

"To save the world, we're going to have to stop working," as the late David Graeber put it, soon before his death in September 2020. "If addressing [this] seems unrealistic, we might do well to think about what those realities are that seem to be forcing us, as a society, to behave in ways that are literally mad."[37] Comedy confronts this madness with its own madness, one that can break our attachment to what is killing us, and perhaps help us find something that won't.

---

34   See Georges Bataille, *The Unfinished System of Nonknowledge*, ed. Stuart Kendall, trans. Michelle Kendall and Stuart Kendall (Minneapolis: University of Minnesota Press, 2001).

35   Bataille, *The Unfinished System*, 135.

36   Anca Parvulescu, *Laughter: Notes on a Passion* (Cambridge: MIT Press, 2010), 98–99.

37   David Graeber, "To Save the World, We're Going to Have to Stop Working," The Anarchist Library, accessed December 31, 2021, https://theanarchistlibrary.org/library/david-graeber-to-save-the-world-we-re-going-to-have-to-stop-working.

Part One

Comedy and the World of Work

"Work, work, proletarians, to increase social wealth and your individual poverty; work, work, in order that becoming poorer, you may have more reason to work and become miserable."

—Paul Lafargue, *The Right to Be Lazy*

CHAPTER ONE

Watching Work on TV

Watching television is often perceived as an escapist or lazy activity, or even as a non-activity. We aren't *working* ourselves to death, apparently, but "amusing ourselves to death," as Neil Postman famously claimed of television viewership, casting a dystopian future of media junkies and mindless consumption from the year 1985. We watch TV as unthinking sheep, the story goes, anesthetizing ourselves to the supposed realities of everyday life. If we are to believe this—that watching TV is escapist, lazy, or anything that characterizes a state of not-working—then it makes sense that *not* watching TV would be imagined, by contrast, in terms of work: as a matter of self-discipline, or an individual's work ethic. What would it mean to think of this state of not-working, instead, as grasping at an antiwork practice of everyday life?

Or how might we think of watching TV alongside all the other daily acts of sabotage in the world of work—all the common practices of taking back our time, comprising our shared yet often individualized forms of resistance? Here, I think of a worker at my local grocery store, who watches TV shows while he stocks shelves, stealthily propping his iPhone against a loaf of bread or a jar of pickles and listening with one wireless earpiece, always glancing around the corner and listening with the other ear for his supervisor. He seems to know that, so long as he stocks the shelves quickly enough, he can probably get away with watching TV as he does it. And why not? Why wouldn't we want this for him? Stocking shelves is boring—not to mention dangerous work during a pandemic. He's paid minimum wage to risk his life so that I can browse different peanut butters. Watching a sit-com seems the least he can ask for. He reminds me of a friend who worked night shifts at the front desk of a hotel and would stay up with coffee and late-night talk shows; or of myself, watching episodes of *30 Rock* and hardly laughing, just trying to stay awake as I breast-pumped enough milk to go to work the next day.

I recently heard about a work meeting on Zoom during which someone forgot to hit 'mute' as they started watching an episode of *Frasier*, and I've come to love the idea that *Frasier* could be antiwork.

While we could think of watching TV as something like an antiwork practice, it is also how we tolerate work, and how we continue working. And for the most part, what we watch reflects back to us the social totality of work—by now, a seemingly infinite swath of serial content, all still somehow tethered to the narrative worlds of our working lives. Just when we're done working, whether waged or unwaged, what is even in the slightest way fathomable as life "off the clock" is life watching work. What does it mean to spend all day juggling one or multiple jobs, come home to do more work as you make dinner and clean up and perhaps take care of others along the way, only to watch a TV show about a workplace or a household (that is: just another kind of workplace)? How do we reconcile with the fact that most of what we are doing when we watch TV is watching work—or that maybe we are even continuing to be at work, even when we think we're done for the day?

A Brief History of Laughing at Work in Sit-Coms in the United States

In 1929, Walter Benjamin wrote of Charlie Chaplin's appeal to "the most international and the most revolutionary emotion of the masses: their laughter."[1] Elsewhere, Benjamin describes this laughter as a "therapeutic release of unconscious energies," specific to the collective body of a cinematic audience.[2] But it is also an experience of catharsis vital to Chaplin's filmmaking and approach to comedy, which extends to an unrelenting critique of work. Most famously in *Modern Times* (1936), a utopian desire drives the crowd's laughter, as The Tramp, Chaplin's iconic character, fumbles through work at the assembly line, sabotaging the entire factory, unleashing chaos through slapstick. The crowd's laughter cuts across anxieties about automation and human labor, out of a joy for watching the world of work as both dysfunctional and irrational, as it is dismantled and seen for the absurdity that it is.

---

1 Walter Benjamin, "Chaplin in Retrospect," in *The Work of Art in the Age of Its Technological Reproducibility, and Other Writings on Media*, ed. Michael W. Jennings, Brigid Doherty, and Thomas Y. Levin, trans. Edmund Jephcott, Rodney Livingstone, Howard Eiland, and Others (Cambridge: Belknap Press of Harvard University Press, 2008), 337.
2 Walter Benjamin, "The Work of Art in the Age of Its Technological Reproducibility, Second Version," in *The Work of Art in the Age of Its Technological Reproducibility, and Other Writings on Media*, 38.

Sixteen years later, when Lucille Ball and Vivian Vance paid homage to Chaplin's assembly line on *I Love Lucy*, a different kind of laughter was at stake. This was not the utopianism of collective laughter, as Benjamin conceives of the cinematic audience, but a critical laughter in the context of the household audience. Besides the change of context, it was a version of the joke which included housework. It was a comedy located not outside of work, as in the exceptional space of the cinema, but immanent to work. In the 1952 episode, entitled "Job Switching," Lucy and Ethel accept a challenge with Ricky and Fred: the women will go to the unemployment office seeking day jobs, while the men stay home. After they struggle to find a job that they're qualified for, Lucy and Ethel end up at a chocolate factory, and hijinks ensue. And yet the punchline of the episode comes from the men's sudden realization that housework is work. Throughout the day, Ricky and Fred discover all that they've failed to recognize in their spouse's working day, and they botch every chore. By the end of the day, they've virtually destroyed the kitchen, with rice overflowing all over the floor, and a chicken exploding from the pressure cooker. It is a joke even more powerful on television, breaking through the atomization of the family household, not only denaturalizing housework but de-isolating it as well, rendering it a source of collective experience, beyond the walls of the living room—and the kitchen.

Since its invention, television has been designed around and for the space of the household. It is a medium uniquely positioned to represent the household as a workplace, but also to conjure a domestic imaginary of leisure, play, and escapism. This tension provided a premise for shows like *Bewitched* and *I Dream of Jeanie*, in which the inside joke between the audience and women in the household is that housework is magic.

My grandma taught me, from an early age, that the secret to housework isn't magic but television. I remember watching her at the ironing table with reruns of *Matlock*, *Magnum P.I.*, or *Murder, She Wrote* in the background. Mysteries were her favorites. Coffee, cigarettes, crossword puzzles, and daytime reruns were all parts of the daily ritual of chores she brought me into as she offered countless instructions on how to make a bed with proper hospital corners, how to launder her brassieres and panty hose, how to iron and fold.

In the late forties, the early years of TV broadcasting, networks learned from the conventions of radio programming to develop daytime content. By the fifties, with national advertising, networks were producing programs that "could be watched in a distracted manner," television scholar Gary Edgerton explains, such that "women could adjust their housekeeping routines to this entertainment by turning the volume up, [and] taking small 'breaks' for favorite programs[.]"[3] As with radio, there were initially concerns that the new medium would divert women's attention from housework.[4] These concerns illustrate the paradox of housework: that it is comprehensible as work only at the risk of not being performed.

In the mid-seventies, feminist theorist Carol Lopate articulated this particular relationship between housework and daytime programming in an incredible essay called "Daytime Television: You'll Never Want to Leave Home." As Lopate suggests, "the heartbreak, confusion, restrained passion, and romance of families in the soaps" provides an anesthesia to the drudgeries of housework, "[filling] out the hollows of long afternoons where children are napping and there is ironing or nothing at all to be done."[5] Lopate traces the temporal flows of the domestic workday through the affective routines of daytime content:

> The morning is geared for energy and hard work, at the same time offering women release through the fantasy of possible TV appearances and free washer-dryers, automobiles, and vacations to Hawaii; the afternoon reminds us that the real adventures and romances take place inside our families. And all the way through the day, time is dotted by enticements of food, laundry soaps, cleansers, toiletries, and shampoos. The synthesis of adventure, love, and security inside the family is to be had through cleaning shirts whiter, preparing glistening foods, and staying young and lovely with stockings, makeup, and shampoo.[6]

TV programming structures the rhythms of daily chores, in this sense, less as a distraction from work and more as a companion. It is content created for a type of work for which, typically, there are no coworkers, "water cooler" discussions, or lunch breaks. Along with this isolation, housework is by nature degrading work—"invisible, repetitive, exhausting,

---

3 Gary R. Edgerton, *The Columbia History of American Television* (New York: Columbia University Press, 2007), 99.

4 Edgerton, *The Columbia History of American Television*, 97.

5 Carol Lopate, "Daytime Television: You'll Never Want to Leave Home," *Feminist Studies* 3, no. 3/4 (1976): 70.

6 Lopate, 70.

unproductive, uncreative," as Angela Davis elaborates.[7] Watching TV can make this work feel less like work, just as the world sees the activity of housework as not-quite-work. At the same time, the companionship of daytime programs becomes an approximate form of payment, for a form of work that is historically low-waged if not unpaid. Just as housework is unquantifiable, the world of daytime TV is seemingly infinite and intensely repetitive—it may be easier to imagine the end of the world than it is to imagine the end of *The Price is Right*.

While soap operas, game shows, talk shows, and cooking shows accommodate and even anesthetize the endless chores which comprise housework, the sit-com has historically had a more complicated relationship to this work, designed for a white, suburban, vaguely "middle-class" family audience during the "after work" hours of primetime. Within this conception of the family audience, the mother/wife is ambiguously positioned. When televisions were initially marketed in the late forties, the cultural anxiety about women's enjoyment of television, as Edgerton suggests, is the underpinning of advertisements "depicting women standing in the kitchen washing dishes while the rest of the family watched the set in the next room," or women "providing refreshments for her guests while the company was engrossed in the program."[8] This marginalization of the wife/mother from the family audience can be tracked in the plot structures of early sit-coms of the fifties as well. In shows like *The Honeymooners*, the ongoing joke is domestic violence. In *Father Knows Best* and *Leave it to Beaver*, the mother is always supportively and unfunnily in the background of the comedy. And by the early sixties, family sit-coms like *The Andy Griffith Show* and *My Three Sons* removed the mother figure entirely, focusing instead on widower fathers.

Throughout their history, traditional sit-coms have drawn much of their plot material from the separation of the household and workplace. *The Dick Van Dyke Show* (1961–1966) strikes a perfect balance between these two seemingly separate realms, as it follows the husband-protagonist Rob Petrie (Van Dyke) from the office to the suburban home. In the show's introductory sequence, Rob trips over the ottoman in the living room when he comes home from work, marking (and mocking) his inability to make this transition from work life to domestic life with any finesse. Comedically, however, much of the show's material is generated from the inseparability of these two realms—whether through

---

7   Angela Y. Davis, *Women, Race & Class* (New York: Vintage, 1983), 222.
8   Edgerton, *The Columbia History of American Television*, 97.

dinner parties, office functions, happenstance meetings, or just bad luck, Rob's work life and home life find ways to collide. At the same time, the domestic imaginary is always at odds with the world of work, but never fully a part of it.

The externality of the household in workplace sit-coms corresponds with a broader process of what Marxist-feminist Maria Mies termed *housewifization*: an imaginary of capitalism which renders the household and household labor a "natural resource," premised on the "total atomization and disorganization of these hidden workers[,]"[9] coinciding with the disappearance of the factory, the Fordist mass workplace. Housewifization accounts for this spatial imaginary of the workplace sit-com, for which the household is somehow outside of work, and housework is miraculously disconnected from formal wage labor. "As the housewife is linked to the wage-earning breadwinner, to the 'free' proletarian as a non-free worker," as Mies explains, "the 'freedom' of the proletarian to sell his labour power is based on the non-freedom of the housewife."[10] In the context of the workplace sit-com, this contradictory freedom, the freedom to be at work, is imagined not just through comedy but *as* comedy. Work is where life is fun, where the laughter is. With few exceptions among sit-coms in the fifties-sixties, the housewife is the perpetual straight man, either not in on the joke or not amused by it, and often (implicitly) having to clean up after it.

In the seventies, among the most significant antiwork sit-coms in the U.S. are those which managed to more deeply trouble this boundary between the household and workplace, along with the traditional genre split into workplace sit-coms and family sit-coms. Some of these shows were integral to the Black sit-com boom of this time, in large part Norman Lear productions that built off the success of *All in the Family* (1971–79) and its social commentary. *Sanford and Son* (1972–77), based on the British series *Steptoe and Son* (1962–65, 1970–74), brings together the workplace and family, taking an orientation toward work as a world of gimmicks and hustles, from the standpoint of Black people marginalized from the labor market. The show follows junk dealer Sanford (Redd Foxx) as he involves his son Lamont (Demond Wilson) in a constant pursuit of the next big score. As a comedy of errors, the show explores the antinomies of labor, time, and value which Sianne Ngai locates in the "gimmick": "The gimmick saves us labor," Ngai explains, "The gimmick

9 Maria Mies, *Patriarchy and Accumulation on a World Scale: Women in the International Division of Labour* (London: Zed Books, 2001), 110.
10 Mies, *Patriarchy and Accumulation on a World Scale*, 110.

does not save labor (in fact, it intensifies or even eliminates it). The gimmick is a device that strikes us as working too hard. The gimmick is a device that strikes us as working too little."[11] *Sanford and Son* wavers in these instabilities, the laughter coming not only from the hijinks, but from a deeper point of recognition in the systemic preposterousness of work. Part of the ongoing joke is that so-called honest work will get Sanford and Lamont nowhere, making gimmicks and hustles always a better bet (not to mention more fun). This antiwork dimension of the show strikes a clear contrast from its contemporary, *The Jeffersons*, in which a Black family "moves on up" from Queens to Manhattan based on the success of their dry-cleaning chain. Where *The Jeffersons* glorifies hard work (and assimilation), *Sanford and Son* makes a joke out of work. Work is the ultimate scam.

Through the seventies, workplace sit-coms also began blending the workplace with the household, constructing a romantic vision of work life. In shows like *The Mary Tyler Moore Show* (1970–1977), or *Taxi* (1978–1983), the workplace comes to resemble a family structure, with the boss as father figure or crazy uncle—surely a reflection of the transition of many women workers from the household to workplace. The best character on *The Mary Tyler Moore Show* is Rhoda, Mary's next-door neighbor, who serves as an intermediary between Mary's workplace, the fictional television station WJM, and her single life in an apartment building in downtown Minneapolis. Like *Laverne & Shirley* (1976–1983), focused on best friends and roommates who work together on the factory floor of a Milwaukee brewery, *Mary Tyler Moore* weaves together visions of young, independent working women with a cozy and joyful domestic life. By contrast, in *Taxi*, much of this home life can be found instead in the taxi company's fleet garage, where drivers catch a break and commiserate with mechanics. Much like *Cheers* (1982–1993), *Taxi* is about workers who are mostly single, sometimes divorced, who maintain their closest personal relationships in a workplace context, whether as workers or customers. Only on occasion do we follow the characters into their actual living situations.

Meanwhile, many sit-coms in the eighties reconfigured the household into different kinds of workplaces. *Benson* (1979–86), *Gimme a Break!* (1981–87) and *Who's the Boss?* (1984–92) take on the household as a workplace most explicitly, through portraits of domestic workers

---

11 Sianne Ngai, *Theory of the Gimmick: Aesthetic Judgment and Capitalist Form* (Cambridge: Belknap Press of Harvard University Press, 2020), 72.

who become part of the family, so to speak; while shows like *Designing Women* (1986–93) and *Newhart* (1982–90) adapt the household into a small business. Each of these series mingles the fantasy of non-work and leisure in the household with an increasingly familial and domestically situated workplace, for the most part envisioning work as love, and losing track of the joke entirely.

With the exception of a few working-class family shows, such as *Good Times* (1974–79) or *Roseanne* (1988–97), the curse of the American sit-com is the American work ethic, a valorization of work that increasingly seeks to understand the workplace as family—making work and dedication to one's employer not just a matter of love, but of moral responsibility. So many of the workplace sit-coms that populated primetime during my childhood in the nineties (*Murphy Brown, Wings, Night Court, NewsRadio, Just Shoot Me!, Spin City*) sought to imagine "the workplace," as this magical space outside of the household, where one is even more truly at home. This was also essential to the workplace "dramedy" industry of the decade to follow (*Ally McBeal, Grey's Anatomy*), which made the workplace not just romantic but sexy. By the 2000s, this compulsion to imagine the workplace as a better home than home is what drives the U.S. adaptation of *The Office* (2005–13), along with contemporaries like *30 Rock* (2006–13) and *Parks and Recreation* (2009–15)—as boss Michael at one point remarks, only half-jokingly, "an office is a place to live life to the fullest, to the max . . . an office is a place where dreams come true."[12]

Seventy years later, what remains quite remarkable about *I Love Lucy*'s antiwork domestic comedy is precisely its insight into the household as the workplace where television is consumed. Formally designed for the household, television has always disturbed the boundaries between what is and is not perceived as work and what constitutes a "workplace" from a few different angles, all of which reflect some of the broader ideological transformations of work in this time. While sit-coms have mystified work throughout their history, making workplaces into families and sites of fulfillment and passion, it's in that mystification that sit-coms appeal to something else—an impulse against work that draws so many viewers in, but that can't be directly articulated within the sit-com's narrative world. In this sense, the sit-com offers up exactly what it forbids: a life against work.

---

12 Jeffrey Blitz, "Stress Relief," *The Office* (NBC, February 1, 2009).

The Serialization of Precarity Comedies

The first time I read Charles Dickens's *Great Expectations*, I was a newly declared English major, assigned to complete the novel and write an essay about it in two weeks for an introductory course. As I rushed through the novel's fifty-nine chapters, I remember struggling to take any of it in, feeling burdened by a sense of hurry, and thinking about the readers of Dickens's time. I wondered whether, in today's terms, this was something to be *binged* in this way. Like all of Dickens's work, the novel was published serially: between the winter of 1860 and late summer of 1861, chapters came out on a weekly basis in magazines like Harper's Weekly. Over 100,000 copies of *All the Year Round* (which Dickens co-owned) were sold each week, with dozens of people reading each copy. Unlike the English major checking off another title from "the canon," these readers experienced the narrative through a delayed gratification, luxuriating in each chapter, more akin to how circles of friends today gather for "*Succession* Sundays."

In the nineteenth century, serial culture "[re-created] capitalism's image," as Jennifer Hayward explains, "by providing what is essentially a payment plan for narrative."[13] Under capitalist development, serialization emerged as the ideal form of representation, institutionalizing a system of delayed gratification. In this sense, we might understand seriality as the narrative logic of capitalism, designed to "perpetually [defer] desire in order to promote continued consumption," as literary theorist Roger Hagedorn suggests.[14] In the twenty-first century, serial culture reflects, perhaps more specifically, the narrative logic of capitalist *crisis*, formally replicating cycles of catastrophe, recuperation, rupture, and revolutionary possibility, all contained by the narrative's serial structure of unendingness. This is what's so provocatory about the closing scene of *The Sopranos*, when the screen cuts to black almost arbitrarily, if not menacingly, before we get to find out what happens—that is, whether Tony Soprano is about to be killed. As the scene builds, Journey's "Don't Stop Believin'" plays—interrupted, in the final cut, after the lyrics "don't stop." The song is about precisely this seriality of capitalist life: "workin' hard to get my fill / Everybody wants a thrill / Payin' anything to roll the dice / Just one more time . . . Oh, the movie never ends / It goes on and on and on and

---

13 Jennifer Hayward, *Consuming Pleasures: Active Audiences and Serial Fictions from Dickens to Soap Opera* (Lexington: University Press of Kentucky, 1997), 29.
14 Roger Hagedorn, "Technology and Economic Exploitation: The Serial as a Form of Narrative Presentation," *Wide Angle* 10, no. 4 (1988): 12.

on." Rather than an ending, the show meditates on the desire for continuation. This desire, mobilizing any serial narrative, is always betrayed by an ending. But over the last two decades, there has been a huge shift towards narratives never having to end—this is the entire formula for the Marvel Universe, for instance. The regime of narrative franchises is by now quite extensive, reaching everywhere from superheroes to *Downton Abbey*.

In the post-financial crisis years, serial comedy was revived from the antiquated conventions of the sit-com by shows like *Broad City* (2014–19), which explored the seriality of precarity in the characters' instabilities, vulnerabilities, and desperation, mostly to find and secure work. The show was part of a cluster of what I'll chronicle as 'precarity comedies' in this time, and it incarnated many elements of this genre. Before it became a Comedy Central series, *Broad City* was an independent web series, filmed between 2009 and 2011 by stars Ilana Glazer and Abbi Jacobson. Issa Rae's HBO series *Insecure* (2016–21) followed a similar trajectory, from an original web series called *Awkward Black Girl* that Rae created and starred in from 2011–2013. These kinds of origin stories are essential to the seriality of precarity comedies: they're scrappy, determined, and won't give up. In *Broad City*, central characters Abbi and Illana are two college-educated twentysomethings who enter the "adult world" at the dawn of the financial crisis. While an older generation taught them values of hard work and paying dues for a comfortable future, Abbi and Illana see only the hope of getting by, as they look to a horizon of financial crisis and privatization, deteriorating career options and prospects of security. The show captures a vision of work life as constant juggling, frantic side-hustling, living off credit cards, family favors, and impossible debts. A stark divergence from the Dickensian world of coming of age and class ascent, this is the anti-bildung trajectory of the precarity comedy, based on the characters' non-growth and socioeconomic descent, in which they churn and churn and never get anywhere. Most of the early episodes of *Broad City* revolve around a mundane task: doing a chore, making some money, buying some weed. All to just get through the day.

While capturing so much of what the precarity comedy stands for, *Broad City* struggles to frame its comedy in these terms, especially as it digresses through the Trump era. The series eventually transforms into more of a liberal feminist narrative of self-discovery and post-Clintonite despair—in its version of jumping the shark, the shark is Hillary Clinton, in an extremely awkward cameo. But at its best, the show is what we might label avocado toast comedy: a middle finger to Australian real estate mogul Tim Garner, who argued that this generation of post-crisis adults would never become homeowners while "spending $40 a day on smashed avocados and coffees and not working."[15] Rather, to the extent that *Broad City* understands itself as a precarity comedy, it is rooted in a sense of capitalist crisis, for which avocado toast is a minor indulgence against the ideological doctrine of self-imposed austerity. This is a narrative world of taking what you can get.

Out of any of the post-financial crisis precarity comedies in the U.S., *Party Down* (2009–10) is the most relentlessly antiwork. In its dark and cringe-inducing portrait of failed or struggling actors working for a Los Angeles catering company, *Party Down* approaches work as an absurd masquerading of power relations and meaningless social interactions. Like any classically antiwork comedy, the central antagonist is the boss, Ron Donald (Ken Marino). The other antagonists are the horrible and extremely wealthy clients. Each episode tells the story of a different terrible gig, with different terrible clients: corporate retreats, fundraisers, a sweet sixteen for a film producer's daughter, an orgy, Steve Guttenberg's birthday party. Meanwhile, the critique is always subtly undermined by the will-they-won't-they plot of workplace flirtation, between Casey (Lizzy Caplan) and Henry (Adam Scott), the straight characters (both sexually and comedically) in the midst of various pathetic show business hopefuls. For the most part, Casey and Henry are heroes in the story, for their slacking, pranking, and general nonchalance toward the life of perpetual gigs and bullshit catering events. Compromising this antiwork ethic, however, is Casey's desire to make it in acting. Her seemingly more authentic ambitions are always counterposed to Ron's ideas of "success" in an era of economic crisis.

A new iteration of the precarity comedy, after the post-financial crisis era, was developing by 2016, in shows like *Atlanta* (2016–) and *High Maintenance* (2016–20). Annie McClanahan has brilliantly defined this as a shift into the "tipwork picaresque," distinct for the representation of subjects "whose working lives are defined by multiple and fragmented social relations and by temporary, uncertain, and fluid working conditions," as McClanahan explains, "characters whose stories are not so easily wrestled into more familiar narratives of development, education, and achievement."[16] Formally, the picaresque, which is a precursor to the

---

15 Sam Levin, "Millionaire Tells Millennials: If You Want a House, Stop Buying Avocado Toast," *The Guardian*, May 15, 2017, https://www.theguardian.com/lifeandstyle/2017/may/15/australian-millionaire-millennials-avocado-toast-house.
16 Annie McClanahan, "TV and Tipworkification," *Post45*, January 10, 2019, https://post45.org/2019/01/tv-and-tipworkification/.

serial, unfolds through episodes that trail or wander beside a protago-nist figure, traditionally defined as a literature of "the rogue's progress."[17] *High Maintenance* captures these picaresque qualities of post-crisis com-edies quite intricately, in its whimsical yet critical portrait of gig work in New York City, following a nameless cannabis bike delivery-person ("The Guy") through a world weathered by debt, unemployment, housing inse-curity, among other forms of disenfranchisement that have come to define today's adulthood. Unlike series like *Girls* (2012–17), which imagine this disenfranchisement through elitist visions of a post-undergraduate life phase, *High Maintenance* projects into the future a sense of everlasting uncertainty, constant risk, and occasional luck. Some episodes bring the critique of work to the foreground, while others tend to romanticize pre-carity, and the life of riding bikes and getting stoned all day, sometimes getting to meet cool people. Far more consistently than antiwork comedy, the show develops and refines the tipwork picaresque aesthetic, moving between narrative worlds and magnifying shared conditions of anxiety, longing, and uncertainty.

Among the most captivating antiwork serial narratives of this period has been *Atlanta*, in which everyday life is about things just not getting worse. Breaking even becomes the tempo of each episode, following the protagonist, decisively named "Earn" (Donald Glover), as he bounces between dead-end jobs and side hustles to provide for his ex-girlfriend, Vanessa (Zazie Beetz), and their young daughter, Lottetia. Earn is smart, well-intentioned, and frequently innovative, with each day facing a dense terrain of risk and instability: somehow paying bills and chipping in for rent, finding places to crash, avoiding cops and incrimination, meeting other family obligations, never catching a break. Throughout the show, work is everywhere, in traditional jobs, unwaged caretaking, career aspi-rations, artistic and creative work, along with the cycle of gigs, scams, and risks.

Boredom is what compels much of *Atlanta*'s antiwork comedy. A trip to jail has the boring, sterile, impersonal atmosphere of the DMV. It's not that jail isn't hellish, but it is the hellishness of the bureaucratized neoliberal state that comes out so clearly in the show's subdued brutality. In the moment, it's hellish because sleeping isn't permitted, because of the lighting and smells and discomfort of the cell, because of the paperwork and phone calls and logistics of getting out. It will continue to be hellish

---

17 See Robert Alter, *The Rogue's Progress: Studies in the Picaresque Novel* (Cambridge: Harvard University Press, 1964).

with an ongoing commitment to meetings, fees, and conditional agreements that only further establish a sense of rightlessness and perpetual criminalization. Beneath the surface of boredom is this neverendingness of getting by and surviving.

The strongest element of *Atlanta* is its titular character, the city itself. The show's labyrinthian portrait of Atlanta conjures elements of Toni Morrison's magical realist depictions of Black social death—what Sharon P. Holland describes as a world in which "there is no full embrace of the margin . . . only the chance to struggle against both a killing abstraction and a life-in-death," and where "neither choice is an appealing option."[18] Earn chases several dreams to get him out of Atlanta. When he graduated from high school, he went to Princeton briefly before dropping out. Now, years later, he's dreaming of another escape managing the rap career of his cousin Alfred (Brian Tyree Henry). Both of these dreams get him out of Atlanta, but they also both put him in closer proximity to white culture, requiring him to perform and participate in a white supremacist, false utopian fantasy of "post-racism." While the show does much to critically negate ideologies of work and anti-Blackness, in its antiwork imaginary of Atlanta there are likewise glimpses of the utopian. Part of the looming uncertainty of the series' narrative world is a sense of spontaneity and even extraterrestriality. Earn's uncle, for instance, always speaks of his pet alligator, who lives in a room in his house. Most people believe he's crazy and that the alligator is not real. Yet for much of an episode, the possibility of this alligator is ever-present. Earn and his friend Darius show up when the police are called about a domestic disturbance between the uncle and his girlfriend, and Earn maneuvers through his interaction with the police, carefully communicating that his uncle is not a threat and suffers from mental illness, holding together a sense of uneventfulness with imminent danger. As one of the show's many depictions of the police's routinized terror over Black neighborhoods, the scene is building towards a sense of escalated violence and trauma. But as they wait for the uncle, beside the police fully armed, what breaks this escalation is the alligator who emerges from the front door. The police are dumbfounded, as the uncle escapes through the back. These moments of absurdity burst into the narrative, throwing everything into disarray, carrying with them fragmentary glimpses of another world quite beautifully.

---

18 Sharon Patricia Holland, *Raising the Dead: Readings of Death and (Black) Subjectivity* (Durham: Duke University Press, 2000), 17–18.

Precarity comedies like *Atlanta* and *High Maintenance* also conceive of antiwork comedy through a stoner aesthetic. This stoniness often takes hold of the narrative, as in the case of Earn's uncle's alligator, or an episode of *High Maintenance* told from the perspective of a dog in love with his dog walker (a friend of The Guy). Most episodes of these shows feature constant weed smoking, more-or-less. In neither show is this framed as a matter of laziness or stupidity—as in nearly every stoner comedy of the decades before. As Glover has argued, in *Atlanta*, "the characters aren't smoking weed all the time because it's cool but because they have P.T.S.D.—every Black person does."[19] The show's representation of smoking weed as an aspect of everyday life isn't just non-judgmental, but political. *High Maintenance* is similarly disinterested in moral judgment. Foregrounding the commodification and circulation of marijuana, the show weaves together a stony imaginary of interconnectedness and collective experience, conjuring, at the very least, the possibilities of a non-capitalist life. These conjurings are momentary and partial, fleeting grasps at somewhere else.

In 2021, *Reservation Dogs* (created by Sterlin Harjo and Taika Waititi) brilliantly explores some of these dream-like, stony and utopian qualities of the precarity comedy, as it charts the daily lives of a group of four Indigenous teenagers—Elora, Bear, Cheese, and Willie Jack—with big plans of someday leaving their reservation in Oklahoma for California. As they chase this fantasy future in a faraway place they've never been to, they drift and wander in their community. They spend a day driving around Elora's uncle, Brownie, who's determined to sell a jar of "ancient weed," and who teaches them how to fight. They share moments of profound comradeship. They learn about each other and their ancestors. Getting to California, in other words, is never quite the point.

Troubling Nihilism in Antiwork Comedies

For far too much antiwork comedy, nihilism is the precondition. That is: access to the possibilities of antiwork are limited to anti-utopianism. And it is with this precondition that, where nihilism is abandoned, too often the comedy goes with it. In unapologetically antiwork series like *Party Down* or *The Office* (UK), the critiques of work and their rigor weaken once the plots slip into sentimentality, steering toward the territory of

---

19 Tad Friend, "Donald Glover Can't Save You," *The New Yorker*, March 5, 2018, https://www.newyorker.com/magazine/2018/03/05/donald-glover-cant-save-you.

romantic comedy, coupling off the mostly boring protagonists. The politics of antiwork comedy are not uncomplicated. Antiwork comedy is an entangled mess of shared longings: a utopian, critical negation of work, never not at odds with an anti-utopian foreclosure of post-work possibility; the crossfires between our compulsion to reproduce ourselves through work and our revolt against it in the name of our true desires. In cultivating a critical sensibility towards work, antiwork comedy often takes as its premise that There Is No Alternative.

Here, I turn to *Seinfeld* (1989–98)—one of the most popular sitcoms of all time, famously dubbed in nihilistic terms as a "show about nothing." Is *Seinfeld* antiwork? A friend, and labor historian, recently answered this question: "no, it's antiworker."[20] I liked this response; but I wondered, could both be true? While it's certainly antiworker, it's also antiboss. The characters on *Seinfeld* are ceaselessly inconvenienced by the eccentricities of seemingly defective workers—taxi drivers, waitresses, mechanics, plumbers, housecleaners, etc. Most every episode revolves, in some way, around an experience of customer dissatisfaction of some sort. At the same time, it is a world in which bosses are either evil, stupid, or otherwise inadequate to the power they hold. While the show romanticizes Jerry's job as a stand-up comedian, which ostensibly enables him to a life of almost full-time leisure, it also degrades Kramer's seemingly post-work existence and continually reinforces the joke that his lifestyle is actually impossible. Of course, in Jerry's case, what is romanticized is more specifically his state of never-quite-working—the ways in which his observational comedy as a stand-up derives from the seeming non-work activities of his everyday life. George is celebrated, but also emasculated, for his lack of ambition and constant desire to maximize his laziness (e.g., secretly napping under his desk at the office). Elaine is at her most hilarious when she finds herself beholden to one of her bosses' unbearable demands. To the extent that the series is antiwork, in this sense, it is not just antiworker, but anti-antiwork.

Still, in most ways, *Seinfeld* is not pro-work. Throughout the show's nine seasons, the world of work appears arbitrary, dysfunctional, and corrupt. None of the characters understand a career as intrinsic to happiness or fulfillment, and those who do are certainly mocked for their earnestness. The dream is for all of them to just be able to sit in the diner, all the time, and complain forever. The dream is contingent, of course,

---

20 Thanks to Zach Schwartz-Weinstein for this insight, and to Jo Aurelio Giardini for this conversation as well.

on other people still having to work. All of this comes into crisis with the moralist turn of the show's last episode, when Jerry, Elaine, George, and Kramer, are put on trial as the "New York Four" in the fictional town of Latham, Massachusetts, after breaking the newly passed "Good Samaritan Law" as they fail to help a man being mugged and instead stand around and laugh at him. Through morality, this narrative emerges from the trap the show found itself in, leading towards the finale: how to still be a "show about nothing," while fulfilling the demands of a series conclusion to culminate and emplot. The show could either, it would seem, reaffirm its nihilism, or bend to the conventions—and either way, it would fail.

Antiwork comedy certainly has the ability to "engage nihilism without succumbing to it," as television scholar Thomas Hibbs writes, but this dance with nihilism often defangs the critique at stake in the comedy.[21] Like *Seinfeld*, most nihilist comedies tend less towards critique and more towards complaint. In *Seinfeld*, if there is a *something* around which the plot orbits, despite its promise as a "show about nothing," it is complaining—and more precisely, it is the voice of dissatisfaction, animating the show's fantasy life of the perpetually not-working customers. In *Party Down*, unswervingly antiwork compared to *Seinfeld*, complaining is a way to gesture at a set of political problems, bringing the audience to the threshold of critique. At that threshold, however, the narrative world of the series begins to collapse in on itself. It hardly knows what to do outside the parameters of insincerity.

In the 2000s, the "cringe comedy" marked an important juncture for nihilist comedies. *Curb Your Enthusiasm* (2000–), as a post-*Seinfeld* meta-comedy, adapts the complaint-driven "observational comedy" of the original series into a cringe-inducing, accelerated nihilism. The cringe-effect functions through identification. I remember showing my dad an episode of *Curb Your Enthusiasm* a long time ago, and watching him squirm and put his hands in front of his eyes, muttering "No! No! No!" as Larry continued to make his situation more painfully awkward. As comedy goes, it's often more stressful than horror. Over the years I've known many to call the show unwatchable because of the cringe. At the same time, "a cringe of mutual embarrassment" produced by this comedy, as Nick Salvato claims, "has the potential to forge communities, however, fragile . . . or toxic."[22]

---

21 Thomas S. Hibbs, *Shows about Nothing: Nihilism in Popular Culture*, 2nd rev. and expanded ed. (Waco: Baylor University Press, 2012), xvii.
22 Nick Salvato, *Obstruction* (Durham: Duke University Press, 2016), 45.

While cringe comedy enacts this sense of mutual embarrassment and collectivity, it also provokes shame in different ways. In the case of *Curb*, it is a shame for which the only way out, ironically, is nihilism. In other cases of cringe comedy, the play with shame can be pedagogical, clarifying the consequences and collective implications of an individual's behavior. The brief and then briefly rebooted satirical HBO series *The Comeback* (2005, 2014) is a cringe comedy that, in its fierce takedown of Hollywood, is also empathic. As the show follows the has-been Hollywood actress Valerie Cherish (Lisa Kudrow) in her often pathetic attempts to revive her career, over and over again, through her forties and fifties, we cringe out of empathy as much as disgust for the power dynamics of Hollywood. The cringe induces shame but also a desire to destroy the entertainment industry, operating as both antiwork and antinihilistic. While I have encountered readings of *Arrested Development* (2003–6, 2018–19) along the same lines—that it is, at its core, fundamentally a story about hating the rich—I am not entirely convinced. Just as we cringe in *Arrested Development* at the mishaps of the Bluth family, certain characters have been celebrated and meme-ified for their abuse of power, as in the 'boss bitch' attitude of Lucille (Jessica Walter). Over the last two decades, cringe comedy has mutated and proliferated, in an ongoing battle with its own nihilistic tendencies.

Another variant of the nihilistic comedy that emerged in this time is what Lauren Berlant identifies as the "traumic," a "genre that milks the formal likeness of trauma and the comedic," which "draws on what's dark about the situation comedy and ludicrous in the situation tragedy."[23] The traumic focuses on "beings under pressure and disturbed by what's happened around them," Berlant explains, "[who] are usually destined not to be defeated unto death but to live with the light and heavy effects of damage, still acting, being acted upon, and trying to keep things moving, which is to say, surviving." Berlant considers these elements of the traumic in the animated comedy *BoJack Horseman* (2014–20), which brings together surrealism, antiwork nihilism, and trauma. Like a cringe comedy, *BoJack* is difficult to watch past one or two episodes at a time (generically antibinge), but rather than a shared sense of awkwardness and humiliation, it drudges up pain, often drifting into melancholy. Its central character, BoJack (a has-been actor and horse), is depressive, abusive, and

---

23 Lauren Berlant, "The Traumic: On BoJack Horseman's 'Good Damage,'" *Post45* (blog), November 22, 2020, https://post45.org/2020/11/the-traumic-on-bojack-horsemans-good-damage/.

self-destructive, and set to ruin all his relationships without any hope of healing. As Berlant emphasizes in their reading, what moves the narrative forward is not healing, but surviving with damage. And the damage may get worse.

Like *Curb Your Enthusiasm*, *BoJack* tells the story of a celebrity living off (and in the shadow of) a sit-com he did in the nineties, and similarly, it seeks to trouble and meditate on the ideological landscape of sit-coms. While the sit-com world is safe, predictable, and familiar, it is built on abuse. Throughout *BoJack*, we encounter drug addiction, sexual harassment and assault, and the exploitation of child actors as integral to the working conditions of the sit-com. Sit-coms are the lies we have been told about work and family. And sit-coms are the lies we continue to tell ourselves. At its best, *BoJack* is a study of the sit-com as this site of collective trauma, as when BoJack goes on a bender with his former co-star Sarah Lynn, who subsequently dies of a heroin overdose.

The final lesson of *BoJack* "is that there is no lesson, no story he can tell later to a friend, no joke he can make to close the moment," writes Stephanie Foote.[24] It is not the nihilism of "No Exit," but as Foote suggests, of no closure. What's most compelling about nihilist comedies, more generally, is their resistance to narrative resolution. In the world of sit-coms, resolutions are silly or cheap. Resolutions are part of the lie. Whether through shame, trauma, or sadness, these attempts to take apart the nihilism at the heart of antiwork comedy exhibit a set of political limitations, along with intense utopian longing. This is not a longing for resolution so much as a longing for a non-nihilistic conceptualization of antiwork—a way to make the critique of work thinkable without, by necessity, thwarting the capacity of comedy to help us imagine what the world could be otherwise.

Laughing at Work

Waged or unwaged, whether as a "job" or as a "labor of love," whether visibly or invisibly, people are working all the time, even when they're watching work on TV. To recognize this is incredibly dystopian—the way that, even when we think we're escaping work to experience pleasure in TV comedy, we're still inevitably never-not-working. As we recuperate from work to do more work, we are still thinking about work, dreaming about

---

24 Stephanie Foote, "No Closure," *Post45* (blog), November 23, 2020, https://post45. org/2020/11/no-closure/.

work, and making ourselves into more compliant and productive workers. Even when we try to conceive of a world outside of work, through activities that seem to be for the sake of our entertainment, we are still in a state of being *lost in work*, as Amelia Horgan describes. "[W]hen we criticise work, we often come up against fear and confusion. This fear is not merely the product of a work ethic promulgated by elites," she explains of this trap. "Given that, under capitalism, work becomes the only avenue for self-development, respect and fulfillment, this is a genuine fear of a loss of self."[25]

That watching work is what many of us do when we think we're not working seems to encapsulate so much about our shared life in the trap. Yet at the same time, what drives many TV comedies about work, however romantic or nihilistic or indistinctly, is a utopian urge to laugh at work. Much of the time, this desire is buried under so much else. There is the compulsion to work, but also to love doing it. There is the hope to find oneself in work, or to derive from work what we aren't able to discover about ourselves in any other terms. And then there are the survival tactics—just treading in this sea, doing our best to make this world feel livable, if not potentially entertaining at times. But to laugh at this world is to grasp at another one.

---

25 Horgan, *Lost in Work*, 13.

CHAPTER TWO

The Stand-Up Artist in the Age of Gigification

Gigs are nothing new to the world of jobs. Yet increasingly the gig has come to characterize our experiences of work: all the short-term contracts or freelancing, moonlighting, side hustles and "one night stands" that comprise an emergent paradigm of work-life. According to some scholars of the "sharing economy," this is an era of microentrepreneurialism, a horizon of possibility for a "generation of self-employed workers," as Arun Sundararajan postulates, to be "empowered to work whenever they want from any location and at whatever level of intensity needed to achieve their desired standard of living."[1] While microentrepreneurialism is certainly the promise of gig work, precarity is the overwhelming reality for most gig workers. In 2017, as the buzz about the gig economy was reaching its peak, the average gig worker was making less than $500 a month.[2] The median earning of Uber and Lyft drivers, for instance, is $3.37 an hour, with 30 percent of drivers actually losing money at an hourly rate in gas expenses.[3] Meanwhile, the ideological narrative of the microentrepreneur who "makes it" remains a dominant force.

Key to this ideological narrative is what Sarah Brouillette has outlined as "the mainstreaming of the figure of the artist as valorized mental laborer,"[4] oriented towards labor as "an act of self-exploration,

---

1 Arun Sundararajan, *The Sharing Economy: The End of Employment and the Rise of Crowd-Based Capitalism* (Cambridge: MIT Press, 2016), 177.
2 Abha Bhattarai, "Side Hustles Are the New Norm. Here's How Much They Really Pay," *Washington Post*, accessed December 31, 2021, https://www.washingtonpost.com/news/business/wp/2017/07/03/side-hustles-are-the-new-norm-heres-how-much-they-really-pay/.
3 "The Economics of Ride-Hailing: Driver Revenue, Expenses and Taxes," accessed December 31, 2021, https://ceepr.mit.edu/workingpaper/the-economics-of-ride-hailing-driver-revenue-expenses-and-taxes-under-revision/.
4 Sarah Brouillette, *Literature and the Creative Economy* (Stanford: Stanford University Press, 2014), 49.

self-expression, and self-realization."[5] Under the guise of artistry, conditions of precarity are romanticized and obscured as part of a creative process—a "reformulation of capitalism," Luc Boltanski and Eve Chiapello argue, "in terms of what [is] exciting, creative, protean, innovative and 'liberating.'"[6] The worker's conceptualization as artist was essential to the post-financial crisis era, instilling a new regime of work. With a vocabulary of "flexibility," "autonomy," and "self-management," this new regime became coded in terms of the worker's discipline and self-imposed austerity. Lauren Berlant points to the surfacing, in this time, of an austere imaginary of "aspirational normativity." What takes hold is a vision of a life "dedicated to moving toward the good life's normative/utopian zone but actually stuck in what we might call survival time, the time of struggling, drowning, holding on to the ledge, treading water, *not-stopping*."[7]

It was in this period that a certain cultural fascination with the stand-up comedian was also reactivated. Madison Square Garden had only sold out three times for comedians before 2009. Between 2009 and 2015, three different comedians sold out the arena multiple times.[8] From 2012 to 2015, Comedy Central's original programming nearly doubled.[9] By 2016, an internal study at Netflix determined that 63 percent of the company's subscribers had watched at least one stand-up special that year.[10] With the vast expansion of niche audiences made possible by online media platforms, more stand-ups were creating comedy specials but also signing contracts for traditional comedian-centered sitcoms. Series like *Louie, Whitney, Mulaney*, and *Difficult People* featured various "sad-com" interpretations of the figure of the stand-up, diverging from the traditional sit-com and towards more of an auteur aesthetic (as in *Louie*'s cringy homage to Woody Allen, which C.K. only further accentuated later on, with the hire of Allen's longtime editor and collaborator

5   Sarah Brouillette, "Creative Labor," *Mediations: Journal of the Marxist Literary Group* 24, no. 2 (Spring 2009), https://mediationsjournal.org/articles/creative-labor.
6   Luc Boltanski and Eve Chiapello, *The New Spirit of Capitalism* (London and New York: Verso, 2005), 324.
7   Lauren Berlant, "Nearly Utopian, Nearly Normal: Post-Fordist Affect in *La Promesse* and *Rosetta*," *Public Culture* 19, no. 2 (Spring 2007): 279, https://doi.org/10.1215/08992363-2006-036.
8   Jesse David Fox, "How the Internet and a New Generation of Superfans Helped Create the Second Comedy Boom," *Vulture*, March 30, 2015, https://www.vulture.com/2015/03/welcome-to-the-second-comedy-boom.html.
9   Fox, "How the Internet and a New Generation of Superfans Helped Create the Second Comedy Boom."
10 . Jesse David Fox, "Is Netflix Hurting Stand-Up?," *Vulture*, September 18, 2017, https://www.vulture.com/2017/09/netflix-comedy-special-domination.html.

Susan E. Morse). This time also saw a surge in documentaries about legends and well-established figures in stand-up,[11] as well as documentaries and docuseries about up-and-coming, aspirational comedians.[12] While the major networks and venues were investing more in stand-up-related content, stand-ups were also taking on microentrepreneurial ventures like web-series. Stand-ups like Jimmy Pardo, Joe Rogan, Greg Proops, Scott Aukerman, Doug Benson, Marc Maron, and Chris Hardwick began their own podcasts, long before many of us knew what podcasts were.[13] Aukerman—who now often, always self-mockingly, refers to himself as one of the heads on "Mount Podcast"—founded the *Earwolf* comedy podcasting network with Jeff Ullrich in 2010, which has produced over one hundred podcast series since. Hardwick, similarly, launched *The Nerdist Industries* based on his initial podcast. Maron began his show out of his garage, with only one sponsor, in an origin story that conjures some of the tropes and fantasies of seventies-era tech renegades and entrepreneurs. The list goes on, and then it goes on some more.

At the heart of this coincidence of financial crisis and comedy boom is a particular fetishization of the *stand-up artist*, an entrepreneurial protagonist in the world of creative aspiration, paying dues, and hard-earned self-actualization. As artist, that is, the stand-up comedian became the paradigmatic worker to this transforming world of work, an era which Annie McClanahan defines in terms of heightened "tipworkification." As McClanahan suggests, tipworkification captures the reduction of labor costs for service-industry employers, but also "yokes these changes in the wage to the increased importance of gigwork." The low wages of tipwork, she speculates, "have arguably provided the gig economy with a population of workers willing to take on second or third jobs doing things like driving for Lyft," while gigwork "borrows many of the formal features of tipwork, including the lack of basic workplace protections and job security."[14]

---

11   See, for example, *Richard Pryor: Omit the Logic, Dying Laughing, When Stand Up Stood Out, Why We Laugh: Black Comedians on Black Comedy, Why We Laugh: Funny Women, The Unbookables, I Am Comic, I Am Road Comic, Conan O'Brien Can't Stop, Knock Knock, It's Tig Notaro, Joan Rivers: A Piece of Work, American: The Bill Hicks Story, Brand: A Second Coming, Tig, Pauly Shore Stands Alone*, etc.

12   *The Comedy Garage, Dying to Do Letterman, Alone Up There, Judy Toll, The Funniest Woman You've Never Heard Of*, etc.

13   Comedy podcasting remains dominated by white men, who represent a kind of macho-entrepreneurialism, and reflect the shock-jocking which many of these comedians brought with them from traditional radio. I discuss some queer and femme-centered podcasts that have diverged from these trends in Chapter 8.

14   Annie McClanahan, "TV and Tipworkification." *Post45*, January 10, 2019, https://post45.org/2019/01/tv-and-tipworkification/.

To the cultural imaginary of tipworkification, the stand-up comedian comes to embody this prevailing work ethic—a key feature of which is an obscuring of work as artistry. This work ethic of the stand-up artist is not just a matter of hiding their status as worker from the audience for the sake of customer satisfaction, but a matter of repressing their own self-understanding as worker in the process.

In the stand-up industry, there is a shared principle of "working for the laughs." The aim is generally to provoke laughter every fifteen seconds on stage.[15] Laughter needs momentum. And maintaining the laughter, if it ever starts, involves a lot of adrenaline. Bombing is a formative experience that never ends—even successful stand-ups face this possibility with every performance. The audience *has* to laugh. "It doesn't matter how long you've been doing stand-up comedy," stand-up international mega-star Russell Peters explains, "you are never exempt from a bad night. Never. It doesn't matter who you are. That's the beauty of comedy is that you're not guaranteed to kill."[16] Certainly audiences will give some comedians more of a chance than others—they come to see headliners, for the most part, but may have little interest in the opener, tasked with "warming up the crowd." Road comics speak of frequent challenges not only in "working for the laughs," but in getting their audience's attention in the first place, as they compete with the sports game that's been muted on the television sets—or even worse, replace the entertainment of the game when it's turned off.

Working for the laughs involves enduring awkward silences—or, for more effective stand-ups, learning to joke about or with the silence—but also facing the nightly possibility of hecklers. Some stand-up comedians speak of getting heckled as a form of initiation. Some take pride in heckling back and incorporating the heckler into their act. To deflect a heckler entails a particular craftsmanship, which some can flaunt. Perhaps a comedian will reach a career point where hecklers are booed or even removed by security, but there is never in a comedian's career a point where the threat of heckling goes away. And nothing is off-limits for the heckler. Sexual harassment, racist hate speech, body-shaming, threats of violence—all of this comes with the territory of a stand-up gig.

---

15 Of course, the more "authentic" the comedian, the less they are beholden to this general rule. I'll get to this in Chapter 4.

16 Lloyd Stanton, *Dying Laughing* (Gravitas, 2017), https://catalog.pcpls.org/kanopy/kan1475657.

In the world of stand-up, it's just the comedian against the world. There are no prospects of safety, just ways to make the system work for you, one performance at a time, working for the laughs. And how to make it work, for you, is what at least the idea of the stand-up exemplifies for contemporary workers.

As an "art form," stand-up operates, indistinctly, within the customer service industry, manifesting this logic of tipwork. Since the fifties, most stand-up has been performed in bars or clubs, and comedy is a way of putting customers in their seats—and ideally, keeping them there. For club owners, most of the revenues come from alcohol sales. While comedians are working for the laughs, the servers are working for the tips. And through the course of the night, as customers drink more, they become more likely to engage in a variety of forms of harassment. In the bar and restaurant industry, there are more sexual harassment claims filed than in any other industry, with 90 percent of women and 70 percent of men reportedly experiencing some form of sexual harassment in their workplace.[17] Some customers even believe that they are entitled to harass, and explicitly state the right to harass as part of what they're paying for. Facing conditions of transmisogyny, not just from customers but a hypermasculine workforce, trans rights activist and bartender Lucky Michaels, a nonbinary trans woman, reflects that in over twenty years working in the industry, "most of the trans people that I find [are] absolutely in the closet, stealth because it's a really toxic environment for people in general."[18] Bar and restaurant workers find themselves endlessly calculating "the tipping equation," as journalists Catrin Einhorn and Rachel Abrams explain: "each shift comes with questions that do not apply to millions of other workers around the country: How much money will I make, and how much will I tolerate to make it?"[19] In the stand-up industry, similarly, sexual harassment is pervasive. Stand-up Kate Smurthwaite recalls being assaulted by a promoter in the kitchen before a performance, and at another club, "guys getting their genitals out and rubbing them against

---

17 See Stefanie K. Johnson and Juan M. Madera, "Sexual Harassment Is Pervasive in the Restaurant Industry. Here's What Needs to Change," *Harvard Business Review*, January 18, 2018, https://hbr.org/2018/01/sexual-harassment-is-pervasive-in-the-restaurant-industry-heres-what-needs-to-change.

18 Jaya Saxena, "For Trans People in the Service Industry, Discrimination Is an Unfortunate Reality of the Job," *Eater*, June 29, 2020, https://www.eater.com/2020/6/29/21304536/trans-workers-struggle-with-discrimination-scotus-ruling.

19 Rachel Abrams and Catrin Einhorn, "The Tipping Equation," *The New York Times*, March 11, 2018, https://www.nytimes.com/interactive/2018/03/11/business/tipping-sexual-harassment.html.

me[.]"[20] Stories like this have long been known as common place, even unremarkable.

As a figure of tipworkification, the stand-up artist of this period is conceived as much through failures as aspirations—a far cry from the *Seinfeld*esque vision of the successful stand-up comedian who works weekends and spends the rest of the time in a diner with friends or at home eating cereal. The HBO series *Crashing*, for instance, is comedian and podcaster Pete Holmes's semi-autobiographical portrayal of his early years in stand-up, during which he was fighting to get stage time and living rent-free by crashing on peoples' couches (hence the title), sometimes staying with well-established comedians who extend life wisdom and career tips. Following what reviewer David Sims calls "a confusing slog of a career,"[21] *Crashing* is still, ultimately, about *becoming*, exploring the world of comedy as a system of "doing your time" and "paying your dues," all the while conjuring a myth of what George Morgan and Pariece Nelligan call the "self-assembled creative career."[22] Part of this process of self-assembly, as the series depicts, is the very unglamorous and unpaid gig of "barking." "Barking" is a system of promotion for comedy clubs, in which comedians earn stage time with the number of people they get through the door, based on long hours on the street handing out flyers and making conversation with strangers. This is literally paying to be able to work. While *Crashing* uncovers some of the most exploitative and degrading elements of stand-up (barking, hecklers, road gigs), the series does little in the way of questioning. It instead idealizes comedy as a world of self-discovery. Despite its emphasis on the low-points in a comic's career, the series presupposes Holmes's ascendance at a meta-level, with the HBO series being undoubtedly a career high-point for any comic (especially with no acting experience and, let's be honest, little in the way of acting talent). The show plays up this metanarrative, crafting in its depiction of Holmes's failures a sense of necessity, tinged with social Darwinism. Even though the show is uninterested in success, success is nevertheless its precondition—a safe

---

20 Rachael Healy, "'I've Had Men Rub Their Genitals against Me': Female Comedians on Extreme Sexism in Standup," *The Guardian*, August 5, 2020, sec. Stage, https://www.theguardian.com/stage/2020/aug/05/creepy-uncomfortable-sexism-harassment-assault-faced-by-female-standups.

21 David Sims, "What 'Crashing' Got Right About Stand-Up," *The Atlantic*, April 10, 2017, https://www.theatlantic.com/entertainment/archive/2017/04/hbo-crashing-season-one-finale-review/522498/.

22 George Morgan and Pariece Nelligan, *The Creativity Hoax: Precarious Work in the Gig Economy.* (London: Anthem Press, 2018), 43.

place from which to meditate on the struggles and corruption encountered in the journey of "making it."

For stand-ups, the status of "working comic" is achieved through years of enforced amateurism. Many stand-ups never become working comedians. Maybe they'll earn as much as $100 a night, but life without a day job of some sort is rare. Most of today's stand-up comedy workers juggle part-time employment and odd jobs to afford their stage time, if they can even get it. Those who are well-known enough can market themselves on Cameo, the personalized video shout-out website and app launched in 2017, where comedians offer customized messages or online chats for as little as $6. These are "comedy workers" as in their comedy is acknowledged as work, but as therein *not-yet-art*. Comedy tours are a rite of passage, while only some of these gigs amount to much more than free food and a motel room with maybe a performer's rate at the bar. Road comics often share motel rooms, sleep on the couch of a backroom at the club, or during the ten-hour drive between gigs. And day jobs are a familiar source of comedy material—comedy workers have always relied on short-term employment, often with merely the hope of breaking even on the rest.

The Workers' Struggle at the Heart of Stand-Up's "Golden Era"

An important aspect of the post-financial crisis comedy boom was a historical revision of the mid-seventies "golden era" in stand-up, a myth that saturates so many comedian memoirs and documentaries from the 2010s. Richard Zoglin's *Comedy at the Edge: How Stand-up in the 1970s Changed America*, Kliph Nesteroff's *The Comedians: Drunks, Thieves, Scoundrels, and the History of American Comedy*, Yael Kohen's *We Killed: The Rise of Women in American Comedy* are among the many popular books written about this romantic period from the vantage of 2008–2016. In 2009, William Knoedelseder published *I'm Dying Up Here*, a best-selling account of this "golden era," at the center of which is an attempt to re-narrate the most pivotal labor struggle in comedy history. Later made into a brief TV series on ShowTime, *I'm Dying Up Here* is a politically fraught, often reactionary account of stand-up history.

Grounded primarily in the Los Angeles scene, Knoedelseder's narrative takes its focus on the Comedy Store, the Sunset district club which continues to thrive, and which started the careers of so many iconic stand-ups. The Comedy Store began in 1972, the same year that *The Tonight Show* moved from New York to Los Angeles. By the mid-seventies the club became known as a pipeline to Johnny Carson. Following the ascent of club regular Freddie Prinze in 1973, as Knoedelseder writes, "the Comedy Store [was] on every comic's map and created a new equation in their heads: One set at the Comedy Store plus one appearance on Carson equals the whole world."[23] Talent agents were in the audience every night, looking to sign new comedians.

Back in the mid-seventies, the Comedy Store was packed with actual starving artists. Comedians performing at the club counted the buffet of olives and maraschino cherries as a consistent source of sustenance. Ambitious comedians from all over the country were moving to Los Angeles to live out of their cars, sublet closets, or share rooms with the hope to get some stage time. Every Monday, fledgling comedians would line up on the street for what was called "potluck night"—a try-out for new talent, in front of club owner and comedy legend Mitzi Shore (and yes, mother of Pauly).

Mitzi Shore was never a comedian, nor was that ever her plan. In August of 1974, she became the owner of the Comedy Store as part of her divorce settlement from previous owner and comic Sammy Shore, to whom she'd been married since 1950. Two years before their divorce, and soon after the club opened, Sammy Shore began to feel overwhelmed by the business—or so the story goes. Knowing that his wife was fascinated by comedians, he asked her to manage the club while he did some shows in Las Vegas. "She said okay with no visible excitement," Knoedelseder writes, "but once he was gone, she jumped on the opportunity"[24]:

> She turned her attention first to the growing number of young comics who'd been coming in night after night and sitting in the back hoping to get on. Under Sammy's whoever's-famous-goes-first rule, they rarely got a chance. But Mitzi saw potential in the youngsters, both as performers and as a labor pool.[25]

As comedian Paul Mooney joked, Sammy Shore's absence at the Comedy Store was "the best thing that ever happened to comedy in Los

23 William Knoedelseder, *I'm Dying Up Here: Heartbreak and High Times in Stand-Up Comedy's Golden Era* (New York: Hachette, 2009), 35.
24 Knoedelseder, *I'm Dying Up Here*, 36.
25 Knoedelseder, *I'm Dying Up Here*, 36.

Angeles."[26] By the time her divorce from Sammy was finalized, Mitzi had developed a new philosophy of management for the club, based on her own distinct theory of comedy. The club, she insisted, had to be envisioned from thereon as "part college and part artist colony."[27]

Shore was known for a frequent "inspiring oration" to new comedians in the club, as Knoedelseder recounts: "This is a college," she would tell them, "I started this for you."[28] Rather than wages, the Comedy Store offered what she claimed to be a "curriculum that allowed young comedians to develop their art."[29] The process began in the amateur potluck nights, then graduated to the regular lineup, with the promise of eventually gaining headliner status as performers. The club became known for Shore's "door guy system," which was understood as something like an apprenticeship for hopeful comedians. Others were assigned with janitorial tasks or answering phones—or whatever else Shore had in mind, including personal errands. In comedian-turned-filmmaker Mike Binder's docuseries *The Comedy Store*, a long list of comedians remember their start through this "system," getting paid little to nothing.[30] Fancying herself as the "head of faculty and dean of students," as Knoedelseder writes, Shore took personal offense when comedians asked for compensation. While headliners got paid, at varying rates, the rest of the comedians were continually reminded by Shore of their status as "students." "They don't deserve to be paid," Shore told comedian Tom Dreesen, "This is a showcase. This is a college."[31]

Shore's supposedly *pedagogical* philosophy of management resembles so much of the post-crisis labor paradigm, from which Comedy Store was re-cast in such romantic terms. Especially in the creative economy, "companies seek to harvest the creative bounty by camouflaging the workplace," as George Morgan and Pariece Nelligan suggest.[32] This camouflaging is most prevalent in the tech "campuses" of Silicon Valley, where CEOs attempt to "recreate both the anarchic spirit of radical experimentation and the ludic aspects of the undergraduate environment."[33] Through a

26 Kliph Nesteroff, *The Comedians: Drunks, Thieves, Scoundrels, and the History of American Comedy* (New York: Grove Press, 2015), 284.
27 Knoedelseder, *I'm Dying Up Here*, 149.
28 Knoedelseder, *I'm Dying Up Here*. 156.
29 Knoedelseder, *I'm Dying Up Here*, 89.
30 Mike Binder, "The Comedy Store" (Showtime, November 1, 2020), https://www.sho.com/the-comedy-store.
31 Nesteroff, *The Comedians*, 307.
32 Morgan and Nelligan, *The Creativity Hoax*, 119.
33 Morgan and Nelligan, *The Creativity Hoax*, 119.

logic of apprenticeship, workers are figured as artists or students as a premise for extracting free labor. In his 2012 book *Intern Nation*, Ross Perlin probes the internship industry boom of this post-crisis paradigm of work, in which the figure of the intern functioned as "a kind of smoke-screen, more brand than job description, lumping together an explosion of intermittent and precarious roles we might otherwise call volunteer, temp, summer job, and so on."[34] In the creative economy and beyond, this internship boom took place "at the nexus of transformations in higher education and the workplace,"[35] muddling the boundaries of worker and student.

Many comedians have attested to the "learning experience" of working for the Comedy Store. The legacy of the club is filled with mentor figures, starting with Richard Pryor. Knoedelseder portrays Pryor as the "emeritus professor" of the Comedy Store, taking residence at the club sometimes spontaneously, staying late after hours and offering feedback to aspiring comedians.[36] "A Pryor appearance," he writes, "had the frenzied feel of a heavyweight title fight in Vegas, with lines stretching around the block as tourists and celebrities jostled for the fewer than two hundred seats per show."[37] It was by the late seventies that Pryor "became the teacher from whom everyone else learned," as Scott Saul suggests in his biography *Becoming Richard Pryor*.[38] While many legends have performed and workshopped at a host of other clubs, what was distinctive to the Comedy Store, especially in the seventies, was this ethos of mentorship. Through the decades, comedians who worked the club spoke of various teacher-figures, but it all began with Pryor.

As a result of her exclusive deal with Pryor, Shore made enough money to put $50,000 into a new showroom with 450 seats. Much of the construction and painting was done by Shore's in-house labor force of aspiring comedians. Shore also bought several condos to house headliner comedians, in town to perform in the newly established

---

34 Ross Perlin, *Intern Nation: Earning Nothing and Learning Little in the Brave New Economy*, rev. ed. (New York: Verso, 2012), xi.

35 Perlin, *Intern Nation*, xi.

36 As Pryor biographers David and Joe Henry write, "anytime Richard wanted to wood-shed new material, all he had to do was let Mitzi know and she would clear the decks for as many nights or weeks as he wanted." David Henry and Joe Henry, *Furious Cool: Richard Pryor and the World That Made Him* (Chapel Hill: Algonquin Books of Chapel Hill, 2013), 161.

37 Knoedelseder, *I'm Dying Up Here*, 88.

38 Scott Saul, *Becoming Richard Pryor* (New York: Harper-Collins, 2014), xvi.

Main Room. It's estimated that during this time she was making about $100,000 a week.[39]

By the late seventies, Shore's managerial style was brewing tensions in the stand-up community. As comedian-turned-author Kliph Nesteroff recalls, comedians couldn't understand Shore's system: "They paid the waiters, they paid the waitresses, they paid the valet, they paid the guy who cleaned toilets. They don't pay the comedians?"[40] While Shore kept insisting that the club was a "college," comedians like Bill Kirchenbauer became more vocal about their outrage. "Tell me what college charges people to come in and watch students," Kirchenbauer jokes in an interview with Nesteroff.[41] By the end of 1978, comedians started secretly meeting and discussing their struggles. So many were working temp or part-time jobs in the day, and then spending every night working for free at the club. They'd seen a few shooting stars who'd launched from the club stage into multi-million dollar contracts, but mostly talented peers would burn out and walk away from their dreams, or much worse, were lost in some way to substance abuse. All the while Shore was paying for ambitious remodeling projects, real estate deals, and vast supplies of cocaine and other high-end drugs. Some of them had already spoken up to Shore about their grievances. One New Year's Eve—usually the most high-earning night of the year for clubs, with revenues from the bar—Dreesen ran into an up-and-coming comedian who'd just finished a set at the Store. The comedian killed that night on stage, but was asking around for $5 for breakfast. "I told Mitzi that story," Dreesen remembered, "and she said 'Well, he should get a goddam job.' I said, 'Mitzi, he has a job. He worked for you on New Year's Eve.'"[42] From the privacy of secret meetings, outside the club, stories like this were circulating more rapidly—and comedians were beginning to realize their power collectively. Soon they were discussing the possibility of a strike.

In the early months of 1979, unwaged workers from the Comedy Store formed the CFC (Comedians For Compensation). Their meetings were chaotic, filled with heavy drinking, joking around, and cocaine breaks in the bathroom. Jay Leno "was behaving like a hyperactive child: jumping up and down, being funny and distracting," David Letterman

---

39 Binder, "The Comedy Store."
40 Nesteroff, *The Comedians*, 307.
41 Nesteroff, *The Comedians*, 307.
42 Richard Zoglin, "The First Comedy Strike," *Time*, February 4, 2008, http://content. time.com/time/arts/article/0,8599,1709866,00.html.

recalls of his later nemesis, "to the point where everybody sort of thought, well, maybe we shouldn't tell Jay about the next meeting."[43] Dreesen, taking a more serious attitude than some of the other well-established regulars, assumed a leadership role. Soon he began meeting and negotiating with Shore, but she refused to compromise. Her lawyers assured her that a strike would be illegitimate. The comedians were not, technically, her employees. They were free agents. Ultimately, however, this made little difference, as they could still stage a walk-out.

The picket line formed on March 27th. By then, the CFC had 137 members, including some of the most prominent regulars at the club.[44] News of the "comedy strike" made national headlines over the following weeks, and Carson brought it up several times on *The Tonight Show*. Towards the end of the strike, Carson asked guest Buddy Hackett what he thought about the labor struggles: "The way it looks to me is, if you've got a place where you can get up and do your stuff—where you can learn your craft, especially with an audience," Hackett explains, "because if you do it in front of a mirror, you don't get much reaction."[45]

The night before the strike began, Letterman guest hosted *The Tonight Show*, with rave reviews. The next night, when Shore drove up to the club and saw the picket line of fifty-nine comedians surrounding the parking lot, it was supposedly the sight of Letterman among the strikers that most upset her.[46] She felt personally betrayed. In the weeks to come, she continued to drum up support from loyalists willing to cross the picket line. Garry Shandling, Howie Mandel, Mike Binder, Argus Hamilton, Lois Bromfield, David Tyree, Ollie Joe Prater, Alan Bursky, Allan Stephan, and Frank Carrasquillo were among the nineteen scab-comedians willing to prove their loyalty. In that time, the atmosphere of the club became more and more toxic. Shore sent some of the tough guys among her loyalists to harass Elayne Boosler, a prominent member of CFC leadership and one of the only women working the club at the time. Shore's loyalists then beat up one of the strikers—a young gay comedian, who could be made an example of.[47] It's also speculated that one of the picket-crossing comedians threw a Molotov cocktail at the roof of the Improv, the Comedy Store's main competitor in

43 Zoglin, "The First Comedy Strike."
44 Knoedelseder, *I'm Dying Up Here*, 232.
45 "The Tonight Show" (NBC, May 8, 1979).
46 Nesteroff, *The Comedians*, 306.
47 Nesteroff, *The Comedians*, 307.

Los Angeles, burning half the building.[48] The striking comedians were starting to panic.

By the sixth week of the strike, the CFC was getting support from the Screen Actors Guild, along with high-profile comedians (Comedy Store emeriti like Pryor and Carlin, as well as legends like Bob Hope). There were a number of sympathetic news pieces. But the panic among the comedians was not subsiding. One night, about fifty members met before joining the picket line. Shore had sent comedian Biff Manard to the meeting to speak on her behalf. As Dreesen recalls, Manard "basically said, comedians don't need to be paid because they're artists, and artists don't need to be paid."[49] Manard had little support in the room and left the meeting in a rage. Soon after that, once everyone had congregated outside the club, Manard drove his car into the picket line, hitting Jay Leno. While Leno was hardly injured, the commotion brought the strike to a fever pitch. People were screaming, an ambulance was called, and the crowd was talking about Manard working as Shore's henchman. It was soon after that when Shore called Dreesen up to her office in the club. They were both sick of the strike, Dreesen explains, and they worried about what would happen if it kept going. That night they called a lawyer and hashed out a compromise into the morning hours.

A deal was finalized after three days. "Against my better judgment," Shore told the *Los Angeles Times*, "I have conceded to pay the comics in the Original Room. It is my third and final offer to them."[50] With the exception of predetermined amateur nights, comedians would be paid twenty-five dollars per show. In 2003, Shore told the Los Angeles Times "I won the strike, but I made it that they won," adding, "I was like Ruth, being stoned to death. I didn't deserve what they did to me."[51]

Through the course of the eighties, the stakes of the strike were steadily reduced to tales of interpersonal conflicts and differing managerial styles by many comedians. "Everybody always has a nasty thing to say about her," comedian Eleanor Kerrigan remarks of Shore's reputation in the years since. "But if it was a man, they'd be like, 'oh he's a great businessman.'"[52] Undoubtedly, this is true—the macho environment among comedians certainly led to Shore, the proto-boss bitch, being caricatured

48 Nesteroff, *The Comedians*, 307.
49 Binder, "The Comedy Store," October 11, 2020.
50 Knoedelseder, *I'm Dying Up Here*, 211.
51 Knoedelseder, *I'm Dying Up Here*, 267.
52 Binder, "The Comedy Store," October 11, 2020.

in misogynist and derogatory ways, having little to do with her principles of management but her seemingly unearned status in the stand-up world. And perhaps these principles would not have been resisted and organized against if Shore had not been a novice club owner, inheriting the business from her ex-husband, after decades of life as a homemaker. All the same, to consolidate all of the political struggle and ideological stakes of the strike into a narrative of Shore's incompetence or the comedians' chauvinism misses the point entirely.

With the resurgent interest in stand-up history in recent years, the labor struggles of 1979 have been politically diffused by narratives like Knoedelseder's *I'm Dying Up Here*. While the strike is certainly pivotal in Knoedelseder's historical account of a "golden era," it marks the end of an age of supposed innocence in the "art" of stand-up. But the countercultural energies of stand-up comedy had already become marketized. It was right around this time that Caroline Hirsch, owner of the New York club, Caroline's, famously predicted that comedy would be "the rock of the 80's."[53] Hundreds of comedy clubs popped up all over the U.S., creating a nationwide circuit of road comics and headliners.[54] This was the era of blockbuster comedians like Jerry Seinfeld, Eddie Murphy, Robin Williams, Andrew "Dice" Clay and Roseanne Barr. The drug scene at many comedy clubs was bleaker than ever, with notorious substance abusers like Sam Kinison dominating the stage at the Comedy Store with reckless and sometimes dangerous behavior. And yet the "toxic" atmosphere recounted by many comedians performing at the Comedy Store in that time is consistently attributed to the strike, and the bad blood and turmoil in the years to follow.

Central to the mythology of the strike is the suicide of comedian Steve Lubetkin. In the weeks after the strike, as comedians were going back to work the stages at the Comedy Store, Lubetkin complained that Shore was retaliating against him. He wasn't getting any stage time, and was visibly distraught, concerning some of those around him. But Shore continued to give him the cold shoulder, claiming that he was taking it all too personally. On June 1, Lubetkin checked into a room in the Continental Hyatt next door to the club and jumped to his death from the fourteenth

---

53   Stephen Holden, "The Serious Business of Comedy Clubs," *The New York Times*, June 12, 1992, https://www.nytimes.com/1992/06/12/arts/the-serious-business-of-comedy-clubs.html.
54   Jason Zinoman, "Comedy Is Booming. I Can't Wait for the Bust.," *The New York Times*, November 22, 2017, https://www.nytimes.com/2017/11/22/arts/television/comedy-is-booming-i-cant-wait-for-the-bust.html.

floor. In his suicide note, he wrote "My name is Steve Lubetkin. I used to work at The Comedy Store." Based on Lubetkin's suicide note and behavior during the last weeks of his life, his death was certainly political. Comedians who accused Shore of retaliating against Lubetkin, however, were retaliated against themselves, scorned for supposed opportunism. In Mike Binder's 2020 docuseries on the Store, numerous comedians dismiss the political significance of Lubetkin's suicide, challenging his claims of retaliation and putting forth a more pathologically-driven account of his demise.

The strike also gets caught up in other mythologies, like that of the "late night wars" of the nineties.[55] Having grown up watching late night talk shows in the nineties, it's hard for me to fathom the comedy strike, when not-yet-rivals Letterman and Leno were not only friends, but comrades at the picket line, standing up to management. In that nineties late night world the culture of comedy had a far different character—it was hyper-competitive and hyper-individualistic, populated by narcissists and adrenaline junkies chasing the spotlight, hoping to land a sit-com or a talk show, whatever the corporate world could offer. The strike and the many stories surrounding it open up questions about what happens when comedians act in solidarity—how they practice their comedy, and how they theorize it. The strike was a critical juncture in comedy history, the nature of which extends far beyond the scope of any individual rivalries.

Revising this history has been essential to the post-financial crisis comedy boom, its ideology of work and dream of the art of stand-up. More than ending an age of innocence, as some have claimed, the strike was the last gasp of something else. Another world of comedy seemed, however briefly, quite possible at the picket line.

It was never just a matter of making gas money or paying for a breakfast after the show. What gets lost in the historical imaginary of late seventies stand-up is the way in which comedians found themselves in a double-bind: were they to recognize their comedy as labor, would that mean denying their comedy as art? Throughout the various conflicts of the strike, this was the false choice posed to the strikers. It was through this collective organizing that the strikers could pull back the façade of a "college" and "workshop space," stop questioning their dedication as artists or students, and really see themselves as workers.

---

55 Much of this mythology is chronicled by author Bill Carter in the 1994 book *The Late Shift*—and revisited in his 2010 sequel *The War for Late Night*.

Road Comics of the University System

> "I'm teaching four classes across two universities this
> semester. It's the adjunct version of an Uber driver hitting
> the max hours and switching over to Lyft."
> —my friend Dakota

Like comedy, teaching is an art that we only know through its commodification, and all the wretchedness that goes along with that. In the post-financial crisis university system, the era of tipworkification has been one of adjunctification: part-time and contingent teaching labor, comprising the majority of undergraduate education today. In the U.S., privatization measures in the university system were dramatic in 2009–2010, resulting in significant tuition increases, mass layoffs, and a greater reliance on short-term academic labor that has only escalated in the years since. As of 2018, approximately 73 percent of all faculty positions in the U.S. were nontenure positions.[56] A more recent study of adjuncts found that nearly a third earned less than $25,000 a year, with another third making less than $50,000.[57] Besides teaching, many adjuncts can only get by with other sources of employment—especially since, no longer in graduate school, they must now pay off massive student debt. Among the adjuncts I know there are people who have worked on the side as baristas, personal assistants, sex workers, short order cooks, translators, bartenders, receptionists, ghost writers, dog walkers, drug dealers, babysitters, editors, housecleaners, waiters, farm stand workers, Lyft and Uber drivers, bakers, eldercare workers, marijuana trim workers, bike messengers, housesitters, DoorDash and Instacart deliverers, strippers, and more.

While I was finishing my PhD, not-yet-adjunctified, I watched as some of the smartest, most high-functioning and professionalized of my peers encountered rejection after rejection for tenure-track jobs. They'd withstand this by telling themselves it was just a matter of building up the resume with more bullet points for next year—academic publications

---

56 Data from AAUP (American Association of University Professors), cited by
Colleen Flaherty, "A Non-Tenure-Track Profession?," *Inside Higher Ed*, October 12, 2018,
https://www.insidehighered.com/news/2018/10/12/about-three-quarters-all-faculty-
positions-are-tenure-track-according-new-aaup.
57 Colleen Flaherty, "Barely Getting By," *Inside Higher Ed*, April
20, 2020, https://www.insidehighered.com/news/2020/04/20/
new-report-says-many-adjuncts-make-less-3500-course-and-25000-year.

(never paid) and conferences (which they'd mostly pay to attend)—while cobbling together teaching gigs at different universities and colleges across the Bay Area. By now, most adjuncts I know speak of tenure as a joke.

Many adjuncts teach at multiple schools, often located hours away from each other. They lead a life of endless highways, power naps, disorientation, and meals from vending machines. At some point, it occurred to me that adjuncts are the road comics of the university system: traveling sometimes great distances from campus to campus as road comics do between clubs, performing their material for an hour at a time. This epiphany probably came during a long chat with Jo, one of my closest friends. In her first semester of adjuncting, Jo taught five classes at three different schools. She was teaching in the classroom 30 hours a week, and driving 30 hours a week. On weekends, we'd do our grading together, and she'd tell me some of her stories from the road and the classroom, always hilarious. Missed exits on the freeway, living off of turkey jerky and Diet Pepsi, forgetting which readings were assigned for different classes— being able to laugh about it seemed like an important relief.

Like any road comic, the typical adjunct got into teaching because, at some point, the idea of the job captured their imagination. But somewhere along the way, for most who pursue it, the dream of teaching gets clouded by the realities of the work—while many of us would be happy to teach a few classes a year, the lucky of us are teaching 3–4 classes per term, if not more, to be able to make monthly payments. At the same time, there are always reminders of how it all started. Teachers can always bomb, but the best can avoid it for the most part and spark an energy so strong for groups of people who've gathered, however willingly, to think about something together. In either case, there's potentially a lot of adrenaline pumping through your veins.

When I started teaching, I was assigned to an upper division Literature course as a graduate student teaching assistant. I was twenty-three, and very nervous. Throwing up before class was a frequent occurrence. I'd never spoken in front of a crowd that big before. Suddenly I was doing this for an hour and a half. I could feel the eyes of each student on every inch of my body most of the time. I struggled to breathe. I had no idea what I was doing and my anxiety ran the show. Eventually, as I was assured would happen by many, I got used to it—but the pressures never fully went away.

As some have noted, what we are seeing today in universities is a paradigm of "yelpified" pedagogy, in which students are positioned as customers in relation to their teachers, who have little to no job security.

For adjuncts, especially when working for a university or college for the first time, there can be a lot of pressure to please the students, in order to avoid any complaints that might impact the prospect of getting rehired. Much of the anxiety is fixated on the student evaluation, a survey taken in the last week of the term (right before final exams), which goes on the instructor's teaching record. I've known adjuncts who bring home-baked goods or buy donuts for the last day of class, right before students fill out evaluations. I know an adjunct who brings a bag of candy to every class, not just for special occasions, but throughout the term. When I substituted for him a few years ago, his students asked me at the beginning of the class, "where's the candy?" and I had no idea. I say this without judgment. The flat-out bribery came from a sense of fear and desperation. The candy should never have felt necessary. But it does.

The sound of a snore in a classroom, I assume, feels something like the sound of a "boo" in a comedy club. When you're teaching a college seminar at 8AM on a Monday, you become familiar with this sound. I've been teaching this timeslot for years, and if I didn't drink an inordinate amount of coffee before each class meeting, I'd be struggling myself. Back when I dreamt of one day teaching at a university, I could never have anticipated how much of my lesson-planning would be focused on just keeping everyone in the room awake. But at 8AM, this is a high priority. Students stay up all night studying, and whatever else, in dorms that never seem to have a quiet hour. When someone falls asleep in class, the class discussion is unavoidably derailed. We can pretend it's not happening, which is its own little game, or someone can nudge the person, and we'll have to all figure out how to move past it, sometimes with a slight chuckle or maybe a joking aside. I've known of professors who wake up sleeping students, sometimes in traumatic ways (like slamming a book shut in front of them)—but of course those professors are tenured, and from the position of being securely employed, are far less concerned about their latest student grievances.[58] Mostly, when I look out to a classroom of drowsy students doing their best to stay awake and care about whatever we're supposed to be discussing that day, while the world feels like it won't stop ending, I find myself trying to be as entertaining as possible. I'll move around the room, and lock eyes with different students when I'm talking. I'll play music during the passing period. I'll joke around.

---

58 Even so, as a tenured friend reminds me, there is an anxiety about course evaluations —of being blamed, for example, for the declining humanities enrollments that will eventually close their departments.

While students submit their evaluations at the end of the quarter, they also write about their instructors online. A friend who teaches in my department often sends me screenshots of things students are saying about us on Reddit—there was a long thread, for instance, speculating about which instructors were going to strike and which were going to scab. On RateMyProfessor, the top descriptors of my profile are currently "inspirational," "caring," and "hilarious." There are thumbs ups and thumbs downs and I'm ranked for quality and difficulty—my classes are like any movie on RottenTomatoes. Before RateMyProfessor took down this feature, I received chili peppers from students ranking my "hotness"; elsewhere on the internet, I've read harsh criticism of my choice of sweaters and shoes, as well as commentary about the way I smell and the tenor of my voice. It's easy to get into the mentality that your students are your customers (and also your harshest critics)—and it's easy for students to get into this mentality too. Our dynamic has been framed by the university, inescapably, as a customer-service relationship, beginning with the online shopping experience of placing classes into a shopping cart icon when they enroll. Too many of my students are hemorrhaging out money, taking on student loans, and looking onto a future of endless debt. What has brought all of us to the classroom, in other words, is the same tragedy.

From what I've observed since I began teaching in 2008, college students have become much more immune to the university's reliance on this customer-service relationship as a way to pit us against each other. At this point, most of my students are young enough that they don't remember the financial crisis, they just know its aftermath. They expect everything to keep getting worse, but not usually from a position of cynicism. Having worked with well over a thousand 18–22-year-olds in the last decade, I'm inspired by the growing majority of my students who have just had enough of all the lies, ranging from climate crisis denialism to racist monuments to university-wide alerts, in which striking workers are characterized as posing a safety threat to the campus community, if not worse. At UCSC, where I have been an adjunct since 2016, undergraduates were vital to the struggle when graduate student workers went on strike in early 2020, demanding a cost-of-living-adjustment (COLA) to meet the rental rates in Santa Cruz (where the median cost for a one-bedroom apartment is $2,242 a month, 123 percent of a Teaching Assistant's yearly salary).[59] Undergraduate students were at the picket line every day,

59 Pay Us More UCSC, "Rent Burden Calculator," 2020, https://payusmoreucsc.com/rent-burden-calculator/.

and many locked arms with their striking TAs and faced the violence of policing. They were outraged at the university's official narratives of the strike throughout. More recently, as my union planned a two-day strike of 6,500 lecturers after two years of bargaining with UC management, many of my students extended their solidarity, cutting through all the nonsense, and seeing our struggle as shared.

The Commedification of Everyday Work

"How should we understand comedy differently, and how does comedy stage its own anxiety-producing/alleviating, social-distance-gauging missions differently," Lauren Berlant and Sianne Ngai ask, "if people are increasingly supposed to be funny all the time?"[60] This is the demand of what they draw from Arpad Szakolczai as the "commedification" of modern social life.[61] For hours each day, sometimes unendingly, precarious workers everywhere are producing content for social media, hoping to go viral and then someday, somehow, get paid for what they love. They're spending their days thinking up tweets, staging photoshoots for Instagram, coming up with new routines for TikTok, doing stuff for free with the tempered expectation that it won't always be like this.

It's in this kind of world that the stand-up comedian, an unlikely hero, appears as a guide of sorts, modeling different styles of self-management in the midst of fans, competitors, and endless hecklers. By its design, Twitter is a perfect platform for stand-up comedians, specialists in distilling a story with a punchline in 280 characters or less. To rise to the ranks of verified blue check accounts involves developing an on-stage persona, endurance, and a drive to entertain, as well as a willingness to bomb. Like the stand-up comedian, the precarious worker learns to develop a schtick—a work persona, which makes work more bearable, but which also becomes a measure of self-worth. The more likes, loves, and shares, the more value a precarious worker derives from this not-yet-waged time.

All these likes, loves, and shares also release dopamine—through the same neural pathways stimulated by laughter.[62] Social media is designed to activate a dopamine reward system for its users, with strong parallels

---

60 Berlant and Ngai, "Comedy Has Issues," 236.
61 Berlant and Ngai, "Comedy Has Issues," 240.
62 See Sören Krach et al., "The Rewarding Nature of Social Interactions," *Frontiers in Behavioral Neuroscience* 4 (2010): 22, https://doi.org/10.3389/fnbeh.2010.00022.

to the "adrenaline rush" of stage time identified by so many stand-ups. Psychologist and comedian Matt Bellace has written extensively about the physiology of laughter. Laughing or making others laugh can induce a "natural high," Bellace explains, but what's distinct about making people laugh is the element of social risk.[63] On Twitter, while operating on the same dopamine reward system, that sense of risk varies among users depending on different factors. In his book *The Twittering Machine*, Richard Seymour examines addiction as the template for his central concept. "Whether or not we think we are addicted," he writes, "the machine treats us as addicts . . . The problem is, no one knows what addiction is."[64] Often this addiction is defined in neurochemical terms. Social media addiction has been compared most closely to gambling addiction in terms of the cognitive and behavioral experience. Culturally, as Seymour explains, this link to gambling is part of a broad imaginary of "life as a lottery."[65] "What we're really asking for when we post a status is a verdict," he argues, "In telling the machine something about ourselves, whatever else we're trying to achieve, we are asking for *judgement*."[66]

Both parts incurably insecure and utterly confident, the stand-up comedian constantly asks for judgement. Inasmuch as stand-up is about seeking approval, it's also about saving face and normalizing rejection. The stand-up is an expert at consolidating and managing attention. More than symbolizing success and ascendance, however, the stand-up personifies the neoliberal work ethic of the precarious worker: resilient, flexibilized, and aspirational.

Jobs can have a way of appearing to be something other than work. That isn't to say that, in the world of work, we aren't sometimes put into contact with what might be discerned as "art." Contemporary capitalism, as Sarah Brouillette writes, idealizes the precarious worker as a "profitable, pervasive, regulated symbol of autonomy from routine, standardized, mechanized production."[67] In the post-crisis paradigm of what Brouillette calls the artist-author, Miya Tokumitsu argues, the idea of the "labor of love" is reconfigured as a labor of *hope*, "[encouraging] the most vulnerable workers to double down on the very system that exploits them. There's little impetus to abandon hope of a good life when it appears just within

63 Matt Bellace, *A Better High: Laugh, Help, Run, Love ... and Other Ways to Get Naturally High!* (Deadwood, OR: Wyatt-MacKenzie Publishing, 2012), 42.
64 Richard Seymour, *The Twittering Machine* (New York: Verso, 2020), 51.
65 Seymour, *The Twittering Machine*, 66.
66 Seymour, *The Twittering Machine*, 66.
67 Brouillette, *Literature and the Creative Economy*, 54.

grasp."[68] The stand-up artist may embody the gigified work ethic of these times, internalizing the conditions of work and transmuting exploitation into artistic aspirations, but not without an undercurrent of antiwork questioning and post-work longing. Stand up may be a hyper-competitive world of comedian frenemies and constant hustling—while it is also a world of rare comradeship between outsiders, misfits, and survivors, working out their traumas through laughter, and dreaming of a life beyond work.

Like all artists, stand-up comedians are told at some point or another—or perhaps repeatedly—that they must suffer for their art. Far more than perceived as work, creativity has been historically linked to madness. As a romanticized gig worker, the stand-up is at the same time a late twentieth century *poète maudit*, living against society. Stand-up comedians are notoriously iconoclasts and martyrs—dying for their artistic and political freedom, or so the legend of Lenny Bruce has it. These cultural narratives of the stand-up comedian perpetuate a much longer tradition of abstracting the *work* of artwork, knotting up creative activity in a myth of necessary pain and art earned through sacrifice.

To this end, a defining moment in stand-up in recent years was Robin Williams's suicide in August 2014. There were tributes to Williams around the world, memorializing the stand-up turned film star and Oscar-winner. Since 2014, these tributes to Williams's comic genius have been ongoing, reflecting specifically on his lifelong mental health struggles and substance abuse issues.[69] Like any suicide, especially in the case of any person perceived as *successful*, Williams's prompted much speculation. Many came to make sense of his suicide in relation to his diagnosis with Lewy body disease, a form of dementia. However, his death also seemed to authenticate a certain cultural narrative of the stand-up comedian as inexorably miserable—the "sad clown," "both wildly outgoing and painfully introverted, at home in a crowd of strangers and desperately alone with the people he knew best," as Williams's biographer David Itzkoff elaborates.[70] Williams was, as fellow comedian Lewis Black put it, "like

---

68 Miya Tokumitsu, *Do What You Love: And Other Lies about Success and Happiness* (New York: Regan Arts, 2015), 118.

69 See *Robin Williams: Come Inside My Mind* (dir. Marina Zenovich, 2018), *Robin's Wish* (dir. Tylor Norwood, 2020), and *Robin* (2018) authored by New York Times writer Dave Itzkoff.

70 Dave Itzkoff, *Robin*, (New York: Henry Holt and Company, 2018), 423.

the light that never knew how to turn itself off."[71] Comedy, according to this broader cultural narrative of the tragic comedian, is a way of chasing off the misery—until it catches up.

This perception of madness in artists has a long history, of course, and it continues to inspire research, more recently geared toward the psychology of creativity. In 2015, researchers in Iceland surveyed 86,000 Icelanders.[72] Based on their profession or hobbies, 35,000 participants were deemed "creative"—and this group was almost 25 percent more likely to carry mental disorder variants including schizophrenia and bipolar.[73] Among comedians, according to a 2014 study published in *The British Journal of Psychiatry*, there are especially high rates of "psychotic" personality traits which "predispose to and mediate the symptoms of psychotic illness," including "moodiness, social introversion and the tendency to lateral thinking."[74] While these research efforts are largely inconclusive, they substantiate some of the assumptions already made of comedians and their motivation to pursue comedy. And yet, out of the recent research on the dominant psychological traits among creative workers, working conditions are hardly differentiated.

The impulse to pathologize artists is its own phenomenon, however, surfacing throughout this research. While the artist has long been cast as a figure of madness, this has been more recently accentuated by the "massive pathologization of human life" today, as psychologist and researcher Svend Brinkmann notes, resulting in "[a breakdown of] distinctions between problems in living and psychiatric disorders."[75] Part of this cultural shift is a tendency toward self-pathologization or diagnosis, as a means to explain and manage conditions of heightened and ongoing crisis, compartmentalizing much broader historical processes like the precaritization of work into matters of individual psychology.

---

71   Marina Zenovich, *Robin Williams: Come Inside My Mind* (HBO, 2018), https://www.hbo.com/documentaries/robin-williams-come-inside-my-mind.

72   Ian Sample, "New Study Claims to Find Genetic Link between Creativity and Mental Illness," *The Guardian*, June 8, 2015, https://www.theguardian.com/science/2015/jun/08/new-study-claims-to-find-genetic-link-between-creativity-and-mental-illness.

73   Robert A Power et al., "Polygenic Risk Scores for Schizophrenia and Bipolar Disorder Predict Creativity," *Nature Neuroscience* 18, no. 7 (July 2015): 953–55, https://doi.org/10.1038/nn.4040.

74   Victoria Ando, Gordon Claridge, and Ken Clark, "Psychotic Traits in Comedians," *British Journal of Psychiatry* 204, no. 5 (May 2014): 341–45, https://doi.org/10.1192/bjp.bp.113.134569.

75   Svend Brinkmann, *Diagnostic Cultures: A Cultural Approach to the Pathologization of Modern Life* (New York: Routledge, 2016).

Artists, including comedians, often endorse this pathologically-driven account of their artistic practice and self-mythology. The drive to produce art is attributed, all too often, to one of two modes of explanation: innate talent (and madness) or trauma. Countless comedians have participated in this self-pathologizing mythology of the comedian figure.[76] More than what makes comedians unique, their shared sense of suffering is what makes them, to the contrary, evermore relatable. The correlation is not between misery and comedy, but between misery and work.

---

76 Many comedians, for instance, provided such accounts in the 2015 documentary *Misery Loves Comedy*. Directed by comedian-actor-podcaster Kevin Pollack, the documentary's thesis is forceful and mostly unconvincing.

Part Two

Gender at Work: Comedy, Work Ethics, and Antiwork Ethics

CHAPTER THREE

Comediennes

> "Woman must write her self: must write about women and bring women to writing, from which they have been driven away as violently as from their bodies—for the same reasons, by the same law, with the same fatal goal. Woman must put herself into the text—as into the world and into history—by her own movement."
> — Hélène Cixous, "Laugh of the Medusa"[1]

The Work of Inclusion

The story of women's inclusion in comedy has many beginnings, each of which tells us a different version of the same point: that comedy is something for which the act of inclusion is necessary in the first place. The other side of this story is lost to history—legacies of women's humor circulated through gossip, private conversations, letters, and diaries, all forgotten, destroyed, or suppressed by official narratives and historical record. This much deeper, more complicated dynamic between women and humor is bound up in different cultural contexts, patriarchal and racial exploitation, and the history of literacy, authorship, and private property. Here, the story I want to track is not about recovering these lost histories but understanding women's inclusion in comedy *as work*.

One of the places to begin is Restoration England. Women's participation in theater was criminalized in England until 1662, with a patent issued under Charles II. While the patent itself was framed in terms of social reform, "the subsequent licentiousness of Restoration

---

1 Hélène Cixous, "The Laugh of the Medusa," trans. Keith Cohen and Paula Cohen, *Signs: Journal of Women in Culture and Society* 1, no. 4 (Summer 1976): 875–893.

drama" has been problematically blamed "on the sexual exploitation of actresses," as theater scholar Elizabeth Howe argues.[2] "The fact that the actresses were utilized primarily as sexual objects suggests something about the Restoration age in general," writes literary historian Elizabeth Woodrough stating that, although women "were permitted to perform alongside men on the public stage, paradoxically this license often merely served to undermine female limitations."[3] And yet in acting, women found rare access to waged-labor, increased mobility and visibility in public spaces, and greater access to other resources and forms of sociality. Specifically as work, acting was imagined as freedom.

On and off stage, actresses suffered incredible abuse. They withstood constant harassment from audiences, sometimes escalating to rape and assault. "Of the eighty or so actresses we know by name on the Restoration stage," writes Howe, "apparently about a mere one-quarter of this number led what were considered to be respectable lives [...] usually married to fellow actors who could presumably protect them to some degree from harassment at the theater." In fact, many actresses were marketed for their sexual availability, as a way for theater companies to attract audiences.[4] It was with the ostensible freedom gained by the right to *play themselves* that women in theater found themselves "to a large extent," as literary historian Harold Weber puts it, "[free] to play the whore."[5]

This predicament of partial freedom, in and through exploitation, is not exceptional to the actresses of the Restoration period, but in many ways fundamental to the history of women's inclusion in workplaces— and moreover, women's inclusion in what counts as work. Through the figure of the housewife, Silvia Federici declared in 1975 that *"for women sex is work,"* arguing that "giving pleasure is part of what is expected of every woman. Sexual freedom does not help."[6] Through the history of the comedienne, we might also assert the inverse: that the presupposition of women's inclusion is that *all work is sex work.*

---

2 Elizabeth Howe, *The First English Actresses: Women and Drama, 1660-1700* (Cambridge: Cambridge University Press, 1992), 26.

3 Elizabeth Woodrough, ed., *Women in European Theatre* (Oxford: Intellect Books, 1995), 21.

4 Howe, *The First English Actresses*, 34.

5 Harold Weber, *The Restoration Rake-Hero: Transformations in Sexual Understanding in Seventeenth-Century England* (Madison: University of Wisconsin Press, 1986), 134.

6 Silvia Federici, *Revolution at Point Zero: Housework, Reproduction, and Feminist Struggle* (Oakland: PM Press; Brooklyn: Common Notions; Brooklyn: Autonomedia, 2012), 25.

The story of women's inclusion in comedy cannot be disentangled from this story of women's inclusion in the workplace—a story that has always been mediated by sexuality. It was not until the twentieth century that women in comedy had any control over the comedy itself as writers. Rather, much like the history of women and literature which Virginia Woolf famously refutes in *A Room of One's Own*, there is no history of women's comedy, merely that of women playing parts in men's comedy. In the comedienne, just as Woolf speculates of the [insert: white, bourgeois] woman-writer, "a very queer, composite being thus emerges":

> Imaginatively she is of the highest importance; practically she is completely insignificant. She pervades poetry from cover to cover; she is all but absent from history. She dominates the lives of kings and conquerors in fiction; in fact she was the slave of any boy whose parents forced a ring upon her finger. Some of the most inspired words and profound thoughts in literature fall from her lips; in real life she could hardly read; scarcely spell; and was the property of her husband.[7]

When women entered the comedy writer's rooms for television in the fifties, freedom was once again the promise of joining the workforce. Still, the vast majority of women's parts were written in all-white male writer's rooms. It would be decades before a comedy show about women would also be, even for the most part, written by women. All the while, there has been a powerful perception of being included, with women on the screen.

In the world of comedy, sketch and improv have historically been the most inclusive of women, however tokenistically. As Andi Zeisler explains, "even with women as a crucial part of the comedy-troupe structure, their contributions have often been perceived as less central than that of their male counterparts," and often assumed to be "a nod to political correctness in casting." No matter how much women in sketch infiltrated "comedy's long-running sausage party," Zeisler writes, "women are still left telling their jokes mostly to each other."[8] In sketches, their function has been to

---

7 Virginia Woolf, *A Room of One's Own and Three Guineas* (New York: Oxford University Press, 2015), 33.
8 Andi Zeisler, "Laugh Riot: Feminism and the Problem of Women's Comedy," in *Bitchfest: Ten Years of Cultural Criticism from the Pages of Bitch Magazine*, ed. Lisa Miya-Jervis and Andi Zeisler (New York: Farrar, Straus and Giroux, 2006), 152.

play the girlfriends, sisters, mothers, waitresses, nurses—supporting characters, always in the service of men's work of comedy. As Frances Gray has argued, women have historically been restricted to the role of "handmaid of laughter, not its creator."[9]

In the history of stand-up, Phyllis Diller and Joan Rivers are often hailed as the first women to enter the scene, but Jackie "Moms" Mabley had been performing what would become understood as stand-up for decades before these white women started working night clubs in the late fifties and early sixties. Mabley is one of the most remarkable figures in twentieth century comedy, whose comedic method innovated techniques from vaudeville and stand-up. In 1908, she began performing in minstrel shows, at the age of fourteen. Her childhood had been quite tragic. By the time she left home to join the minstrel shows, she had given birth to two children, both conceived from rape. Her first pregnancy was at the age of eleven. The rapist who caused her second pregnancy, when she was thirteen, was the white sheriff of the town Brevard, North Carolina, where she lived with her family.[10] Performing in minstrel shows, Mabley became incredibly successful (though still modestly paid) by her twenties—after doing a show at Connie's Inn in Harlem, she started working with the Chitlin' Circuit, a cluster of venues for Black entertainers in the South and parts of the east and Midwest. Within a few years into touring in the Chitlin' Circuit, at the age of twenty-seven, she was known among other Black performers as a lesbian. Decades after Mabley's death in 1975, Whoopi Goldberg discovered private photos of Mabley from the thirties-forties, performing comedy in men's clothing on stage. In a documentary she produced about Mabley's life, Goldberg speculated "I think everybody was like, 'OK'. . . I think she was a woman among men and who was equal to those men. And they treated her like a man. And I think that is what helped give her longevity."[11] By the sixties, however, when Mabley began performing for more white audiences on the *Ed Sullivan Show* and the *Smothers Brothers Hour*, Mabley "cultivated a mask

9 Frances Gray, *Women and Laughter* (Charlottesville: University Press of Virginia, 1994), 21.

10 Daryl Cumber Dance, ed., *Honey, Hush!: An Anthology of African American Women's Humor* (New York: W.W. Norton, 1998), 637.

11 From Whoopi Goldberg, *Whoopi Goldberg Presents Moms Mabley: The Original Queen of Comedy*, documentary (HBO, 2013), https://www.hbo.com/documentaries/whoopi-goldberg-presents-moms-mabley-doc; see also Lou Chibbaro Jr, "Meet the Legendary Queer Comedian 'Moms' Mabley," *LGBTQ Nation*, August 8, 2017, https://www.lgbtqnation.com/2017/08/meet-legendary-queer-comedian-moms-mabley/.

of physical ugliness" in her performances, Eddie Tafoya suggests.[12] She would wear unflattering clothing, mess up her hair, and contort her face. When she was older she would take off her dentures before getting on stage. She continued to sexualize her comedy, often building her routines around innuendo toward younger men and positioning herself as the butt of the jokes. While sexualization was always a precondition of Mabley's inclusion as a performer, self-deprecation was her ticket to working in the white, patriarchal world of comedy. At the same time, and despite these compromises, Mabley experienced a form of autonomy rare for women in comedy, and throughout her career she continued to write her own material.

As opposed to stand-up, improv and sketch comedy have always depended more on women's participation at some level. When Elaine May began working with Mike Nichols in Chicago in the early fifties, she was perceived as a hot commodity in the comedy world. By the late-fifties, the pair began performing together exclusively, becoming the legendary improv duo Nichols and May. A few years before he died, "sit down" comedian Shelley Berman explained how he first conceived of his signature act of a one-sided phone conversation in the mid-fifties. "Well, I went to Elaine May and I said 'I've got an idea,'" he recounted, "She said 'fine, it's a good idea, but I'm doing a thing with Mike Nichols.' But I could not give that up. But how can I do an act if I don't have a way?"[13] When May rejected him, Berman interpreted this as Nichols's possession over her, plain and simple. While Nichols was undoubtedly possessive of his incredibly talented partner, what May got from her collaboration with Nichols was in turn an actual creative partnership. She had her pick of comedians to work with, and Nichols was the only one she could truly *work with*—however possessive, he was different because he saw her as a partner, not as a muse. As May recalls, "we found each other hilarious." But it was more than that—her talent, and the way in which it could be put on display, were specific to the conditions of improv. May was known especially for writing comedy on her feet and shining particularly as an improv comedian. "The improv invariably showcased the two of them at their most relaxed and connected," writes Nichols biographer and cultural critic Mark Harris, but "Nichols would have to fight to keep from

---

12 Eddie Tafoya, *Icons of African American Comedy*, Greenwood Icons (Santa Barbara: Greenwood, 2011), xvii.

13 Marc Maron, "Episode 332: Shelley Berman," *WTF with Marc Maron*, November 5, 2012.

breaking character and cracking up."[14] Instrumental to the duo's success was May's writing herself into the comedy, not just playing out some man's scripted lines.

While women have found more inclusion in sketch and especially improv, the joke of women's expendability has also had a long history in these sectors of the comedy world. Famous all white male sketch comedy groups like Monty Python, Kids in the Hall, and many more extending to current groups like Tim and Eric, avoided the inclusion of women with cross-gender acting. The gender politics of Monty Python's *Flying Circus*, more generally, have been debated for decades. Most of the women characters on the show were played in drag by men in the group, with the exception of Carol Cleveland, who was often featured in minimal speaking parts with minimal clothing. Cross-gender acting in the series has been celebrated for mocking "institutionalized representations of gender and sexuality," as Marcia Landy suggests, in an argument strawmanning "supporters of identity politics" for taking issue with the ways in which the Pythons' caricatures of femininity "do not present 'desirable' and affirmative gender images to emulate."[15] Landy and others have thoroughly discounted valid queer and feminist critiques of Python out of a distinct sense of fandom, reducing this question of gender to a matter of supposed oversensitivity. Quite consistently, the rule of casting was, if the woman's part was sexy, give it to Cleveland, and if the part was funny, give it to one of the men. The terms of women's participation were sexually exploitative, but they also reinforced the conception of women as merely proximate to comedy, and never quite funny themselves.[16]

The comedienne's predicament, as many have bemoaned, is stuck between these imperatives to be sexy and funny. And historically these imperatives have been at odds: the comedienne's inclusion in comedy

14 Mark Harris, *Mike Nichols: A Director's Life* (New York: Penguin, 2021), 70.

15 Marcia Landy, *Monty Python's Flying Circus* (Detroit: Wayne State University Press, 2005), 79.

16 While in their time, Monty Python's cross-gender caricatures of women might have been conceived as a rebellious response to homophobia in the UK, Python alumnus John Cleese has been among the many vocal antitrans celebrities who have spoken up in support of J.K. Rowling in recent years. However jokingly, Cleese continues to assert his authority over who gets to be a woman: "When a woman who was once a man is competing against women who have always been women," he tweets, "I think she has an advantage, because she inherited a man's body, which is usually bigger and stronger than a woman's[.]" "I'm afraid I'm not that interested in trans folks," he replied to his critics. See Ryan Lattanzio, "John Cleese Accused of Transphobia After Tweeting 'I Want to Be a Cambodian Police Woman,'" *IndieWire*, November 22, 2020, https://www.indiewire.com/2020/11/john-cleese-defends-jk-rowling-accused-transphobia-twitter-1234600163/.

comes through her sexualization, just as that sexualization has also, paradoxically, discounted her abilities as a maker of comedy. Linda Mizejewski has called this a binary of "pretty" versus "funny" for which "women comics, no matter what they look like, have been located in opposition to 'pretty,'"[17] leading to a "suspicion about women comics as gender outlaws[.]"[18] Crucially, Mizejewski draws a distinction between "attractive actors with good comic timing" and "women who write and perform their own comedy."[19] Actresses have been praised for comedy to the extent that they are not seen as the authors of comedy, often figured instead as *muses*: the inspiration and vessel of comedy, stripped of agency.

In navigating this impossibility of the pretty versus funny binary, women in stand-up have found ways to write and perform their own material with a few strategies. "I came out as a clown," Phyllis Diller once explained of her entry into comedy, "a clown is androgynous. They didn't worry if I was a man or a woman."[20] Much like Moms Mabley's comedy, Diller's sense of raunchiness often counteracted this clownish desexualization—an approach many contemporary comediennes continue to take, either to refute or circumvent the pretty/funny binary. Throughout the stand-up comedy boom of the eighties, some of the most successful women in comedy were perceived as asexual, self-masculinizing / butch, or queer: Roseanne Barr, Sandra Bernhard, Brett Butler, Ellen DeGeneres, Whoopi Goldberg, Rosie O'Donnell, Paula Poundstone, among others. In the nineties, another comedienne archetype emerged in the fag hag (Margaret Cho, Kathy Griffin), whose sexuality is defined in relation to gay men. It was in the nineties that women in stand-up also began engaging their sexualization more directly, often joking about their bodies and bodily experiences, including sex but also periods, abortions, and rape (Janeane Garofalo, Sarah Silverman). At every step, however, and no matter the strategy, sexualization was an unavoidable factor—a part of the job.

As late as 2005, cultural critic Dana Goodyear named comedy "the last remaining branch of the arts whose suitability for women is still openly discussed."[21] Part of this is the ideological fixation on stand-up comedy in

---

17 Linda Mizejewski, *Pretty / Funny: Women Comedians and Body Politics* (Austin: University of Texas Press, 2015), 5.
18 Mizejewski, *Pretty / Funny*, 16.
19 Mizejewski, *Pretty / Funny*, 1.
20 Dana Goodyear, "Quiet Depravity," *The New Yorker*, October 17, 2005, https://www.newyorker.com/magazine/2005/10/24/quiet-depravity.
21 Goodyear, "Quiet Depravity."

the U.S. as a domain of free speech, making it a hotbed of hate speech. In addition, and more pervasively, there is an illusion that comedy is simply a meritocracy. The laughs don't lie, as many established men in the industry insist. According to this logic, if you can get the laughs then you get the stage time. But of course the precondition of getting stage time, whether explicitly or implicitly, has largely been a matter of *hanging with* daily sexual harassment or worse, from audience members or fellow comedians. Soon after she started headlining at a comedy club she'd worked at for years, Amy Schumer recalls overhearing a security guard saying "Amy's so successful now. I wonder how she got that?" while pantomiming a blow job.[22] In 2015, Schumer spoke of this as typical behavior in the comedy industry. By 2017, these dynamics both on and off stage made comedy especially vulnerable to the critical interventions of #MeToo, while entertainment faced the most pressure as an industry based in the business of public opinion. Some of the issues that were already hotly disputed within comedy—rape jokes, what to do about the legacy of Bill Cosby, antitrans and antifeminist humor, etc.—quickly became incorporated into the cultural debates of #MeToo.

Overwhelmingly, the stories that came out of #MeToo with the most legibility to public discourse were situated in traditional workplace contexts. Harvey Weinstein's unambiguous leveraging of his power as head of Miramax to perpetually assault aspiring actresses became a template for #MeToo as a movement against bosses. In entertainment, this led to a ripple-effect of cases against industry bosses like CBS CEO Les Moonves, President of the Academy of Motion Picture Arts and Sciences John Baily, Chief Creative Officer of Pixar and Walt Disney Productions John Lasseter, Amazon Studios head Roy Price; and directors like Brett Ratner, Bryan Singer, Oliver Stone, James Toback, and Quentin Tarantino. The critique of power dynamics in the workplace was central to #MeToo, which at its most effective pronounced some of the ways that sexual harassment and assault have been conditional to women's inclusion across workforces.

In comedy, #MeToo's critique of the workplace was what differentiated Louis CK's pattern of sexual abuse towards women in comedy from Aziz Ansari's sexual misconduct with a date who he brought back to his apartment. Ansari's case soon became exemplary of #MeToo "going too far," while CK's treatment of fellow comedians came to stand for a

---

22 Colin Gorenstein, "Amy Schumer: Death Threats Have Made Me Want to 'Use My Voice Even More,'" *Salon*, July 7, 2015, https://www.salon.com/2015/07/07/amy_schumer_death_threats_have_made_me_want_to_use_my_voice_even_more/.

systemic crisis in comedy culture. Debates over Ansari's "cancelation" (followed by a new comedy special, a year and a half later, and a renewal of his series on Netflix) signify the limit-point of #MeToo: specifically, the misrecognition of the household as a non-workplace. The dividing point of these debates is over the context: Ansari brought a date home, and acted coercively, while at least seemingly outside the power dynamics of a workplace relationship. A similar debate was launched over comedian and *The Nerdist* CEO Chris Hardwick, whose ex-partner Chloe Dykstra, an actress and performer, published an essay detailing consistent experiences of emotional and sexual abuse. After an enforced hiatus from his job as host of *Talking Dead* on AMC, Hardwick returned to his job after a network statement which claimed "given the information available . . . we believe returning Chris to work is the appropriate step."[23] In her essay, Dykstra goes into detail about how she was "expected to be ready for him when he came home from work," and how playing the part of his partner was a job that entailed dieting, limited social interactions, housework, and sex work. After she left him, Dykstra explains that Hardwick "made calls to several companies where I received regular work from to get me fired by threatening to never work with them. He succeeded. I was blacklisted . . . he steamrolled my career."[24] Stories like Dykstra's merely pluck at the strings attached to being included.

The story of women's inclusion in comedy is a story about compromises, and beneath each compromise lies a history of violence. To the violence of exclusion, inclusion has seemed like the only possible antidote. What it means to be included, however, often means more violence.

In late 2017, crucial questions of inclusion were raised among feminists, in response to #MeToo. "Clearly our absence from movements against sexual violence isn't simply due to a lack of public attention," as Natalie West writes of sex workers, arguing that dehumanization "makes us impossible to victimize, or else it can render us the ultimate victims."[25] Key to sex worker exclusionary radical feminism (SWERF) and trans-exclusionary radical feminism (TERF) is a shared project of reversing the logic of inclusion, based on a violent policing of the

---

23 Sandra Gonzalez, "Chris Hardwick Returning as Host of 'Talking Dead' Following Investigation," *CNN*, July 25, 2018, https://www.cnn.com/2018/07/25/entertainment/chris-hardwick-talking-dead/index.html.

24 Chloe Dykstra, "Rose-Colored Glasses: A Confession.," *Medium*, July 7, 2018, https://medium.com/@skydart/rose-colored-glasses-6be0594970ca.

25 Natalie West, "Introduction," in *We Too: Essays on Sex Work and Survival*, ed. Tina Horn, Selena, and Natalie West (New York: Feminist Press, 2021), 7.

boundaries of gender and work. "[W]hether rad-fem or anti-feminist, pro- or (avowedly) anticapitalist," Sophie Lewis contends, "most of the people who abhor sex work and reject trans-ness share the belief that the matter of 'being a woman' isn't agentive, isn't work, isn't a performance, and isn't a relation."[26] The disacknowledgment of sex work as work fulfills this logic of "inclusion," for which sexualization and risk of sexual violence have always been unspoken stipulations. "Being practically all of us whores," as Lewis concludes, "it's about time we learned to fight as such, especially for our trans sisters, and against the tyranny of work."[27]

Whether in traditional waged forms, or in informal, emotionally and physically ambiguous forms, seemingly unmediated by the market, work has been the underlying conflict of #MeToo—and the way in which #MeToo has found its most effective vocabulary of struggle. While the office assistant harassed in the workplace may seem different from the domestic partner assaulted at home, work is their mutual condition. So much domestic violence, for this very reason, is instigated over domestic chores, regardless of how this might be seen as workplace dynamics specifically.

Throughout the entertainment industry, the mythic "casting couch" has long symbolized the sex work implied by work—a part of the job left out of the job description, notoriously for office assistants, nannies, nurses, and most other traditionally feminized workforces. This was why, as a college student, I did everything to steer clear of working as a waitress or barista, like so many of my friends. One of my close friends constantly dealt with sexual harassment at the coffee shop where she worked, especially from regular customers. She explained that the more she not just accepted the harassment from regulars, but even normalized it, the better her tips got. When a job at the coffee shop opened, the prospect of applying for it stressed me out. But my time substituting for a friend, working a cushy job at the front desk of the Sociology department (where I mostly answered phones and shredded paper), was about to run out. I decided to advertise myself as a dog walker in the neighborhood, and within months I had some steady clients, and got to spend most of my time with dogs—it was the best (but lowest paying) job I ever had.

Nearly every job involves some negotiating with the prospect of sexual harassment if not violence. Some jobs are more explicit about

26 Sophie Lewis, "SERF 'n' TERF," *Salvage*, February 6, 2017, https://salvage.zone/in-print/serf-n-terf-notes-on-some-bad-materialisms/.
27 Lewis, "SERF 'n' TERF."

this—and, in some cases, can be imagined as wages *against* work. In 1974, Silvia Federici re-articulated the demand of wages for housework as "wages against housework" in this spirit. While demanding inclusion in the wage system, this orientation *against* is also a negation of this system. It is not just a gesture, but a way to antagonize the wage from the bottom up. Today, marital rape and spousal abuse remain legal throughout the world, more or less as an extension of housework. Similarly crucial to the SWERF ideology is the assertion that sex workers cannot be raped. Experiences of sexual violence from sex workers have been systematically delegitimated, both legally and ideologically, because of the perception of a direct transactional agreement. Part of this delegitimization is the unsee-ing of indirect transactions—all the ways in which, for instance, the most heteronormative gender relations are based in such implicit agreements.

Like work, sex work is an expansive concept, a way to understand not only conventional forms of prostitution, based in direct transactions, but a wide range of other activities associated with work. Just as for the comedian, for the sex worker "there is something disruptive about getting paid to give and receive pleasure," as Heather Berg writes of the politics of calling sex work "work": "from an antiwork position, [this is] not to bid for respectability or repudiate pleasure. It is, instead, to refuse that pleasure be appropriated and bled dry as yet another site of extraction."[28] As Berg suggests, "pleasure makes work livable but also gets us to do more of it,"[29] looking to porn work to trouble the ways in which sex work is excluded from conceptions of work, alongside conceptions of sexual violence, and the sexual violence intrinsic to so much work.

To the extent that comedy reveals this world of work, in which so much work is to varying degrees also sex work, comedy also distorts work in political ways—romantically, antagonistically, ambiguously. The story of women's inclusion in comedy is about moving through the political possibilities of this distortion.

The Comedienne Boom at *Saturday Night Live*

In her 2013 memoir *Bossypants*, Tina Fey depicts a "cosmic shift" in the gender dynamics at *Saturday Night Live*, catalyzed by Amy Poehler:

---

28 Heather Berg, *Porn Work: Sex, Labor, and Late Capitalism* (Chapel Hill: The University of North Carolina Press, 2021), 184.
29 Berg, *Porn Work*, 2.

> ...Poehler was new to SNL and we were all crowded into the seventeenth-floor writers' room, waiting for the Wednesday read-through to start. There were always a lot of noisy "comedy bits" going on in that room. Amy was in the middle of some such nonsense with Seth Meyers across the table, and she did something vulgar as a joke. I can't remember what it was exactly, except it was dirty and loud and "unladylike."
>
> Jimmy Fallon, who was arguably the star of the show at the time, turned to her and in a faux-squeamish voice said: "Stop that! It's not cute! I don't like it."
>
> Amy dropped what she was doing, went black in the eyes for a second, and wheeled around on him. "I don't fucking care if you like it." Jimmy was visibly startled. Amy went right back to enjoying her ridiculous bit.[30]

As Fey recalls, Poehler "made it clear that she wasn't there to be cute. She wasn't there to play wives and girlfriends in the boys' scenes." Some would describe it as the era of the *SNL* "girls' club"—a time of not taking it anymore, in inspiring ways. But this was also, in comedy, the birth of the (mostly white liberal feminist) contemporary comedienne: a figure exemplifying the corporate work ethics and career oriented "feminisms" of the years to come.

The *SNL* girls' club began with Fey's promotion to head writer in 1999. This was the first time that a woman had taken that position since the show premiered in 1975. After a year on staff, Fey lost thirty pounds and suddenly, as she recalls, "there was interest in putting me on camera."[31] After that, she became the co-anchor of *SNL*'s signature news feature "Weekend Update," paired with Fallon, and her promotion to head writer happened soon thereafter. Over the next decade, the show was celebrated for its comedienne cast that included Fey and Poehler, as well as Rachel Dratch, Ana Gasteyer, Maya Rudolph, Molly Shannon, and Kristen Wiig. This was a moment long-awaited in the history of *SNL*.

During the late seventies, *SNL* was "the show that finally opened the door to women trying to break into sketch comedy on-screen and

---

30 Tina Fey, *Bossypants* (New York: Back Bay Books/Little, Brown, 2012), 143.
31 Alex Witchel, "'Update' Anchor: The Brains Behind Herself," *The New York Times*, November 25, 2001, https://www.nytimes.com/2001/11/25/style/counterintelligence-update-anchor-the-brains-behind-herself.html.

behind the scenes," as comedy historian Yael Kohen claims.[32] However, as many women in comedy from that time have since attested, the atmosphere at *SNL*, especially in the early years, was outright chauvinist, and often abusive. "There was a lot of misogynist stuff that I considered to be demeaning to women—or to any group—on Saturday Night Live," as Lily Tomlin remembers of that period. "It was not my style . . . It was too limited to me. It was too easy in some sense."[33] A number of Tomlin's comedy specials in the early seventies were produced by *SNL* creator and producer Lorne Michaels.

Michaels's particular role in the workplace dynamics at *SNL* has always been a matter of ambiguity and suspicion. As original cast member Laraine Newman argues, "Lorne was really a champion of the women writers and gave them an even break . . . He is not one of those people that thinks women are not funny."[34] And yet, as Newman recalls, "the boys got away with a lot." She adds: "They were bad and we were good. We were punctual and they were late. We were clean and they were dirty. We were prepared and they weren't—it was that stuff." Fellow original cast member Jane Curtin has spoken out about the show's extreme chauvinism during the early years as well: "John [Belushi] didn't like being in sketches with women. He told me women were not funny. Actually, Chevy [Chase] said it to me as well," Curtin explains, adding "it was ridiculous. It was just insane. There's no way you can respond to that, so you just have to learn to live with it, plod on."[35]

What's striking about Curtin's remarks is the way that enduring this workplace misogyny was so crucial to the comedienne's work ethic on the series. Years later, this mandate for women in the cast to "plod on" was reinforced by the chatter around cast member Nora Dunn's departure from the series in 1990. While Dunn was already preparing to leave the show at the end of the season, she and the musical guest Shuhada Sadaqat (formerly known as Sinéad O'Connor) decided to boycott an episode, in a refusal to work with that week's host, comedian (and legendary chauvinist) Andrew "Dice" Clay. In an interview in 2015, following the 40th anniversary of *SNL*, Dunn explained that her objection to "Dice" Clay

32 Yael Kohen, *We Killed: The Rise of Women in American Comedy* (New York: Farrar, Straus and Giroux, 2012), 95.

33 See Tom Shales and James Andrew Miller, *Live from New York: The Complete, Uncensored History of "Saturday Night Live" as Told by Its Stars, Writers, and Guests* (New York: Little, Brown, 2015), 44.

34 Shales and Miller, *Live from New York*, 58.

35 Shales and Miller, *Live from New York*, 56.

was that "his character was only about one thing: abusing women and laughing about abusing women."[36] As a result of the boycott, Dunn was dismissed early from the show—and made an example of for women in the years to come.

Throughout the accounts of women who've worked at *SNL*, there are copious stories of sexual objectification, each of which illustrates the ambiguities of consent under pressures to be a competent and dependable worker—not to mention the prospect of getting your script on the air. "My first time on the show, I was in a G-string," recalls Ana Gasteyer, who joined the cast in 1996, "we were in G-strings and practically nude and covered in bubbles [as] these, like, body girls . . . it was the first thing I'd ever done so I was kind of like, 'This is icky and embarrassing but it's also a part of your job[.]'"[37]

Part of the formula for *SNL* has been to disproportionately rely on the schticks of the drugged-out and/or charming lazy white man on cast. John Belushi, Chris Farley, Adam Sandler, and now, Pete Davidson all follow this trajectory—and perhaps they do work hard, as there are certainly countless stories of their contributions to *SNL* history, but they get to wear sweatpants and/or do lots of drugs as they do it. By contrast, the founding comediennes of *SNL*'s girls' club (Fey, Poehler, Rudolph, Gasteyer) took the much more demanding (and corporatizing) work ethic that it had always required of women in that boys' club, and they turned that into their schtick.

Towards the end of this 2000s era of the girls' club, which has since been revived by the show's casting, Fey and Poehler made use of this idealized perception of the comedienne's work ethic to voice their support of Hillary Clinton's first presidential campaign in 2008. "What bothers me the most is when people say Hillary Clinton is a bitch," Fey remarks, "Yeah, she is. And so am I. And so is this one [pointing at Poehler]. You know what? Bitches get stuff done."[38] Nothing summed up the girls' club more than "bitches get stuff done"—it was the closest they got to just taking a megaphone and declaring "we're the best at capitalism!" Fey had already left the show in 2006 (though she made frequent guest appearances).

---

36 Kera Bolonik, "Nora Dunn: 'SNL Is a Traumatic Experience. It's Something You Have to Survive,'" *Salon*, April 8, 2015, https://www.salon.com/2015/04/07/nora_dunn_snl_is_a_traumatic_experience_it%e2%80%99s_something_you_have_to_survive/.
37 Yael Kohen, "'Saturday Night Live': The Girls' Club," *The New Yorker*, October 16, 2012, https://www.newyorker.com/books/page-turner/saturday-night-live-the-girls-club.
38 Alex Abad-Santos, "SNL's 2008 'Bitches Get Stuff Done' Sketch Foreshadowed Trump Calling Clinton a 'Nasty Woman,'" *Vox*, October 20, 2016, https://www.vox.com/2016/10/20/13346106/hillary-clinton-nasty-woman.

Later, in 2008, Poehler would leave the show, a vision of "bitches get stuff done": at nine months pregnant, she performed a parody rap song about Sarah Palin, in front of Sarah Palin. The next week, she went into labor during rehearsal, despite her best efforts, and couldn't make the show.

The comedienne of this era is the super mom and super worker: the career woman who can have it all but also have a good time doing it. She works because she loves it, and she never complains. She works and never questions why, just how. She works so that she can love herself, and so that she can be loved. She is lean in feminism *avant la lettre*.

In 2013, Corporate Operating Officer of Facebook Sheryl Sandberg published what would become one of the most influential texts in the self-help boom of the post-financial crisis years. In keeping with this genre, *Lean In* addresses a set of systemic social problems and shared struggles, while offering solutions which place total responsibility on the individual: the book contends that "women are hindered by barriers that exist within ourselves. We hold ourselves back in ways both big and small, by lacking self-confidence, by not raising our hands, and by pulling back when we should be leaning in."[39] Throughout *Lean In*, there are traces of "the cultural changes jumpstarted by the second wave," as Nancy Fraser writes, which "have served to legitimate a structural transformation of capitalist society that runs directly counter to feminist visions of a just society."[40] In this process, female leadership—as in the big picture of inclusion in representational politics, one woman at a time—became synonymous with feminist empowerment, a trope that extends from Margaret Thatcher to Sandberg to today's obsession with girl bosses and boss bitches. Precisely in the name of feminism, "leaning in" enacts a politics of antifeminism.

Of course this is all well-trodden territory. But what's often overlooked about *Lean In* is that its co-author, Nell Scovell, cut her teeth in the world of comedy. In 2009, four years before the book came out, Scovell published an essay in *Vanity Fair* about her experiences as one of the few women to ever write for *Late Night with David Letterman*. In all of Letterman's career, there were seven women "who spent a total 17 years on staff *combined*," Scovell explains, while "male writers have racked up a collective 378 years writing jokes for Dave."[41] Of her short time on staff,

39 Sheryl Sandberg, "Foreword," in Nell Scovell, *Just the Funny Parts: And a Few Hard Truths about Sneaking into the Hollywood Boys' Club* (New York: Dey Street, 2018), 8.
40 Nancy Fraser, *Fortunes of Feminism: From State-Managed Capitalism to Neoliberal Crisis* (New York: Verso Books, 2020), 210.
41 Nell Scovell, "Letterman and Me," *Vanity Fair*, October 27, 2009, https://www.vanityfair.com/style/2009/10/david-letterman-200910.

the comedy writer recounts a hostile work environment which forced her to "[walk] away from my dream job."[42] As Scovell would later contend in her 2018 memoir, *Just the Funny Parts*, these were simply the only conditions for women to work in the world of comedy writing. In her foreword to the memoir, Sandberg writes that "Nell didn't just help me write *Lean In*, she lived it."[43] One of Scovell's career highlights was working on the writing staff for *Murphy Brown*, the sit-com that spoke for this career-oriented brand of feminism.

Scovell and her legacy lurk in the background of an early episode of *30 Rock*, in which Carrie Fisher guest stars as Rosemary Howard, an aging feminist comedy writer and the childhood idol of Tina Fey's alter-ego, comedy writer Liz Lemon. Soon after hiring Howard in her writer's room, Lemon is told by her boss Jack Donaghy (Alec Baldwin) "Fire her, and don't ever make me talk to a woman that old again."[44] Years later, Fey moved from satire to direct critique, in a memorable confrontation with Scovell's old boss, Letterman, on his post-*Late Night* interview series on Netflix, called *My Next Guest Needs No Introduction*. "When I had a television show," Letterman explains to Fey, "people would always say to me . . . 'well why don't you have women writers?' and the best I could come up with was 'I don't know.' I didn't know why there were no women writers." As he recalls, "I always thought well, jeez, if I was a woman I'm not sure I would want to write on my little nickel-and-dime dog-and-pony show anyway, 'cause we were on at 12:30–" and then Fey interrupts him: "yeah, yeah," she says, "yeah, we do want to write on it though."[45] To this interjection, the audience responds with a huge applause.

In the interview, which is otherwise very friendly, Fey goes on to tell Letterman how the system at *SNL* is "actually very fair," based on the

---

42 Scovell's critique of Letterman, and his treatment of women in comedy, is further complicated by the case of Merrill Markoe, who was in a romantic relationship with Letterman from 1978–88, and also for much of that time his head writer. Many have claimed that Markoe was the brains behind the operation, having created some of Letterman's signature segments like "Stupid Pet Tricks" and "Stupid Human Tricks," along with the remote shoots. Whether this partnership would have worked without the romantic aspects is one question, but another is about the degree to which Markoe can lay claim to her contributions, as a creator of comedy herself.

43 Sandberg, "Foreword."

44 Michael Engler, "Rosemary's Baby," *30 Rock* (NBC, October 25, 2007).

45 Michael Bonfiglio, "Tina Fey," *My Next Guest Needs No Introduction with David Letterman* (Netflix, n.d.).

midweek table reading which determines the content for the show. Of this table reading system, she explains, "You always get to write whatever you want and you pretty much always get your shot to perform it, and if it plays, it will go." During the girls' club era, she remembers, "the chemistry of that room slowly became more diverse, other things played better."

The metaphor of the comedy writers' room table is an organizing principle in *Lean In*. Intrinsic to what Sandberg characterizes as the "will to lead" is the process of getting a seat at the table. Sandberg writes of an epiphany she had after watching as four women who, "because of their seating choice . . . seemed like spectators rather than participants" at an important meeting:

> I knew I had to say something. So after the meeting, I pulled them aside to talk. I pointed out that they should have sat at the table even without an invitation, but when publicly welcomed, they most certainly should have joined. At first they seemed surprised, then they agreed. It was a watershed moment for me. A moment when I witnessed how an internal barrier can alter women's behavior. A moment when I realized that in addition to facing institutional obstacles, women face a battle from within.[46]

Framed as a work ethic, the feminism concocted by *Lean In* takes this "battle from within" as its political horizon, rather than ever pondering a transformation of women's working conditions on a broader scale. Workplace reforms and structural inequality are deemed simply a matter of individual responsibility. It is always ultimately up to the individual worker to work harder, sacrifice more, and put everything on the table.

If we are to understand leaning in as feminism, let it be clearly an anti-utopian feminism—one that takes settling with what exists as its first principle. The figure of the comedienne has been central to this "transformation of feminism into an accepted part of institutional 'common sense,'" as Eileen Meehan writes, "which works through the neoliberal emphasis on individualism." The logical conclusion of this transformation is that "if equal advancement is now open to formerly marginalized groups of women, then feminist critique of institutions and cultural objects becomes unnecessary, and, to a degree, shameful and retrogressive," Meehan argues,

---

46 Sheryl Sandberg, *Lean In: Women, Work, and the Will to Lead* (New York: Knopf, 2013), 27–28.

such that "individuals under neoliberalism are responsible for their own success or failure on the job, and in their personal lives as well."[47] The struggle is about getting a seat at that table, never about taking a chainsaw to it and everything it represents.

One of the best sketches I've ever seen on *SNL* was the cold open when Kerry Washington hosted in 2013. Despite the last decade of praise *SNL* had received for its almost all white girls' club, the show was getting some bad press for adding five white men to its cast that season. In the sketch, Washington begins in the role of Michelle Obama, but is soon pushed out of the scene for a costume change to play Oprah Winfrey. When she is pushed out of the scene again, in order to return as Beyoncé, a flock of Matthew McConaugheys swarm the stage, played by only *some* of the white men on cast. As Washington moves frantically between characters, a message appears on screen, supposedly from the show's producers:

> [We] would like to apologize to Kerry Washington for the number of black women she will be asked to play tonight. We made these requests both because Ms. Washington is an actress of considerable range and talent and also because "SNL" does not currently have a black woman on the cast. As for the latter reason we agree that this is not an ideal situation and look forward to rectifying it in the near future . . . unless, of course, we fall in love with another white guy first.[48]

In its spoof of the white masculine excess of the show's brand of sketch comedy, the cold open also highlights the ways in which the ethos of "bitches get stuff done" places even greater pressure on non-white performers, while the terms of their work ethic are idealized and dictated by white comediennes.

For the first two decades of *SNL*, the show's cast featured about one Black comedian at a time if at all—notably, Garret Morris from 1975–80, Eddie Murphy from 1980–84, Damon Wayans from 1985–86, and

---

47 Eileen R. Meehan, "A Legacy of Neoliberalism: Patterns in Media Conglomeration," in *Neoliberalism and Global Cinema: Capital, Culture, and Marxist Critique*, ed. Jyotsna Kapur and Keith B. Wagner (New York: Routledge, 2011), 63.

48 Don Roy King, "Kerry Washington," *Saturday Night Live* (NBC, November 2, 2013).

Chris Rock from 1990–93. Yvonne Hudson had a stint on the show from 1980–81, and Danitra Vance was on the show briefly in 1985, but then it was not until Ellen Cleghorne joined the cast in 1991 that a Black woman was hired to do much more than background appearances, when not being asked to perform offensive racial stereotypes. Before he quit the show to go to *In Living Color*, Chris Rock reached a point, as he later recalled, when he "wanted to be in an environment where I didn't really have to translate the comedy I wanted to do," and he wasn't going to be asked to play "whatever slave sketch or banging tribesman."[49] Maya Rudolph was the first Black woman to have a significant presence on the show, at the outset of the girls' club era, from 2000–2007. Yet after she left the show, the cast had been without a Black woman for six years before Washington's interventionary cold open.

The week that Washington hosted in 2013, the civil rights group ColorOfChange.org wrote an open letter to producer Michaels which quickly made headlines. The letter reads: "Your decision to tap Kerry Washington, the breakout star of ABC's tremendously popular *Scandal*, to host this week's show at least acknowledges that TV viewers want to see dynamic, multidimensional Black women characters on screen." It continues, "But it's scandalous that after Ms. Washington's episode wraps on Saturday, this season is unlikely to feature any Black women characters at all."[50] As the letter conveys quite persuasively, the show's casting is not just a matter of diversifying a workplace. Casting has limited the show's representational capacity, as sketch comedy—though this has often been addressed as a matter of who can do the job. As a result, *SNL* has a long history of Black women played by Black men. Soon before Washington's appearance, cast member Keenan Thompson told the press that he refused to play Black women on the show anymore, stepping away from some of his high-profile roles like Oprah, which were all primarily derogatory. The show also has a long history of blackface, which never actually ended. When these issues were being raised in 2013, a recurring character on the show was what ColorOfChange interpreted as a "large, non-functional (i.e., overweight and lazy), unmistakably 'Black' Starbucks coffee barista," played by white cast member Cecily Strong.[51] Though the character has

49 Marc Maron, "Episode 224: Chris Rock," *WTF with Marc Maron's WTF*, November 3, 2011.

50 See Aaron Couch, "Civil Rights Group to Lorne Michaels: Why Doesn't 'SNL' Cast Black Women?" *The Hollywood Reporter*, November 1, 2013, https://www.hollywoodreporter.com/tv/tv-news/snl-lorne-michaels-asked-by-652441/.

51 Couch, "Civil Rights Group to Lorne Michaels."

not reappeared, Strong continued to play many Latina characters, in the absence of a Latina cast member until Melissa Villaseñor joined the cast in 2016. Villaseñor was the first Latina cast member in the show's entire history, joining in its forty-first season. In 2019, *SNL* hired Bowen Yang, the show's first Asian-American cast member, after decades of Asian characters being limited to roles played by white cast members.

Since the white feminist ascendance of the girls' club in the 2000s, the *SNL* writers' room has diversified and adapted throughout the 2010s and especially the Trump years, though never without a fight. While who has a seat at the table may be different, this is what it's always meant to sit there.

Feminism Can Be More Than a Work Ethic

> "[R]efuse the myth of liberation through work . . . For we
> have worked enough."
> —Mariarosa Dalla Costa, "Women and the Subversion of
> the Community"

What's been obscured throughout the history of feminist interventions within and outside of the working world of comedy is the possibility of a feminist comedy at all, unless it is warped and made imaginable as a work ethic. The comedienne, it would seem, has always had to *work for it*. But another feminist comedy is possible, beginning with the refusal to pretend that that work isn't work.

London Hughes's 2020 stand-up special *To Catch a D*ck* helps us to understand what a feminist antiwork ethic in comedy might look like. As the special begins, Hughes sits at her dressing room mirror, talking herself up as "comedy Beyoncé." Much of her material is about being a Black British woman who moved to Los Angeles weeks before everything shut down in February 2020 and not being able to "catch a dick," while Hughes is at her most remarkable in her accounts of all relationships—like all work—as sex work. "Men, you don't have kids. You get kids," she says, continuing, ". . . I think babies are disrespectful to women":

> As a woman, you catch a sudden case of dick, it results in
> a pregnancy? Nine months. NINE MONTHS. NINE MONTHS.
> Making a human in your guts. Making eyes, ears, and
> elbows in your guts. Making a human in your guts. Can't

even drink to get yourself through it . . . Fully formed. A fully formed human. Not like an Ikea. Fully formed. Nine months. Nine months. Nine months . . . Then you've gotta push that fucker out. You gotta push it out. It might take two days. It might take two fucking days. It will rip your vagina. Rip it out. Ruin it, ruin it, ruin it . . . and then blood, blood, blood, blood. Blood, all over the place.[52]

The routine goes on much longer, with Hughes ingeniously pantomiming the excruciating ordeal (and work) of pregnancy and childbirth. Throughout her special, Hughes makes the most out of these descriptions of work—showing things that are otherwise called "love," that is, to be work even still. Upturning the notion of a "labor of love" is intrinsic to her approach to comedy.

Hughes's *To Catch a D*ck* in many ways elaborates what Maya Andrea Gonzalez and Cassandra Troyan brilliantly characterize as the labor conditions of "the girlfriend experience." "Girlfriending as a form of commodified pseudo-experience entails a discreet work relation between a 'provider' of romantic experience—or 'sugar baby'—and its/ their consumer, the 'hobbyist' or 'sugar daddy,'" they explain, unpacking the transactions at the heart of this dynamic: "Over the duration of an individual encounter or throughout an ongoing engagement, this work-relation appears as the non-consumption of an experiential commodity, whilst taking place in an actual labor process of providing intimate services."[53] Hughes creates a hilarious portrait of girlfriending, for which much of the comedy draws its energy from revealing this commodified, exchange-based interaction in romantic experiences. At one point in *To Catch a D*ck*, Hughes tells the story of her brief relationship with a foot fetishist, who she met online. The first week was spent sending him photos of her feet in different positions. "He liked toes up high, toes down low, toes by the seat, toes on the window ledge," she recalls. Then after, they arranged to meet. She was wearing Ugg boots—"OK, let me not lie," she interjects, "I was broke and I was wearing *flugg* boots." However, her date was horrified. "Why are your feet in those furry shoes?" he asked. "I'd love it if you just took the shoes off . . . take them off and I'll buy you shoes." From the train station where they

52 Kristian Mercado, *London Hughes: To Catch a D*ck*, stand-up special (Netflix, 2020).
53 Maya Gonzalez and Cassandra Troyan, "Heart of a Heartless World," *Blind Field: A Journal of Cultural Inquiry*, May 26, 2016, https://blindfieldjournal. com/2016/05/26/3-of-a-heartless-world/.

met, they went directly to purchase some shoes—"they cost twelve hundred pounds. They were rent. He bought me rent shoes!" By the time he brought her to his place, she explains, she realized "I'm ready! I'm ready to suck dick for shoes." She brags that "after the sex, he gifted me a pair of shoes," and ends the story explaining "I was with him for six weeks and I got twelve pairs of shoes!"—to which the audience claps, roaring with laughter.

The refusal of work is a consistent theme through Hughes's stand-up: "What is this shit, exercise?" she asks, "Exercising on purpose? . . . Running? . . . White privilege is running even when no one's chasing you." Her comedy doesn't need to talk about feminism to be feminist—it unfolds through a feminist practice, no matter its content, as a comedy of exposing work as work.

Hughes's comedy resonates, in some ways, with that of Ali Wong, whose comedy is also about the refusal of work. In her 2016 comedy special *Baby Cobra*, Wong interrogates the ideology of lean in—and with it, the work ethic of the white comedienne. "I don't want to work anymore," Wong tells her audience, as she details the professional credentials of her husband. "I don't feed him out of the goodness of my heart, I do it as an investment in my financial future." Of Sandberg, Wong explains, "her book is called *Lean In*," continuing:

> . . . well I don't want to lean in, I want to lie down. I want to lie the fuck down . . . . Our job [as women] used to be no job. We had it so good. We could've done the smart thing, which would have been to continue playing dumb for the next century, and be like "we're dumb women, we don't know how to do anything, so I guess we'd better stay at home all day and eat snacks and watch Ellen, because we're too stupid to have any real responsibility." And then all these women had to show off and be like "we can do it! We can do anything!" *Bitch shut up!* ... They ruined it for us, and now we're expected to work.[54]

Moments like this highlight the limit-point of Wong's politics, as she deals in misogynist tropes which erase work historically performed unwaged or underpaid by women. It's possible to make a joke without doing this—or even, to make a joke out of doing this.

---

54 Jay Karas, *Ali Wong: Baby Cobra*, stand-up special (Netflix, 2016).

As Wong saunters across the stage, ridiculing the ambition and careerism of lean in feminism, she is also, and quite notably, late into her third trimester of pregnancy. Regardless of her punchlines about lying down, she could not be a more picture-perfect version of the ideology of work that she half-heartedly mocks. Two years later, Wong filmed a second stand-up special, *Hard Knock Wife* (2018), towards the end of her second pregnancy. While her comedy, in many ways, is working with a fascinating schtick, it's her leanin-ism, not her pregnancy, which remains the elephant in the room. There's just so much potential, all the while unmet, in her comedy of pregnancy on the job.

These missed opportunities in Wong's comedy beg the question of what an antiwork feminist approach to comedy could be instead. Wong is an incredibly talented performer, whose commitment to the job could not be more evident. Yet her unwillingness to critique her own work ethic distinguishes her comedy from that of Hughes, for instance, whose material is based on recognizing the preposterousness of work. Most of the stories in *To Catch a D*ck* are about what Hughes does to be able to earn—whether through cash, shoes, meals, drinks, Uber fares, etc. In her portrait of *girlfriending* as fundamentally sex work, Hughes participates in a long tradition of raunchy comedienne humor, foregrounding her sexuality throughout, but the joke always orbits around the work of it all. She extends her critical comedy to the unrelenting racism and sexism that are seemingly unavoidable elements of her job as a stand-up comedian—a job which is never at any point hidden as a job, or romanticized as "art," a masquerade which is always in some ways thought to be a part of the job. Wong's comedy, to the contrary, understands comedy much like housework and childcare, as part of an imaginary of jobless non-work: comedy isn't work, she seems to insist—it's a hobby that happens to pay her very well. Whether or not Wong's comedy glorifies the seeming slackerdom of "lying down," it is all the while embedded in a valorization of leaning in.

What would an antiwork feminist approach to comedy look like? Along with Hughes, I turn to River Butcher's recent stand-up as a place to start imagining. Years before their transition in 2021, Butcher took to the stage to process their day-to-day experiences of gender, at times framing this process in antiwork terms. "I don't honestly, at this point know, what my gender identity is. Honestly it feels like, 'do you work here?' they explain on stage, pretending to be a customer. "Because that's what most people call me . . . 'you work here, right?' usually my answer is 'no,' and then their follow up is, 'are you sure?'" Much of the time, Butcher's comedy is about gender being this job you don't want to be at—but that you're somehow always working. And part of this is an active troubling of the politics of inclusion which have riddled the history of feminism and comedy. As Butcher jokes, "realistically though, I identify as the 'and' in 'ladies and gentlemen,' that way I'm included even when I'm not, you know what I mean?"[55]

Maria Bamford is a stand-up whose material often scratches at the possibilities of an antiwork feminist comedy. For decades, she has consistently linked her mental health struggles to her experiences as a worker, both before and after she could rely on comedy for paychecks. In her early years as a stand-up, Bamford worked as an office temp, along with other gigs—for a while she played a Bajoran character in a *Star Trek* touring show that mostly did mall and fast food restaurant openings in the South. In 2010, severe anxiety drove Bamford to audition for (and later accept) the role of a manic shopper for a Target ad campaign. After a while, she began to "obsess about the ethic[s] of advertising something, and consumerism," she later recalled, "I was working a lot more than I ever had . . . but it was also very stressful." Soon thereafter, Bamford was hospitalized. A few years later, she looks back on this experience of becoming the iconic "Crazy Target Lady" in her pseudo-autobiographical series *Lady Dynamite*. At the beginning of the series, Bamford tells her manager Bruce (Fred Melamed) "I would like to do less, not more—that's the thing." Concerned that she'll have another breakdown, she explains "I want to work a little, just smaller things, less pressure. Maybe stand-up at a bookstore, or alone in my living room, or a vintage eyeglass shop?"[56] Far more than present a perfect picture of antiwork critique, Bamford meditates on antiwork impulses and longings. Hesitant to theorize these tendencies, her comedy opens a space for questioning.

The utopian elements of Bamford's antiwork comedy emerge from dystopian feelings. In *Lady Dynamite* and elsewhere, her experiences of suicidal ideation and mania are reconfigured as *zany*, often parodying the mental health stigma of the "Crazy Target Lady." In her account of the "zany" as a key aesthetic category of contemporary capitalism, Sianne Ngai suggests that zaniness is what makes play into a matter of work, as part of a broader set of transitions in affective labor in late capitalism. "For all their playfulness and commitment to fun," Ngai writes, "the zany's characters give the impression of needing to labor excessively hard to produce our laughter, straining themselves to the point of endangering

---

55 Matthew Klauschie, "River Butcher: Gender Normativity & An Accidental Catcall," *Comedy Central Stand-Up* (November 27, 2019).

56 Mitchell Hurwitz, "Pilot," *Lady Dynamite* (Netflix, May 20, 2016).

not just themselves but also those around them." Zaniness in this sense "flatters the spectator's sense of comparative security," she explains, "by turning the worker's beset, precarious condition into a spectacle for our entertainment[.]"[57] In *Lady Dynamite*, this narrative trope operates in terms of Bamford's psychological instability, as the story jumps timelines between moments of job insecurity and relative success. Throughout all this Bamford wears zaniness like an itchy sweater—always scheming for a way to escape, but also, hopefully, survive.

There are also glimmers of antiwork feminist comedy throughout Issa Rae's series *Insecure*, which explores awkwardness as a zaniness systemically linked to Blackness. As the token Black woman among her coworkers at a non-profit, We Got Y'All, the protagonist Issa is constantly dealing with awkard situations. Like many jobs, Issa's far exceeds its job description. Much of her energy day to day is exerted toward withholding her frustrations, biting her tongue. She is constantly performing these micro-tasks that are not only invisible, but consciously hidden—and she actively hides this non-stop work to avoid further awkwardness, and even more work. She neutralizes the low-key racism of her workplace and coworkers, accommodating, internalizing, mediating, compensating for the white guilt of the non-profit system one interaction at a time. "Being aggressively passive is what I do best," she explains at one point. Throughout *Insecure*, these everyday experiences break away at the myth of the "unshakeable" Black woman—what Charisse Jones and Kumea Shorter-Gooden define as a caricature of Black women as "tough, pushy, and in charge rather than soft, feminine, and vulnerable … someone to be feared rather than someone to be loved." [58] Caringly, and insistently, the series works against this idea of unshakeability, as well as the awkwardness of work as an ongoing, painful relationship to whiteness.

Outside her work at We Got Y'All, Issa experiences euphoric moments of solidarity with her friends Molly, Kelli, and Tiffany, a cohort of professional Black women who share war stories. At work, Molly discovers that a white man at her office, who's been there as long as she has, earns significantly more than her while slacking off most of the time. "What am I supposed to do?" she asks her friends. "I'm not one of these work twice as hard pay me half as much bitches." At the same time, the group of friends hardly entertains any illusions about their ability to

---

57 Sianne Ngai, *Our Aesthetic Categories: Zany, Cute, Interesting* (Cambridge: Harvard University Press, 2012), 10-11.
58 Charisse Jones and Kumea Shorter-Gooden, *Shifting: The Double Lives of Black Women in America* (New York: HarperCollins, 2004), 19.

reform their workplaces. "This is so typical," Tiffany complains, "My aunt found out she made less than some of her white employees. Spoke up about it. Nothing happened. She still has to work there." In their workplaces, all of these women find themselves performing what Adia Harvey Wingfield and Renee Skeete conceive as racial tasks in the workplace that, while reinforcing a white hierarchy, "are a type of work that is frequently hidden from white colleagues but that remains essential for minority workers within an organization."[59] In foregrounding these tasks, along with moments of commiseration between these characters, *Insecure* can be understood, consistently, as a comedy with a critique of work. And inconsistently, but quite beautifully, it veers towards an antiwork utopianism—not in the moments when we find ourselves rooting for Issa to take on her workplace, but in the moments when she gets to carve out some space from that world and laugh with her friends.

These are just a few examples of utopian gestures, indistinct expressions of how an antiwork feminism might be cultivated in comedy. It requires a critical utopianism, one which can cut through the false freedoms promised by work. None of these stand-ups or comic actors (Hughes, Butcher, Bamford, or Rae) offers a perfect vision of this feminism. Yet each in their own way develops an approach to feminist comedy that challenges the gendered and racialized capitalist work ethic, so pervasive to the legacy of comediennes.

---

59 Adia Harvey Wingfield and Renee Skeete, "Maintaining Hierarchies in Predominantly White Organizations: A Theory of Racial Tasks as Invisible Labor," in *Invisible Labor: Hidden Work in the Contemporary World*, ed. Winifred Poster, Marion G. Crain, and Miriam A. Cherry (Oakland: University of California Press, 2016), 50.

CHAPTER FOUR

The Trouble With "Authenticity"

"If this was a normal office where, on your first day, someone higher up than you goes: 'Here's a list of guys in the office who might rape you,' you would go straight to HR," Laura Duddy remarked in an interview, a year into working as a stand-up comedian. "But there's no HR—there's nowhere we can go to say this is happening."[1] In so many ways, this was the hope that emerged from #MeToo—or more precisely, the threat. If only possibilities could be imagined further, past the dream of HR-mediation, and toward more revolutionary prospects of collective care.

By now #MeToo conjures an imaginary of cultural upheavals, seismic shifts in the social and political landscape, and specifically, the workplace. When Louis C.K. became the first of a string of prominent comedians to "get #MeToo'd," the comedy industry was still mired in rape joke debates.[2] Despite the fact that stand-up comedy was among the most vulnerable industries, precisely because of its fetishization of "artistic freedom," the supposed threat of "cancel culture" distorts, in many ways, what actually changed in comedy. Less than a year after he was "canceled," C.K. returned to stand-up and released a special a year and a half later. Having lost an estimated $35 million in 2018, C.K. claimed in his first set back at the Comedy Cellar that he'd been to "hell and back."[3] Soon he began selling

1   Rachael Healy, "'I've Had Men Rub Their Genitals against Me': Female Comedians on Extreme Sexism in Standup," *The Guardian*, August 5, 2020, https://www.theguardian.com/stage/2020/aug/05/creepy-uncomfortable-sexism-harassment-assault-faced-by-female-standups.

2   I'll return to this in Chapter 6.

3   See Zack Sharf, "Jerry Seinfeld: Why Louis C.K. Isn't Making His Comeback in the Right Way," *IndieWire*, October 26, 2018, https://www.indiewire.com/2018/10/jerry-seinfeld-louis-ck-comeback-interview-1202015667/; and Zack Sharf, "Sarah Silverman Says Louis C.K. Used to Masturbate in Front of Her With Her Consent," *IndieWire*, October 22, 2018, https://www.indiewire.com/2018/10/sarah-silverman-says-louis-c-k-masturbate-in-front-of-her-consent-1202014148/.

out theaters again. In 2021, he won a Grammy for Best Comedy Album of the Year. While the comedy world has taken a lot of hits in this time, it has more than doubled down. Little has shifted in terms of comedy's power structure, remaining one of the most male-dominated facets of the culture industry. In 2019, among the top ten highest earning comedians in the U.S., the only woman was Amy Schumer.

Today's favorite comedian of the alt right, C.K. rose to success as part of a long tradition of masculinity in stand-up, which by now preserves and legitimates white patriarchal power through a mythology of *authenticity* in comedy. Intrinsic to the myth of authenticity is a particular work ethic, a will to *tell the truth* no matter the consequences. The irony of how this authenticity was jeopardized by the truth-telling of #MeToo, and later, the George Floyd uprisings, should not be lost on us.

Since the stand-up comedy renaissance of the fifties and sixties in the U.S., this myth of "authenticity" emerged and transformed with the political changes of the decades to follow. The prototypical "authentic" stand-up is certainly Lenny Bruce, who was arrested on charges of obscenity several times between 1961–1964 and became a martyr of artistic freedom in comedy. As the authentic, truth-telling stand-up artist, Bruce was a tragic figure—long before his early death, at the age of forty, from a drug overdose in 1966—who stood up against censorship laws for the remainder of his life. Blending social criticism and commentary with storytelling, his comedy diverged in crucial ways from the more formulaic stand-up of the fifties comedy clubs, and inspired some of the best comedians of the sixties-seventies.

Part of the story of "authenticity" since Bruce is the story of how, as Luc Boltanski and Eve Chiapello write, "capitalism incorporated much of the *artistic critique* that flourished at the end of the sixties."[4] What they describe as the "new spirit of capitalism" drew from and redirected revolutionary and countercultural energies of the sixties toward the project of re-imagining capitalism in terms of liberation and the demand for authenticity. "[C]apitalism's assimilation of the demand for authenticity," Boltanski and Chiapello suggest, has "introduce[d] into people's relationship to goods and persons *rapid cycles of infatuation and disappointment.*"[5] Mirroring these cycles, stand-up comedy is one of the defining emergent art forms of this time. And the proliferation of raw, truth-telling, vulnerable artist figures in stand-up comedy since the end of the sixties unfurls

---

4 Boltanski and Chiapello, *The New Spirit of Capitalism* (New York: Verso, 2005), 419.
5 Boltanski and Chiapello, *The New Spirit of Capitalism*, 445.

from the intensive commodification of authenticity, a driving force of this new spirit of capitalism.

This chapter is about this myth of authenticity, its mutations through the years, and how it eventually became the defining feature of stand-up's reactionary turn in the Trump era.

The Poetics of Richard Pryor and the Politics of Being "Un-Phony"

Richard Pryor "was not just a comedian but also an artist and a revolutionary," as Cathy Park Hong writes: "He got rid of the punchline to prove that stand-up could be anything, which is what geniuses do: they blow up moth-balled conventions in their chosen genre and show you how a song, or a poem, or a sculpture, can take form."[6] Pryor's comedy was shaped as much by Malcolm X and the Black Panthers as by his contemporaries in stand-up. After moving to Berkeley in 1969, Pryor began to learn from revolutionaries like Huey P. Newton, studying the Haitian Revolution, reading Frantz Fanon, and experimenting with his comedy. Fellow comedian Cecil Brown, close to Pryor during this period, remembers a show when a white guy in the audience began heckling Pryor. "[The white guy] goes 'you oughta be glad I got a sense of humor,'" Brown recalls, "and Richard said, 'yeah, you know I am glad you got a sense of humor, 'cause I know what you do to us n*ggers.'"[7] During that time, Pryor began not only pushing back against racism he encountered in the clubs, but making the racism he experienced non-stop into his stand-up material. It was this period in the late sixties that forever altered Pryor's comedy, and what made Pryor's method so brilliant was particularly its capacity to speak the unspoken. It wasn't a matter of shock value, but truth value.

But this wasn't always the case. When Pryor started out in comedy, he was packaged by the comedy establishment (talent scouts, managers, and club owners) as "the next Bill Cosby." He began working the New York club scene in the early sixties, when Lenny Bruce was modeling a new kind of stand-up—focused less on punchlines, timing, and most importantly, crowd-pleasing. By the time Bruce died in 1966, Pryor's career was skyrocketing. He landed a contract at the Aladdin, in Las Vegas. By all

---

6   Cathy Park Hong, *Minor Feelings: An Asian American Reckoning* (New York: One World, 2020), 38.
7   Marina Zenovich, *Richard Pryor: Omit the Logic* (Showtime, 2013), https://www.sho.com/titles/3361052/richard-pryor-omit-the-logic.

accounts he'd "made it" not only as a comedian, but as a Black comedian in a time when the stand-up industry was especially dominated by white men. Then in 1967, he experienced what he would later call a nervous breakdown. After years of feeling like "Bill Cosby lite," as Darryl Littleton writes, Pryor was in crisis. In the middle of his performance, as the legend has it, Pryor asked himself in front of the audience, "What the fuck am I doing here?" and then walked off the stage.[8] From that point on, Pryor would become something like the anti-Cosby: a version of Black masculinity in comedy which was decidedly un-phony—and *not* white.

Pryor's antiracism was also explicitly anticapitalist: "It's part of capitalism to promote racism, in order to make things work . . . and that separates people," he explained to journalist Bill Boggs in a 1977 interview. "So they keep people separated and that keeps them from thinking about the real problem. That's as simple as I see it."[9] Hilton Als calls Pryor the first Black spoken-word artist to break out of a certain conception of Blackness in the U.S. that "has almost always had to explain itself to a largely white audience in order to be heard," and the general assumption is that there is "only one story to tell—a story of oppression that plays on liberal guilt."[10]

More and more through the years, the stories about Pryor told among comedians and cultural critics revolved around his *authenticity*. It's hard to find an account of his on-stage presence without encountering this idea of his authentic approach to comedy. He wasn't working for laughs, he was doing something else. "You feel, in the audience," Scott Saul writes, "that you're plugged into the socket of life—that you're seeing not a single man onstage but rather an entire world in roiling motion, animated through a taut experiment in creative chaos and artistic control."[11]

At the heart of these stories about Pryor's authenticity is a particular work ethic, similarly ascribed to Lenny Bruce, and later, to George Carlin—a vision of the stand-up comedian as a philosopher and martyr-figure who cannot help but speak truth to power, and indeed, to express his *authentic self*. But for Pryor, the reality of this myth of

---

8   Darryl Littleton, *Black Comedians on Black Comedy: How African-Americans Taught Us to Laugh* (New York: Applause Theatre & Cinema Books, 2006), 132.
9   See Janice Williams, "Richard Pryor's 1977 Speech about Capitalism Leading to Racism Is Striking a Chord Decades Later," *Newsweek*, July 24, 2020, https://www.newsweek.com/richard-pryors-1977-speech-about-capitalism-leading-racism-striking-chord-decades-later-1520293.
10   Hilton Als, "A Pryor Love," *The New Yorker*, September 13, 1999, https://www.newyorker.com/magazine/1999/09/13/a-pryor-love.
11   Saul, *Becoming Richard Pryor*, 5.

authenticity was a constant battle with the specter of phoniness. After he walked off stage in Vegas, Pryor broke apart his conceptions of comedy in the Bay Area. During that time, he repurposed some of the techniques and insights he'd gained in the years before. He hadn't quit comedy, as some claimed—he was rethinking comedy. He became fascinated by the Black Panthers' emphasis on education, which he applied to his stand-up material.[12] "[Having] come to Berkeley without a clear sense of his future," Saul explains, Pryor "had absorbed the countercultural energies of his new home and tried out different versions of himself: serious actor, guerrilla filmmaker, poet, political satirist. His struggle was that of an artist searching for his true medium, not of a comedian polishing his material."[13]

Pryor re-invented himself as part of his artistic process—in some ways, a relentless shirking off of authenticity, as the work ethic ascribed to his comedy. After committing what many thought was career suicide in Vegas, he re-emerged from his time in the Bay Area with confidence in his new philosophy of comedy. In the early seventies, he transitioned to the Los Angeles club scene, and began workshopping his material to great success, including two Grammy awards in 1974 and 1976 for Best Comedy Album of the Year. While his comedy was gaining mainstream recognition, Pryor kept transgressing boundaries, always with a sense of unease about the specifically white-supremacist conventions of stand-up.

During those years of climbing the ranks of comedians in the seventies, he used the n-word as a political weapon against whiteness, quite often directed at white members of his audience. All this changed in 1979, however, when he visited Kenya. In his autobiography *Pryor Convictions*, he remembers leaving with the regret of "ever having uttered the word . . . on stage or off it. It was a wretched word. Its connotations weren't funny, even when people laughed."[14] While he had once believed in the power of reappropriating the language of hate, he eventually lamented the ways in which the political interventions of his comedy were still embedded in a racist power structure. He became consumed by the question of how to do comedy without compromise.

The year after his trip to Kenya came another pivotal transformation in Pryor's life and comedy. On June 9, 1980, he nearly died during a fire at his house in Northridge, California. Found running down the

---

12   David Henry and Joe Henry, *Furious Cool: Richard Pryor and the World That Made Him*, First Edition (Chapel Hill: Algonquin Books of Chapel Hill, 2013), 118.
13   Saul, *Becoming Richard Pryor*, xiv.
14   Richard Pryor and Todd Gold, *Pryor Convictions, and Other Life Sentences* (New York: Pantheon Books, 1995), 175.

street, he was quickly brought to the hospital in critical condition. It's said his chance of survival was one in three. Rumors circulated about the cause of the fire and whether it was drug-related, arson, or accidental, and more. Ultimately, there was some consensus that Pryor was suffering from drug-induced psychosis at the time. Perhaps he poured rum all over his body and lit a match, or he might have been free-basing cocaine. In an interview following his recovery, he called it suicide. It wasn't an attempt, he insisted, as the suicide "worked": "That person's dead . . . and he was a horrible man."[15]

However bound up in some idea of authenticity, Pryor's approach to comedy lays bare a consistent tension with that idea—the struggle to not be a phony. Authenticity, as Walter Benjamin suggests, is that which eludes reproduction:

> In even the most perfect reproduction, one thing is lacking: the here and now of the work of art—its unique existence in a particular place. It is this unique existence—and nothing else—that bears the mark of the history to which the work has been subject . . . The here and now of the original underlies the concept of its authenticity, and on the latter in turn is founded the idea of a tradition which has passed the object down as the same, identical thing to the present day.[16]

Rather than as a "work ethic" per se, we might understand this as Pryor's comedic method, which involved constant workshopping. Pryor would draft and revise different routines until they reached a point of closure. Then, instead of continuing to perform and polish the routine as a final product, he moved on to whatever was next. Some call this the "raw material" of his stand-up—a phrase that lingers with any mention of *authenticity*.

What is ultimately most *authentic* about Pryor's comedy is what others attempt to copy, or more precisely, what others can only fail to emulate. Just as he was pressured to promote himself as the "next Cosby" in his early years, many comedians since Pryor have tried to replicate his persona but also his method. This legacy in Pryor's career "reveals the inherent

---

15 Footage featured in *Richard Pryor: Omit the Logic* (1:02).

16 Walter Benjamin, *Illuminations: Essays and Reflections*, ed. Hannah Arendt, trans. Harry Zohn (New York: Mariner Books, 2019), 169.

pitfalls of authenticity, but also the necessity for oppressed bodies and communities to hold onto the cultural products that are theirs," as Justin Hogg suggests, pointing to different modes of resistance to the predation of whiteness, expressed as an assumption of universal ownership.[17]

Authenticity is the story about Pryor. It describes the way he continues to be fetishized in comedy. But it is a story he never told—he never claimed to be authentic. That was always about what other people wanted him to be for them.

Searching for Andy Kaufman

What was most authentic about Andy Kaufman's comedy was his inauthenticity. Take his notorious "Mighty Mouse" routine, in which he stood nervously beside a record player, listening to the theme song of the famous cartoon. As the audience waited for him to do something—*anything*—he lifted his arm as the song's chorus arrived, pantomiming Mighty Mouse's declaration "Here I come to save the day!", only to step back and keep listening. Was he serious about any of this? Never. But that didn't stop others from taking it seriously.

Throughout the thirteen years he performed comedy, Kaufman would often insist that he wasn't a comedian. "Andy couldn't tell a joke to save his life. Wouldn't want to," recall his close friend Bob Zmuda and his partner Lynne Margulies in their biography of Kaufman. As they remember, Kaufman was "a bullshit artist, a master in the art of the humbug or 'put-on,' a prankster."[18] Kaufman's jokes were meta-jokes—part of a broader practice of joking about joking, and critically re-imagining comedy through the unraveling or even sabotaging of the audience's expectations. While seeking out what might be considered a more authentic experience of comedy, distinct from the robotic, impersonal conventions of a stand-up "routine," his comedy was premised in an assemblage of distinct characters. Andy Kaufman was the absent center, unknowably shifting between these alter egos. "Kaufman created a hall of mirrors," as Philip Auslander explains, "in which no persona ever turned out to be a dependable representation."[19]

---

17 Justin Hogg, "Between Two Worlds: Race and Authenticity in Cover Songs," *Blind Field: A Journal of Cultural Inquiry*, June 2, 2017, https://blindfieldjournal. com/2017/06/02/between-two-worlds-race-and-authenticity-in-cover-songs/.

18 Bob Zmuda and Lynne Elaine Margulies, *Andy Kaufman: The Truth, Finally* (Dallas, Texas: BenBella Books, 2014), 7.

19 Philip Auslander, "Postmodernism and Performance," in *The Cambridge Companion to Postmodernism*, ed. Steven Connor (Cambridge: Cambridge University Press, 2004), 108.

In his first appearance on Johnny Carson's *The Tonight Show*, in 1976, Kaufman came as his character Foreign Man. He spoke in a vaguely non-American accent, with an endearing cadence and a sense of earnestness that was, beneath the surface, utterly insincere. In the years to follow, he was celebrated for his bad impersonation of Elvis, and for his more defined iteration of Foreign Man as "Latka Gravas" on the ABC sitcom *Taxi*, starting in 1978. The most notorious of his characters, however, was Tony Clifton. As Clifton, Kaufman was virtually unrecognizable, under a fake mustache, wig, and dark glasses. For a period, Kaufman was able to convince some that he and Clifton were different people, hiring Zmuda or his brother to play him during joint appearances designed to elevate the prank. Clifton's stage presence was volatile—a clear contrast from the quiet passivity of most of Kaufman's characters. Clifton would storm onto stage and yell at the audience, and most of his act was an attempt to sabotage Kaufman's career. Clifton's brand of comedy could be characterized as aggressively unfunny, reliant not only on the audience's dissatisfaction but outrage.

"The starting position of the trickster," Helena Bassil-Morozow suggests, "is always that of imprisonment, constraint and limitation."[20] For Kaufman, this constraint was authenticity. To whatever extent "authenticity" has been ascribed to his comedy, this was all based on his persistent, even compulsive drive for inauthenticity. Kaufman's trickster inauthenticity was his artistic strategy and work ethic: in tirelessly resisting the conventions of "comedian," "artist," "genius," he nevertheless drew more and more of these ascriptions to his work. To keep up this momentum, he had to continue coming up with ways to refuse to embrace the conventions he taunted.

The most fascinating part of Kaufman's career began in the late seventies, once he had become something of a household name. Facing some obligation to make appearances *as himself*, Kaufman experimented with ways to deflect his reputation. In a 1977 performance at The Improv, Kaufman begins, "Thank you very much. Right now I'd like to do a comedy routine. Up until now, you know, every time I've appeared some place, I always do that Foreign Man character that I do. And I'd like to branch out and, you know, do myself."[21] After performing a few minutes of stale, clichéd bits, he pauses and says to the audience, in seeming sincerity, "I

---

20 Helena Victor Bassil-Morozow, *The Trickster in Contemporary Film* (New York: Routledge, 2012), 24.
21 *Andy Kaufman Performance at the Improv*, 1977, https://www.youtube.com/watch?v=fzKbqbjEjEE.

don't understand one thing. No seriously. Why is everyone going 'booo' when I tell some of the jokes, and then when I don't want you to laugh, you're laughing. Like right now. I don't understand." After apologizing to the audience and telling them that he had more material but it just won't work now, he excuses himself, only to return a minute later for another routine with the conga drums he brought to stage. As the demand grew for Kaufman to be himself, his comedy pivoted from positioning him as the butt of the joke, and into something like becoming the joke itself.

In the early eighties, Kaufman continued expanding on this self-portrait as joke. He began challenging women to wrestle him in fully equipped amateur wrestling matches, rendering himself a mockery of male chauvinism. Whether this was antipatriarchal or antifeminist (or both) depended entirely on how the mockery was interpreted. But who was to decide? Turning to the author, there was no there there. Who he really was, what he really wanted—these were all unknowable factors, stripping down the experience to the audience's reaction. When Kaufman died in 1984, many believed it was just another prank. Some continue to believe.

But in the years before his death Kaufman was, in many ways, the living death of the author. His comedy, especially in its reliance on participation and interaction, enacted what Roland Barthes conceived as the "multiplicity of writing," in which "everything is to be disentangled, nothing deciphered[.]"[22] Besides reinforcing this fantasy of authentic comedy, Kaufman's refusal of authorship can be read, likewise, as an insistence on taking comedy more seriously as an object of interpretation. He danced around the interpretability of his real intentions, but also around the fantasy of those intentions having any correlation with the meaning of his comedy. He evaded authenticity at every step. At the same time, this inauthenticity preyed on the sincerity of others—whoever was not in on the joke, including those who were being joked upon. These are latent aspects of Kaufman's comedy, often diffused by self-deprecation, but which have endured as his legacy.

§

After he played Andy Kaufman in Miloš Forman's 1999 biopic *Man on the Moon*, Jim Carrey managed to achieve what many deemed impossible in Hollywood, transitioning from his slapstick persona from early

---

22 Roland Barthes, *Image, Music, Text*, trans. Stephen Heath (New York: Hill and Wang, 2009), 148.

nineties roles in *Ace Ventura* and *Dumb and Dumber* into more dramatic roles that brought him critical praise and award nominations. Carrey won a Golden Globe for his performance as a fairly subdued, kind-hearted version of Kaufman, with numerous tear-jerking moments. Through Kaufman, it would seem, Carrey found his way as a "serious actor."

The attempt of *Man on the Moon* was a truthful depiction of Kaufman's life, stripped of all the hijinks, getting at the authentic core, not to mention Carrey's soft side. Throughout the film, Forman's story-telling plays with these layers of meaning—this intertextuality between Kaufman and Carrey, as well as between Kaufman's partner Lynne and Courtney Love, experiencing her own renaissance as an actress, while grappling with the fate of being forever known as Kurt Cobain's widow. More layers were added eighteen years later, by the 2017 pseudo-documentary (or, perhaps, mockumentary) *Jim & Andy: The Great Beyond*. Framed as an account of the making of *Man on the Moon*, *Jim & Andy* claims to uncover what really happened when Carrey played Kaufman—which the studio supposedly kept secret, perceiving the actor's on-set behavior as a liability.[23] These refracted narratives are set into motion with Carrey's recollection of being cast by Forman. Pupils fully dilated, his beard grown to outrageous volume, present-day Carrey explains, entirely straight-faced, that in the late nineties he communicated with Kaufman telepathically. "That's the moment when Andy Kaufman showed up, tapped me on the shoulder, and said 'sit down, I'll be doing my movie.' What happened afterwards was out of my control."[24]

Central to the fantasy of artistry in *Jim & Andy* is Carrey's total relinquishing of his own accountability, armored by authenticity. "It's as if I went into a fugue state, and Hyde showed up," Carrey recalls, "I have a Hyde inside me that shows up when there are people watching . . . sometimes, afterwards. I feel like 'damn, I lost control again . . . to him.'" Throughout the behind-the-scenes footage, Carrey sabotages the filmmaking with drunkenness, harassment of crew members, prop and set destruction, and manic outbursts. As part Kaufmanesque prank,

23 This section has been adapted from a longer piece I published in *Blind Field* in January 2018, "The Artist in the Age of Meta-Masculinity," in which I further explore this juncture of crisis in the masculine figure of abusive artistry in other films such as James Franco's *The Disaster Artist*. See Madeline Lane-McKinley, "The Artist in the Age of Meta-Masculinity," *Blind Field: A Journal of Cultural Inquiry*, January 16, 2018, https://blindfieldjournal.com/2018/01/16/the-artist-in-the-age-of-meta-masculinity/.
24 Chris Smith, *Jim & Andy: The Great Beyond*, mockumentary (Netflix, 2017).

part method acting, the film quickly reaches a point where authenticity doesn't matter—in its place, laid bare, is simply narcissism.

Jim & Andy taps into a mythology of method acting which, in the film industry, has evolved as a long tradition of workplace abuse. Method actors are not only authentic, according to this mythology, but brave—with their artist practice always packaged in terms of their ability to go without "breaking character," and their willingness to go further than others. Of course nowhere in this mythology is the bravery or endurance of those who withstand the constant on-set harassment of these actors. Daniel Day-Lewis is perhaps most celebrated among contemporary actors for his on-set personae, often credited for going beyond method acting and toward a form of transcendence. On the set of *My Left Foot* (1989), Day-Lewis broke his own ribs and would not leave a wheelchair, to purify his performance of cerebral palsy. For *The Last of the Mohicans* (1992), he lived in the woods for a week, hunting and skinning animals. During the filming of *Lincoln* (2012), rumors circulated that he was sending text messages to co-star Sally Field signed "Abe." The story of each of Day-Lewis's performances builds on a certain masculinist conception of artistry, for which art is achieved only through reckless self-absorption, eclipsing all the labors required to accommodate these extreme measures: the film crew members who spoon-fed him during *My Left Foot*, the tailors who custom-designed his clothing for *Gangs of New York* with the most historically accurate fabrics, the actor replaced after being traumatized by the actor's intensity on the set of *There Will Be Blood*, and on and on.

Women using the same "method" tactics to prepare and develop performances are rarely glorified for their practice. Marilyn Monroe's pursuit of method acting has long been a cautionary tale for actresses, Rosemary Malague argues,[25] referring to Monroe's deeply troubled relationship to method acting pioneer Lee Strasberg, which she outlines as a system of emotional control and dependency. While Malague sees a clear-cut exploitative dynamic between the Strasberg school and Monroe, "the ultimate commodity," Shonni Enelow pushes against the conception of method actresses as "passive victims," suggesting that the hysterical caricature of Monroe has overshadowed the history of method actresses.[26] This hysteria is the feminine foil to masculine authentic-

---

25 Rosemary Malague, *An Actress Prepares: Women and "The Method"* (London: Routledge, 2012), 62.
26 Shonni Enelow, *Method Acting and Its Discontents: On American Psycho-Drama* (Evanston: Northwestern University Press, 2015), 48.

ity, glorified as a genius and excusing all transgressions—because transgression is the brand.

By contrast, for hyper-masculine figures like Marlon Brando, method acting is absolutely indistinguishable from abuse. Since directing Brando in *The Last Tango in Paris* in 1972, Bernardo Bertolucci spoke for decades of the film's authentic performances. Of the most controversial scene, in which Paul, played by Brando, uses a stick of butter to anally rape his lover, played by then 19-year old Maria Schneider, Bertolucci would recall in 2013 that "[the sequence was] an idea that I had with Marlon in the morning before the shoot," prompted by Brando's desire for Schneider to react "as a girl, not as an actress."[27] Excluded from the decision-making, Schneider felt "a little raped, both by Marlon and by Bertolucci," as she later reflected.[28] As the actress explained, "Marlon said to me: 'Maria, don't worry. It's just a movie,' but during the scene, even though what Marlon was doing wasn't real, I was crying real tears."[29]

Bringing together the traditions of method acting and authentic comedy, *Jim & Andy* uneasily glorifies Carrey's craft (or supernatural possession?). At the same time, it reads as the ultimate prank—a deeply inauthentic, Kaufmanesque meditation on authenticity. However elaborate the prank might have been, none of this seemed to matter by the time the film came out in late 2017. Four weeks beforehand, the hashtag #MeToo began spreading, and the Time's Up movement in Hollywood was launched soon thereafter. Either way there was little willingness to celebrate the kind of behavior Carrey flagrantly exhibits throughout the film: yelling at workers on set, sabotaging rehearsals and filming schedules, insulting the film crew, all in the name of authenticity.

By now, Kaufman's comedic method is hardly distinguishable from what Fintan Walsh calls the "jackassification of masculinity," a more recent fantasy "giving men access to a power they otherwise lack"—or fear they are losing—as a "celebration of the omnipotent male."[30] This fantasy is cranked to eleven in *I'm Still Here*, a perfect double feature with *Jim & Andy*, as a "mockumentary" of Joaquin Phoenix's supposed retirement

27 Bonnie Malkin, "*Last Tango in Paris* Director Suggests Maria Schneider 'Butter Rape' Scene Not Consensual," *The Guardian*, December 4, 2016, https://www.theguardian.com/film/2016/dec/04/last-tango-in-paris-director-says-maria-schneider-butter-scene-not-consensual.
28 Lina Das, "I Felt Raped by Brando," *Mail Online*, accessed December 31, 2021,
29 Das, "I Felt Raped by Brando."
30 Fintan Walsh, *Male Trouble: Masculinity and the Performance of Crisis* (New York: Palgrave Macmillan, 2010), 181.

from serious acting.[31] *I'm Still Here* begins with Phoenix explain-whining about his decision to retire from the film industry, coated in questions of authenticity:

> "I'm just stuck in this ridiculous self-imposed prison of characterization . . . I don't want to play the character Joaquin anymore, like, I want to be whatever I am, and my artistic output thus far, when I'm really fucking honest with myself, has been fucking fraudulent. And now for the first time I'm doing something that is—whether you like it or not—it really represents me . . . hate me or like me, just don't misunderstand me. That's it."[32]

This is how he sets up his next move, a career in hip hop. Exploring this joke entails plenty of moments of humiliation (as when Phoenix tries to work with P Diddy, or parties too hard in almost every other scene)—but this humiliation spreads across the film, to the working conditions of everyone involved. Following the release of the film, a producer and cinematographer sued director Casey Affleck for sexual harassment and intentional infliction of emotional distress. Both women complained that Affleck referred to them as "cows," and subjected them to a "nearly daily barrage of sexual comments, innuendo and unwelcome advances."[33]

The terms of authenticity continue to mutate, masquerading as individual (and hyper-masculinized) artistry, while extending itself to the entire workplace. Its toxicity is immeasurable. Who gets to claim this behavior as their art is the trouble with authenticity. But the joke is also, at this point, turning in on itself in critical ways.[34]

The Deceit of "Authenticity"

Louis C.K. 2017 is probably the worst title in the history of comedy specials, but Louis C.K. had no way of knowing that when the special came

---

31 We might think of this, likewise, as a precursor to Phoenix's Oscar-nominated, method-tinged performance in *Joker* (2019).

32 Casey Affleck, *I'm Still Here*, mockumentary (Netflix, 2010).

33 Ben Child, "Casey Affleck Settles Sexual Harassment Lawsuits," *The Guardian*, September 15, 2010, https://www.theguardian.com/film/2010/sep/15/casey-affleck-settles-harassment-lawsuits.

34 Michael Schulman's controversial *New Yorker* profile of *Succession* star Jeremy Strong is a great example of this joke becoming legible.

out that March. By November, the year 2017 came to mark something other than just one more career pinnacle for the blockbuster comedian, when five women made public testimonials illustrating a pattern of sexual abuse well-known within the comedy industry. All of the women described C.K. intimidating them or attempting to coerce them into watching him masturbate. In his special, C.K. pretends to jerk off onto the crowd while joking about how men instinctually want to spread their cum everywhere "without judgment," and how "it's her job to go 'that's enough of you, I think'... that's really enough."[35] One can only imagine how this joke would manifest differently, behind the comedy club curtain.

Amid the debates provoked by #MeToo, the demand to "separate the art from the artist" became one of the rallying points against "cancel culture" in late 2017 and early 2018. "What is to be done about monsters? Can and should we love their work?" asks author Claire Dederer. In her widespread #MeToo think piece, published in *The Paris Review*, Dederer claims that an integral element of artistry is monstrosity: "the artist must be monster enough not just to start the work, but to complete it. And to commit all the little savageries that lie in between."[36] Dederer illuminates some of the contradictions at stake in performing this separation between art and artist—or however the popular mandate would put it. At the same time, she articulates a defense of this monstrosity, as part of the *process*. Whether in method acting or in "authentic" stand-up comedy, we encounter this fixation on process everywhere, continually defending, legitimating, and even venerating abusive behaviors which are inseparable from their artistic practice, and foundational to the working conditions of their art.

In comedy "authenticity is a cultural logic used by those with the social and economic capital to validate talent and belonging," Stephanie Brown argues. Authenticity "sustain[s] masculine dominance in the industry" of stand-up especially, she elaborates, through informal gatekeeping practices which are both gendered and racialized.[37] While much of the tirade against "cancel culture" in comedy has focused on the supposed taking control of social and cultural norms and sabotage of artistic freedom

35 Louis C.K., *Louis C.K. 2017* (Netflix, 2017).

36 Claire Dederer, "What Do We Do with the Art of Monstrous Men?," *The Paris Review*, November 20, 2017, https://www.theparisreview.org/blog/2017/11/20/art-monstrous-men/.

37 Stephanie Brown, "Open Mic? The Gendered Gatekeeping of Authenticity in Spaces of Live Stand-Up Comedy," *Feminist Media Histories* 6, no. 4 (October 20, 2020): 42–67, https://doi.org/10.1525/fmh.2020.6.4.42.

by an era of "wokeness," the crisis in comedy is more precisely that the white masculine dominance in the industry has deteriorated, ever so slightly. To be "authentic," in this sense, is available to some and not others—whomever aligns most with the social norms of the comedy world. The supposed freedom of expression inherent to stand-up comedy, then, provides a "permission [which] becomes prohibition," Sara Ahmed writes, "something that we should not speak about, given that we have been given the freedom to think about it."[38] Similarly, the "cancel culture" invoked as a constant threat to stand-up comedy's *authenticity* merely threatens the culture that has reigned for so long: a system of silencing and disappearing those who destabilize the power structure.

Authenticity in stand-up comedy can also be conceptualized as a matter of audience trust. "The audience has a say in the trusting relationship, and their expectations determine how the comedian has to respond to earn that trust," writes Daniel Abrahams, which presents a problem:

> The comedian must be seen as authentic, but that is not the same as being authentic. This can leave the comedian in a precarious position: either their authentic self just so happens to line up with what the audience expects, or she is caught having to fabricate an inauthentic stage persona just to be accepted as authentic.[39]

Like authenticity, audience trust is cultivated, collaborative, and more easily acquired through *relatability*. "In an industry/subculture hybrid space where comics are friends (who are largely straight white men)," Brown writes of her ethnographic research of Chicago comedians, "womxn, queer people, and people of color—in addition to older comics, comics who are parents, or comics who don't drink—find it harder to fit in."[40]

Up until November 2017, C.K.'s comedy was frequently praised for its confessionalism and vulnerability. While foregrounding his own willingness to humiliate himself, C.K. also vacillates between derogatory impressions of gay people, women he's had sex with, and even his children. Because he does not exclude himself from a comedy based in shame and judgment, but rather centers himself in it, he takes liberties to extend this

---

38   Sara Ahmed, *On Being Included: Racism and Diversity in Institutional Life* (Durham: Duke University Press, 2012), 154.

39   Daniel Abrahams, "Winning Over the Audience: Trust and Humor in Stand-Up Comedy," *The Journal of Aesthetics and Art Criticism* 78, no. 4 (2020): 499.

40   Brown, "Open Mic?"

loathing to the rest of his subjects, *most of whom he has power over*. Much of C.K.'s comedy is about how people, including him, are awful. Throughout his narrative-driven stand-up, people complain; they're ignorant, inconvenient, and lazy. C.K.'s critique isn't driven by righteousness, but what he explores in his 2015 special as a rage against "overthinking": "just get food and put it in here" he jokes, pointing to his mouth, "later, when you feel pressure, just shit out the shit in here," he continues, pointing to his ass.[41]

By early 2020, C.K.'s comeback tour was a testament to this ideology of "authentic" comedy. His comedy special, aggressively titled "Sincerely," reveals a clear understanding of his newfound audience of the alt right. Conservative media outlets like National Review celebrated the comedian's defiance of "cancel culture" and refusal to be "silenced": "He is sincerely trying to tell something like the truth about what it's like to be the person he is, a severely flawed man of the early twenty-first century," writes right-wing journalist Kyle Smith, "Louis C.K. has always invited us to consider the comedy payoff of rolling with our worst thoughts instead of cutting them off before they get disturbing."[42] Through this comedic tactic of disturbance, what C.K. seeks to affirm is by now loud and clear: *yes, white men are awful. Get used to it.*

Shortly after C.K. began making unannounced appearances in comedy clubs in August 2018, some industry powerhouses, like Judd Apatow, voiced their sense that this comeback was "too soon." Jerry Seinfeld, in typical contrarian fashion, claimed that the problem wasn't that C.K. came back but how he did it: "We know the routine: The person does something wrong. The person's humiliated. They're exiled. They suffer, we want them to suffer," Seinfeld expounds, "We love the tumble, we love the crash and bang of the fall. And then we love the crawl-back. The grovel. Are you going to grovel? How long are you going to grovel? Are you going to cry?"[43] I'll note here that in 1993, when Seinfeld was 38, during the fourth season of his sitcom, he began dating seventeen-year-old high school student Shoshanna Lonstein Gruss, and hardly anyone batted an eye—nor did he ever respond to any public criticism. (The story is also eerily similar to the romantic plotline between Woody Allen and Mariel Hemingway in *Manhattan*). Seinfeld speaks as an authority on C.K.'s situation not from an ethical standpoint, but from a position of power in the

---

41 Louis C.K., *Louis C.K.: Live at the Comedy Store* (Netflix, 2015).

42 Kyle Smith, "Louis C.K. Remains Brilliant," *National Review*, April 8, 2020, https://www.nationalreview.com/2020/04/review-sincerely-louis-c-k-comedian-remains-brilliant/.

43 Sharf, "Jerry Seinfeld."

industry. Yet again, authenticity is the lynchpin. Accountability, however that might be conceived, drifts out of the picture. The more authentic the groveling, the more an apology simply doesn't matter.

In all of C.K.'s comedy specials, he simulates orgasms, gesticulating toward the audience with graphic sounds. He modifies these routines ever so slightly through the years. And ultimately, this is what is most *authentic* about C.K.: his desire to masturbate, literally and figuratively, in front of people. The discomfort from these moments in C.K.'s comedy generates more for the comedian to improvise with. However, this is all contingent on the audience's trust, which is to say, their consent. Many of C.K.'s defenders would claim his critics were moralistic, even kink-shaming. As Ben Burgis claimed, "*whatever* you make of this tangle of ethical issues, the bottom line is that Louis C.K.'s sins involved masturbation."[44] In asserting this as the bottom line, quite absurdly, Burgis strategically blurs between the language of ethics and morals, obfuscating questions of consent, along with the workplace context of C.K.'s pattern of abuse. These situations cannot be confused with the logic of audience consent. Audiences choose to be there[45] and they can leave at any point—that's why C.K.'s audiences haven't gone away, disappearing into the cancel-ether, they've just transformed. In 2016, the comedian voiced his support of Hillary Clinton's presidential campaign, appealing to his base of liberal (and self-loathing) men; and now, there are MAGA hats scattered through his crowds. This consensual agreement with the audience has been equivocated with the testimonies of sexual harassment and assault that emerged from within the comedy world, by defenders of C.K. like Burgis. But the testimonies that emerged in November 2017 unveil a far different context of consent, illustrating a repeated leveraging of power (however implicitly) in the industry to coerce comedy workers into sexual favors. In one of these testimonies, comedy duo Dana Min

---

44 Ben Burgis, *Canceling Comedians While the World Burns* (Ridgefield: Zero Books, 2021), 13.

45 The importance of audience consent was highlighted by a more recent incident in stand-up, when John Mulaney surprised his Columbus, Ohio audience on May 20, 2022 with an unannounced opening act from Dave Chappelle, who delivered his signature antitrans material. Mulaney was criticized for "surprising" his audience, and LGBTQ fans spoke publicly about feeling trapped, endangered, and harassed at the show. After Chappelle had ended his latest special *The Closer* with a vow to move on from this material, he instead raised the stakes, moving from the terrain of consenting audiences. Non-consent was exactly the point, as my friend Amanda Armstrong-Price remarked the next day: "the words are supposed to hurt, and if people can opt out, they lose a lot of their sting."

Goodman and Julia Wolov recall C.K. asking if he could masturbate in front of them in a hotel room during the Aspen Comedy Festival in 2002. They remember not knowing if C.K. was joking or not—what were the boundaries of "doing comedy" in this context? What were the boundaries of work? Goodman and Wolov were working comedians, struggling for stage time and hoping to make connections at the festival. While he could *jokingly* ask, it wasn't clear whether they could *jokingly* say 'no'—and what the consequences might be. "We too work in comedy," writes Wolov, in a 2019 essay about the experience with C.K. As Wolov makes clear, "what C.K. did was not done with consent": "We never agreed nor asked him to take all his clothes off and masturbate to completion in front of us," she explains, "But it didn't matter because the exciting part for him was the fear on our faces."[46]

In terms of public perception, there are two factors that differentiate C.K.'s hotel room meeting with Goodman and Wolov from the pattern of hotel room meetings between Harvey Weinstein and numerous high-profile actresses who reported sexual assault. The first factor is fame: most of the women who eventually stepped forward about Weinstein were well-established, and in solidarity. Salma Hayek, Angelina Jolie, Ashley Judd, Heather Graham, Uma Thurman, Mira Sorvino are all among the list of over a hundred well-known in entertainment who have spoken publicly about harassment or assault by Weinstein, spanning decades. That doesn't mean it was easy to break their silence—but we can assume that there are many more women in the industry who had similar experiences with Weinstein and remained silent in order to keep working. Similarly, C.K.'s behavior received far more attention once high-profile comedians like Tig Notaro started publicly urging C.K. to address concerns that were well-known. Notaro was not referring to her own experiences of harassment or assault, but to her awareness of an open secret in the comedy world. In 2015, comedian Jen Kirkman spoke of being mistreated by the "known perv," along with her fear that her career would be over if she named him.[47] This is the real cancel culture—the one that always existed, before powerful abusers came to fear consequence.

---

46 Julia Wolov, "Counterpoint: I Didn't Consent to Louis C.K. Masturbating in Front of Me," *The Canadian Jewish News*, November 12, 2019, https://thecjn.ca/perspectives/opinions/counterpoint-i-didnt-consent-to-louis-c-k-masturbating-in-front-of-me/.
47 Matt Wilstein, "Tig Notaro: Louis C.K. Needs to 'Handle' His Sexual-Misconduct Rumors," *The Daily Beast*, August 23, 2017, https://www.thedailybeast.com/tig-notaro-louis-ck-needs-to-handle-his-sexual-misconduct-rumors.

The second factor differentiating public perceptions of Weinstein's more clear-cut sexual violence from what some have referred to as C.K.'s "weird fetish"[48] is of course C.K.'s claim to "authentic" comedy. This claim to comedy, and this particular brand of comedy, gives C.K. power but also a rhetorical excuse to fall back on, enabling him to argue that he was "just joking." Such a claim holds particular power over comedians, for whom the charge of not being able to "take a joke" can actually upend your career. Who gets to make claims to comedy often has little to do with being funny, and everything to do with being powerful—blurring the lines between work and non-work, a workplace and a non-workplace, consent and coercion, authenticity and inauthenticity. It even extends to what counts as joking and what counts as sexual violence.

Comedy muddies our perception of power and how it works, in other words. Some have called the fellow comedians C.K. harassed or assaulted his "colleagues," precisely to discount critiques of power dynamics within the industry. Burgis insists "these women" (always unnamed) "weren't his co-workers or subordinates," and that as comedians, "everyone involved was essentially a self-employed small businessperson."[49] But for this reason especially, power is incredibly disproportionate in the world of comedy— where "self-employed small business people" range from pay-to-play gig workers to megastars with multi-million dollar contracts, like C.K. With these distinctions aside, Rebecca Corry, one of the women who came forward about C.K. in the fall of 2017, was actually describing an interaction that happened at her workplace, while she and C.K. were writers for a show. In a rather earnest attempt to respond to the situation with nuance and thoughtfulness, Sarah Silverman drew distinctions between some of the cases she'd heard about and made a public statement about how C.K. used to masturbate in front of her, with her consent. "I'm not making excuses for him, so please don't take it that way," Silverman explained, "We are peers. We are equals."[50] Soon after that, Corry responded to what she saw as problematic implications in Silverman's language of "peers" and "equals": "To be real clear, CK had 'nothing to offer me' as I too was his equal on the set the day he decided to sexually harass me. He took away a

48   Mark Breslin, "Breslin: Why I Brought Louis C.K. Back from the Dead," *The Canadian Jewish News*, November 8, 2019, https://thecjn.ca/arts/breslin-why-i-brought-louis-c-k-back-from-the-dead/.
49   Burgis, *Canceling Comedians While the World Burns*, 14.
50   Sharf, "Sarah Silverman Says Louis C.K. Used to Masturbate in Front of Her With Her Consent."

day I worked years for and still has no remorse."[51] With grace, Silverman apologized, and modeled a kind of listening and self-criticism that seems rare in these debates in the comedy world. As Corry later made clear, C.K. harassed her while she was doing her job, and for twelve years afterward, she did her best to stay out of the "C.K. masturbation narrative," "but no matter how hard I tried, it kept finding me—at work-related events, on TV sets, social settings, and comedy clubs. I'd hear people defending him while unabashedly tearing apart the women who'd tried to bring what he was doing to light."[52] After Corry decided to come forward with her story, she was harassed online, and even received death threats. The day he harassed her and every day since, Corry explains, C.K. put her in a "lose-lose situation."

Perhaps creating a toxic work environment was not what C.K. had in mind as he approached one of his coworkers to watch him masturbate in their shared workplace. Perhaps he even imagined sexual harassment as part of his artistic process. But that doesn't change the impact.

Whose "Authenticity"?

The problem with this ideology of authenticity in stand-up comedy began to unfold in the end of the sixties. It has transmogrified through the decades since, just as capitalism has steadily sapped the counterculture of its utopian energy. Since the days of Lenny Bruce, the problem has always been that not everyone gets to be authentic—but also, as in Pryor's case, that authenticity is not always a matter of choice. For Pryor, authenticity was the stranglehold he felt for most of his career. It's the other side of what some characterize as *vulnerable* about his work. Today, authenticity is a fascistic force in stand-up comedy, for which the claim to authenticity renders hate speech a matter of artistic freedom. This is a purely anti-utopian comedy based in the propagation of fear and violence, and it insists that this is what comedy is all about—what it always has been, and what it always should be. It taunts those who question it. None of this has much to do with comedy, but everything to do with power.

---

51 Rebecca Corry, "To Be Real Clear...," tweet, *Twitter*, October 22, 2018, https://twitter.com/HippoloverCorry/status/1054471083967959040.
52 Rebecca Corry, "Louis C.K. Put Me in a Lose-Lose Situation," *Vulture*, May 24, 2018, https://www.vulture.com/2018/05/louis-c-k-put-me-in-a-lose-lose-situation.html.

Today there's much talk of being "brave" in stand-up, and confronting the "woke mob" with a middle-finger. What an insult to the legacy of Bruce, who was targeted by police in comedy clubs and arrested, and whose stand-up was undeniably a form of political protest. Carlin and Pryor, even after obscenity laws had been overturned as unconstitutional, were arrested as well. This is not the same as being criticized on Twitter or having to reconstruct one's fanbase.

Far before this myth of authenticity emerged in the sixties, the origins of stand-up are rooted in a constant push and pull over what is and isn't funny. This questioning is essential to stand-up, and where stand-up draws much of its energy. Since the minstrel shows of the 1830s, when the song and dance routine "Jim Crow" was first popularized, comedy has provoked public debate, and for important political reasons. Again and again throughout this history, as comedy historian Kliph Nesteroff remarks, comedians have complained "you can't joke about anything anymore."[53] This is what this complaint has always been: a cheap line, a plea for audience sympathy, a victim-posturing that is always done most effectively from a position of power. But through the years, more and more, getting the laughs has gotten further and further from the point.

---

53 "Episode 1,278: 'Canceled Comedy' w/ Kliph Nesteroff and David Bianculli," *WTF with Marc Maron*, November 11, 2021, http://www.wtfpod.com/podcast/episode-1278-canceled-comedy-w-kliph-nesteroff-and-david-bianculli.

CHAPTER FIVE

On Jokesterism

> "The next time you hear your voice bleat, 'it was just a joke,'
> ask yourself: Who made you the boss of genre?"
> —Lauren Berlant, "The Predator and the Jokester"[1]

Regarding the process of adapting his BBC series *The Office* for NBC in 2005, Ricky Gervais explains that there were crucial adjustments to be made for an American audience, beginning with the figure of the boss. "We had to make Michael Scott a slightly nicer guy, with a rosier outlook to life" than his British counterpart, the office boss David Brent, Gervais writes: "He could still be childish, and insecure, and even a bore, but he couldn't be too mean."[2] Played by Gervais, David is slimy and insulting. Steve Carell, by contrast, strikes a tone of innocence as Michael. He's always unintentional in his misbehavior. What remains consistent between these boss figures, however, is their jokester philosophy of management.

"[Some of you] didn't like some of the jokes I told earlier," David announces to his employees, in one of his signature outbursts. "You've got to chill out, yeah, trust me, this is what I do, alright?" he continues, "You will never work in a place like this again. This is brilliant. Fact. And you will never have another boss like me. Someone who's basically a chilled-out entertainer."[3] While David forces everyone to listen to his badly-written pop songs, sauntering through the office with an acoustic

---

1 Lauren Berlant, "The Predator and the Jokester," *The New Inquiry*, December 13, 2017, https://thenewinquiry.com/the-predator-and-the-jokester/.

2 Ricky Gervais, "The Difference Between American and British Humour," *Time*, November 9, 2011, https://time.com/3720218/difference-between-american-british-humour/.

3 Ricky Gervais and Stephen Merchant, "The Merger," *The Office* (UK) (BBC, September 30, 2002).

guitar, Michael, the American boss, fancies himself an improv comic. As managers, David and Michael constantly exhibit emotionally abusive behaviors in the workplace, including sexual harassment, racial discrimination, homophobia, and fat shaming. Sometimes, there are mild consequences from HR or corporate. After one such reprimanding, Michael tells his workers, self-pityingly, "you can consider this my retirement from comedy . . . in the future when I want to say something funny, or witty, or do an impression, I will no longer ever do any of those things."[4] Within a minute, of course, he can't stop himself from using his favorite catch-all reply: "that's what she said!"

Throughout both versions of *The Office*, the workers rarely believe that filing a complaint will amount to much, other than the situation getting utterly worse. When Oscar discloses his homosexuality to HR after Michael jokes that he's "faggy for liking *Shakespeare in Love*," Michael calls an emergency conference meeting to prove that he isn't homophobic, and forces Oscar to accept a kiss on the mouth in front of the rest of the office. When corporate intervenes, Oscar is offered a three-month paid vacation and a company car. "Kids, sometimes it pays to be gay," he tells the camera, satisfied with the outcome, but without much hope for anything to change in the office culture. Instead, like everyone else in his workplace, he interacts with Michael's joking misbehavior as unintentional and unavoidable—that is, unavoidable because it is unintentional.

Whether as a traditional boss figure or not, power is what determines the boundary between the joke and non-joke. The jokester, as Lauren Berlant suggests, asserts "control over time and space," framing the parameters of what constitutes *joking* along with "consequences in domains of capital, labor, institutional belonging, and speech situations where the structurally vulnerable are forced to 'choose their battles' or just act like a good sport."[5]

As portraits of jokester managerialism, each version of *The Office* features a competing philosophy of humor. In the BBC version, David Brent descends from the long western tradition of superiority theory in humor—in Brent's case, rooted in Thomas Hobbes's account of laughter in *Leviathan*, as a "sudden glory" and a passion caused "either by some sudden act of their own, that pleaseth them, or by the apprehension of some deformed thing in another, by comparison whereof they suddenly applaud

---

4   Ken Kwapis, "Sexual Harassment," *The Office (US)* (NBC, September 27, 2005).
5   Berlant, "The Predator and the Jokester."

themselves."[6] Superiority theory in humor focuses on "the pleasure experience when one is the agent rather than the target of laughter," Cynthia and Julie Willett explain: "This pleasure, the theory maintains, stems from an increase of one's power, status, or reputation at the expense of others."[7] What's driving most of David Brent's "chilled-out entertainer" managerial practices is this ambition to feel superior, for which joking becomes weaponized to maintain dominance. Michael Scott's jokesterism, on the other hand, is more in keeping with the relief theory of humor, conceiving of the joke as a "release of the liberated inhibitory charge," as Freud claims.[8] As opposed to David's punching down, Michael's jokesterism is verbal diarrhea, coming from a place of sincerity, and a pathetic yearning to be likeable. Where David is abusive, it would seem, Michael is simply *compulsive*.

These competing jokesterisms shape the antiwork dimensions of both series—which, in the case of the U.S. version, transform into an idealized fantasy of the workplace as family. By Michael's departure in the seventh season, he has been reconfigured so extensively from the David Brent prototype that he is a beloved not-quite-father or wacky uncle. Betraying his British analogue, Tim, who sustains a critical antagonism towards his boss, Jim is key to Michael's redemption in the American series, often feeling sorry for his boss, while aspiring to join the managerial class himself. When he and Michael co-manage the office later in the series, Jim sums up a difficult day at work with a new appreciation for Michael: "I think today was a good day to have two managers," he explains, "if you're a family on a lifeboat in the middle of the ocean, one parent might want to keep rowing. But if the other parent wants to play a game, it's not because they're crazy. It's because they're doing it for the kids. And I get that now."[9] Michael's jokester managerialism never ceases, enabling him to call his final emergency conference meeting, just before leaving the company, to say "one last goodbye," in which he makes racist impressions of a Chinese man named Ping.[10] At this point in the series, this jokesterism extends to everyone around Michael as well. And in many ways, the idealized work ethic of the American version is based on this unspoken

---

6   Thomas Hobbes, *Leviathan: With Selected Variants from the Latin Edition of 1668* (Indianapolis: Hackett, 1994), 32.

7   Cynthia Willett and Julie A. Willett, *Uproarious: How Feminists and Other Subversive Comics Speak Truth* (Minneapolis: University of Minnesota Press, 2019), 17.

8   Sigmund Freud, *The Joke and Its Relation to the Unconscious*, ed. John Carey (New York: Penguin Books, 2014), 147.

9   Seth Gordon, "Double Date," *The Office* (NBC, November 5, 2009).

10   Paul Fieg, "Goodbye, Michael," *The Office* (NBC, April 28, 2011).

responsibility to diffuse, redeem, or forgive these power dynamics, without the hope that they'll ever change. The workers just have to get used to it and learn to get their work done anyway.

Meanwhile, since the success of *The Office* (UK), Ricky Gervais has steadily become his own, unironic version of David Brent. Of his characteristically offensive brand of comedy, he declares, "You have to know that art is being brave." In a fit of self-righteousness in 2013, he tweeted "Just because you're offended, doesn't mean you're right." This of course begs a question for which these jokes *presume* to have an answer: who gets to be "right" about comedy? Who gets to be offended? In a 2019 interview with *The Spectator*, Gervais explains that he wants "people to stop saying 'That joke is offensive,'" along with his refusal to ever apologize—claiming this would be the "end of satire and the erosion of freedom of speech."[11] His stand-up leans into hatred and anger, because that's what his crowds have wanted from him through the course of a global right turn in the last decade, during which he has insisted that his comedy *isn't political*. How and why he yields his power is simply a matter of *just joking*.

§

The greatest jokester boss of all time is surely Tony Soprano. In *The Sopranos*, mob boss Tony (James Gandolfini) deals in jokes to assert himself, but also to keep others in line. He tells Bobby, one of his men, who's overweight (just like him), "I think it's time you seriously consider salads."[12] After his cousin and next-in-line gets out of rehab, in recovery from heroin addiction, Tony jokes that he should have a drink—he's tired of Christopher's AA lingo and being serious all the time. These casual jabs accelerate through the series, and the stakes are raised just as Tony's jokester managerialism devolves into tragedy.

So many of the murders in *The Sopranos* are catalyzed by jokes, sometimes quite directly. When New York mobster Johnny Sack finds out that members of the New Jersey family laughed at a joke about his wife's weight told by Sopranos family member Ralphie—that she was having a ninety-pound mole removed from her ass—Johnny attempts to wage a war between the families, leveraging as much of his own power as a matter of honor. In some ways, this is the beginning of the end for the

---

11 Andrew Doyle, "Ricky Gervais: Why I'll Never Apologise for My Jokes," *The Spectator*, accessed January 1, 2022, https://www.spectator.co.uk/article/ricky-gervais-why-i-ll-never-apologise-for-my-jokes.
12 Martin Bruestle, "Do Not Resuscitate," *The Sopranos* (HBO, January 23, 2000).

Soprano family. Whether or not jokes are taken as *just jokes* is a matter of life or death. Likewise, the more power is imposed through joking, busting balls, and wise-cracking, the more a joke can be asserted as "just a joke"—through the sheer, violent force of not joking at all.

However, *The Sopranos* also makes a joke of the idea of the family, in its depiction of the corruption of work. While it can certainly be read as an affirmation of family life—along with the capitalist work ethic, with the seeming virtuousness of being "self-made" reverberating throughout its seven seasons—the series relentlessly mocks itself, often heavy-handedly pointing to the ways in which its central characters conflate notions of family with money and violence, and more generally, control.

In recent years, *The Sopranos* has found a resurgence in popularity, based on a new generation of viewers along with many, like myself, who have rewatched it multiple times since it began in 1999. Some have wondered why a series so packed with depictions of racism, sexism, homophobia, and nationalism would speak so much to this new audience, otherwise caricatured for its naïve "wokeness." Young queer audiences have shown particular interest in the show, and its depiction of fragile heterosexual men—as Chingy Nea, queer writer and comedian declared, "*The Sopranos* belongs to the gays now."[13] An aspect of this mass appeal, it would seem, is that in a world currently obsessed with "getting canceled"—though what that even means is often unclear—the show's narrative world of getting whacked is concrete and undeniable. But the renewed interest in the show is also clearly a matter of comedy. In its time, the series was praised for its dark, often highbrow intervention to television. It's not that the comedy went unnoticed, but it was always subservient to the tragedy. Perhaps now more than ever before, we are able to laugh at *The Sopranos*, and there is a freedom in that.

Part of this freedom is to see Tony as the jokester that he is—as the "crying clown," as he sometimes portrays himself to his therapist, Dr. Melfi, but also as the self-loathing authoritarian jokester, who must be laughed *with* and never *at*. There's a catharsis in not having to take Tony's narcissism and self-conception as a persecuted subject so seriously, if we ever did.

In *The Sopranos*, the comedy bends towards tragedy, and then springs back again. Late into the fifth season of the series Tony's other cousin, also named Tony (Tony B., played by Steve Buscemi), tests the boundaries

---

13   Chingy Nea, "'The Sopranos' Belongs to the Gays Now," *MEL Magazine*, August 13, 2021, https://melmagazine.com/en-us/story/sopranos-queer-culture.

between joking and dedication to the family. After Tony B. gets out of prison, he is the ultimate symbol of family loyalty, having been put away for seventeen years. On the night his cousin was busted, Tony was supposed to be there too, but he had a panic attack during a fight with his mother and cracked his head open. Tony struggles with his sense of indebtedness, at times lashing out in the cruelty of jokes. Tony B., in turn, makes his own jokes, always behind Tony's back, like some cracks about Tony's weight to Christopher. On account of his "sense of humor," Tony B. is gifted a plaque from outside the family that reads "BECAUSE I'M THE BOSS . . . THAT'S WHY!",[14] which he places "in a position of prominence," just before he makes a deal stepping out from Tony's authority—leading Tony to "have to" kill him.

§

Besides setting the boundary between what is and isn't joking, the jokester manipulates distinctions between abuse and conflict. The jokester's rationality is that "conflict is not abuse," which Sarah Schulman premises on the ambiguous discrepancy between abuse as "power over" and conflict as "power struggle."[15] The problem with Schulman's distinction, as Aviva Stahl clarifies with incredible care, is that it obscures the way that "to be believed is fundamentally a question of relative power."[16] "Power is exerted in a multitude of ways," Stahl explains, "some of which may seem insignificant to the outside world, and may not even be consciously registered by the abuser."[17] Similarly, a joke can enact harm, regardless of the joke-teller's intention. While the boss or office manager is indisputably operating from a position of having "power over," the rhetoric of conflict frequently obscures how power works, even in such traditional workplace contexts, but especially interpersonally. Despite offering itself as a point of clarification, this differentiation between conflict and abuse perpetuates the rhetorical slippages which maintain power through these tensions of interpretation and intentionality, often in the service of neutralizing and managing the terms of critique. Just as "abuse" can be re-articulated into the dynamic and mutualism of "conflict," harmful behaviors can be

---

14 Allen Coulter, "The Test Dream," The Sopranos (HBO, May 16, 2004).
15 See Sarah Schulman, Conflict Is Not Abuse: Overstating Harm, Community Responsibility, and the Duty of Repair (Vancouver: Arsenal Pulp Press, 2016).
16 Aviva Stahl, "Trust in Instinct," The New Inquiry, May 9, 2017, https://thenewinquiry.com/trust-in-instinct/.
17 Stahl, "Trust in Instinct."

negotiated into "just joking"—and in this way, jokester managerialism flattens even the most unambiguous dynamics of power into matters of interpersonal differences of experience and opinion.

The "alt right"—or better yet, the fascists—laid claim to the rhetoric of joking for exactly these reasons. The fascist-jokester can act out of violent rage at his whim, ranging from microaggressions to physical assault, hiding like a coward behind the language of joking. The fascist-jokester seizes on comedy's signature alibi, which can be so powerful it can "drag errors and faux pas into the realm of respectability, enabling even the most egregious ethical or aesthetic failing to pass for . . . well, *passing*," as William Cheng puts it.[18] On his radio program which ran from 2015–2017 on the "free speech network" Compound Media, Proud Boys founder Gavin McInnes spewed hate-filled rants, regularly dropping the n-word throughout the hour. When asked by a listener calling into the show about his marriage to publicist Emily Jendrisak, the daughter of Christine Whiterabbit Jendrisak, born to the Ho-Chink Nation, McInnes *joked* that by impregnating his wife he was "cleaning up the races." In another episode, McInnes *joked* that he "used to fuck a lot of rice balls," and gave *joking* tips for "[getting] in a chink's pants." When asked in an interview about this and other racist diatribes, he *jokingly* remarked, "explaining jokes is a comedy sin[.]"[19] This is how the joke works.

As an expression of both superiority and relief, the jokester's joke has been defined by pick-up artists as the art of negging: a way to "hand pick the girl you want and turn her into your loyal girlfriend," as pick-up artist Jesse Charger explains. [20] The "neg" is a strategy of "[undermining] a woman's confidence by making backhanded or snide remarks," Nicky Woolf elaborates: "give a compliment with one hand, and take away with the other." [21] This is of course not the invention of pick-up artists, but engrained in the patriarchal fabric of western heterosexual culture—the plot of courtship that can be traced through any Jane Austen novel, for instance. What's specific about negging is the way in which it absorbs the logic of "just joking" as an explicit strategy of patriarchal control.

---

18 William Cheng, "Taking Back the Laugh: Comedic Alibis, Funny Fails," *Critical Inquiry* 43, no. 2 (Winter 2017): 528–49.

19 Amanda Marcotte, "Gavin McInnes and the Proud Boys: 'Alt-Right without the Racism'?," *Salon*, October 17, 2018, https://www.salon.com/2018/10/17/gavin-mcinnes-and-the-proud-boys-alt-right-without-the-racism/.

20 Jesse Charger, "Negging Women—10 Awesome Negs That Work," *Seduction Science*, 2010, https://www.seductionscience.com/2010/negging-women/.

21 Nicky Woolf, "'Negging': The Anatomy of a Dating Trend," *New Statesman*, May 25, 2012, https://www.newstatesman.com/politics/2012/05/negging-latest-dating-trend.

As Benjamin Noys writes, negging can be understood as a "counter counter-culture," amplifying "the worst elements of the counter-culture (sexism, a de-linked vision of life, radical individualism, etc.)" for the purpose of "[neutralizing] any thinking of freedom as a social form by confining freedom to the freedom to enjoy on the sexual marketplace."[22] In being framed as "freedom of speech," more precisely, the neg-joke works instead towards this un-thinking of freedom.

In manipulating the boundaries between joking and harm, the jokester's rejoinder of "just joking" operates by producing a hysterical subject out of the interpreter. The problem isn't the joke, the jokester claims, but how it was heard. "There are acts of cruelty," writes Jacqueline Rose, "which wipe out—seem at least partly aimed at wiping out—all freedom of mental health."[23] This is how the joke works.

While the jokester corners the interpreter into hysteria, the jokester easily shapeshifts into a figure of persecution and innocence. To the extent that the jokester scorns "victim politics," as one jokester once put it to me, jokesterism seeks to assert itself through a narrative of reverse victimhood. Whereas the act of weaponizing the joke goes unseen as harm, the joke's interpretation—that is to say, the jokester's feeling of being misinterpreted—is rendered a source of harm instead.

It is in this sense that, while in many ways a precarious societal outcast, symbolizing the antithesis of jokester-managers like David Brent, the Joker is also a jokester, in the 2019 Todd Phillips film. As the film follows this Travis Bickle-esque rendition of the Batman villain through his first killing spree, what makes Joker (Joaquin Phoenix) most abusive is his complete inability to see himself in these terms. At the time of *Joker*'s release, a mishmash of social democrats and anti-identitarian leftists celebrated the film as "a harsh indictment of neoliberalism,"[24] while "free thinkers" of the alt right saw the film as a rallying cry against woke culture. Although in seeming opposition, these readings of *Joker* serve a similar purpose for each audience, to validate a jokesterism that brings them together. On both sides, crucially, Joker was perceived as the *real* victim. The way in which the authoritarian wing of the left and the alt

22 Benjamin Noys, "He's Just Not That into You: Negging and the Manipulation of Negativity," *Manipulations*, accessed January 1, 2022, http://www.manipulations.info/hes-just-not-that-into-you-negging-and-the-manipulation-of-the-negativity.

23 Jacqueline Rose, *Women in Dark Times* (London: Bloomsbury, 2014), 19.

24 See Chauncey DeVega, "'Joker': A Harsh Indictment of Neoliberalism and Gangster Capitalism," *Salon*, October 9, 2019, https://www.salon.com/2019/10/09/joker-todd-phillips-indictment-neoliberalism-violence/.

right found this uneasy alignment over the film captured so many of the political contradictions of late 2019, a time that in hindsight seemed to culminate the cultural climate of the Trump years. And perhaps this was the inevitability of a jokesterist presidency.

§

Jokesterism is a disease that has spread throughout the left like everywhere else, often posturing as a crusade against "cancel culture" that is virtually indistinguishable from the rhetoric of alt-right figureheads like the "free speech" warrior and neo-Nazi Milo Yiannopoulos. This jokesterism is not unique to workplace tyrants or to the alt right's most despicable idols—it pervades everywhere, without exception. Wherever there are dynamics of power, however formalized or politically legible, this jokesterism can be maneuvered. It works in the ways that left authoritarians like Ben Burgis attribute, instead, to the spectre of "cancelation": "Cancelation spreads. To be a logic nerd about it, cancelation is 'transitive,'" Burgis writes. "You can be deemed worthy of cancelation for not canceling someone deemed worthy of cancelation—never mind whether you've done anything at all."[25] Of course this is how another version of cancel culture has always functioned—disappearing, silencing, or slandering those who make attempts to challenge the abuse of power.

A couple years ago a tenured professor complained to his social media followers that he had been canceled, after his loyalty to a known sexual harasser became the topic of wider dialogue and outrage. He retained his well-paid position at a prestigious private university, along with his book deal, his positions in editorial boards, and his ranking in a net-work of powerful academics. Plenty of his followers liked the tweet. I thought about this as I watched *The Chair*, along with all the other academic workers I know, in August 2021. The series follows the chaotic, incredibly demanding work-life of Professor Ji-Yoon Kim (Sandra Oh), the first woman appointed to chair of the English department at the fictional Pembroke University. Since its premise was announced by Netflix, the workplace satire of academia was the topic of much speculation. After it came out, there were a lot of debates about the show's representation of adjunct and graduate student labor, and of women and especially Asian and Black women in academia, as well as ageism and the Title IX system and a range of other issues. But what most of my friends seemed to agree

25 Burgis, *Canceling Comedians While the World Burns*, 84–85.

on was the weakness of a particular storyline dealing with cancel culture on university campuses. When Bill Dobson (Jay Duplass) satirically enacts a Nazi salute during one of his lectures, his students misinterpret this satiric gesture, circulating a video of the incident on social media that is rapidly decontextualized (and de-satirized). Soon the university suspends him, and his tenure is put into jeopardy. As the series unfolds, Bill vacillates between a martyr figure and a toxic white man. In the first episode, he shows up to work drunk and stoned, exploits a graduate student who's working as his TA, and accidentally plays on the classroom projector an intimate video of his late wife, naked and pregnant, at the start of a lecture. There are plenty of other ways in which he's vulnerable to Title IX investigations—yet he's "canceled," specifically, as a jokester-professor. The lecture was actually quite good. The problem, as the show sometimes has it, was the earnest, literal-mindedness of the students, who just can't take a joke.

The Chair inspired plenty of reviews and think-pieces that took on this figure of the toxic slacker white man in various academic departments—the kind who barely shows up to meetings, who cannot be trusted with any departmental responsibilities, and who generally makes more work for others, primarily women. These were compelling critiques of the character and how he is problematically redeemed, though only partially, by his desire to get his job back. I myself was hung up on the simple fact that in the eighteen years since I entered academia, as a college freshman, I had mostly seen or heard of controversies surrounding tenured professors going quite differently.[26]

Take the case of Franco Moretti—still on payroll as an emeritus faculty member at Stanford University, and still frequently published by the *New Left Review*. While Moretti was a professor at UC Berkeley,

---

26 It seems worth mentioning that the controversy at the center of the show resembles the case of Ben Frisch, a math teacher who lost his job at a private Quaker school in Manhattan, after thirty-four years of teaching there. During a class Frisch claims he found himself inadvertently in a Nazi salute while explaining how to calculate angles of depression and elevation. To deflect the awkwardness, he joked, "Heil Hitler!" and was mortified "that his stab at Mel Brooks-style parody hadn't landed," as a *New York Times* feature on the incident put it. Frisch is Jewish, and the son of a Holocaust survivor, and not a very good comedian, as many said in his defense. He has also become a paradigmatic figure for a new era in the classroom, in which students, supposedly, can't take jokes. See Jonathan Mahler, "A Teacher Made a Hitler Joke in the Classroom. It Tore the School Apart," *The New York Times Magazine*, September 5, 2018, https://www.nytimes.com/interactive/2018/09/05/magazine/friends-new-york-quaker-school-ben-frisch-hitler-joke.html, https://www.nytimes.com/interactive/2018/09/05/magazine/friends-new-york-quaker-school-ben-frisch-hitler-joke.html.

Kimberly Latta, then one of his graduate students, recalls being sexually stalked, pressured, and raped. In a letter sent to Stanford which she later made public on Facebook, Latta also states that Moretti would "frequently push me up against the wall in his office ... and push up my shirt and bra and forcibly kiss me, against my will."[27] In her account of their relationship, Latta characterizes Moretti's behavior in jokester terms, as "jovial bullying."[28] Later, as a professor at Dartmouth, Moretti assaulted Jane Penner, an English graduate student attending a summer seminar. "There wasn't an obvious channel [to report]," Penner reflected in 2017, adding that Moretti "was a brilliant and powerful scholar. As a mere grad student beginning her dissertation, I couldn't risk inviting his enmity."[29] In 1997, when Moretti visited Johns Hopkins for an informal job talk, a graduate student reported that he touched her inappropriately. When I attended a conference at Stanford in 2015, a cluster of graduate students spoke, huddled in a corner, of several rumors they'd heard—the kind of joking-warning that takes place throughout academia, just like most workplaces.

However problematized and nuanced, the reverse victimhood and professorial martyrdom at the center of *The Chair* seemed to advance this kind of narrative, and maybe even against its better instincts. For me, it brought to mind more than a decade of exchanges among students and student-workers about who to avoid and why, or what to expect if you have to work with or under so and so. Some of these forewarnings regarded a well-known sexual abuser on the academic left. When undergraduates, graduate student workers and adjuncts came together to demand that this tenured professor be fired, providing numerous testimonials of harassment and assault, the struggle was dismissed by many left-academics as an appeal to identity politics. The university's Title IX office had received numerous complaints going back to 2009, but these were variously dismissed until political pressure and independent journalism forced a

---

27 Sean Guynes, "Kimberly Latta Statement," *Twitter*, November 9, 2017, https://twitter.com/saguynes/status/928725320794083328/photo/1.
28 Fangzhou Liu and Hannah Knowles, "Harassment, Assault Allegations against Moretti Span Three Campuses," *The Stanford Daily*, November 16, 2017, https://stanforddaily.com/2017/11/16/harassment-assault-allegations-against-moretti-span-three-campuses/.
29 Liu and Knowles, "Harassment, Assault Allegations."

reconsideration.[30] Similarly, union leadership was dismissive, based on the unwillingness of complainants to consent to a process involving some of the professor's students and close friends. "This is bad for the left," a member of my union's leadership told me. Meanwhile graduate student workers and adjunct lecturers faced retaliation, all mandatory reporters with some obvious labor grievances. It was hard not to notice that what was "bad for the left" was also bad for a boss, and for the university. When graffiti began appearing on campus, in response to the university's failure to address growing concerns among students and workers about sexual violence,[31] four senior professors wrote an open letter of support for the accused abuser, which they sent to the entire Humanities faculty list, which incidentally includes many graduate student workers and adjunct lecturers who do a substantial portion of the division's teaching. In the email they "urge the administration to join us in condemning actions such as these and to take steps to defend us against such assaults." Numerous high-ranking professors and emeriti replied all, voicing their support for their tenured colleague as well. The initial email's posturing, and its claim that calls for accountability amount to "assault," seemed all the more grotesque in the months to come, as journalists began uncovering this professor's long history of abusive behavior toward students and student-workers.

Let it be clear: sexual violence is and has always been bad for the left. Sexual violence isn't specific to the left, but the left is also not exceptional to it. People get hurt from every angle of these conflicts,

---

30 Nidhi Subbaraman, "Some Called It 'Vigilante Justice.' But An Anonymous Campaign Triggered A Real Investigation Into A UC Santa Cruz Professor," *Buzzfeed News*, May 22, 2018, https://www.buzzfeednews.com/article/nidhisubbaraman/gopal-balakrishnan-sexual-harassment-investigation.

31 This concern was in response to multiple Title IX investigations, including a case which was kept completely confidential, leaving many students and colleagues in the dark, until the media broke the news that the professor had been fired for raping a student the night before her graduation in 2015. The campus had also seen a significant spike in Title IX reports, going from 181 reports and 22 investigations in 2014–2015 to 233 reports and 46 formal investigations in 2015–2016. For more on each of these cases, see Brianna Sacks, "University Awards Student One Of The Largest Rape Settlements Ever," *BuzzFeed*, January 31, 2017, https://www.buzzfeednews.com/article/briannasacks/uc-santa-cruz-lawsuit-settlement; Subbaraman, "Some Called It 'Vigilante Justice.' But An Anonymous Campaign Triggered A Real Investigation Into A UC Santa Cruz Professor"; Nidhi Subbaraman, "UC Santa Cruz Has Fired A Professor After He Violated The University's Harassment Policy," *BuzzFeed News*, September 24, 2019, https://www.buzzfeednews.com/article/nidhisubbaraman/gopal-balakrishnan-fired-santa-cruz.

and people make mistakes from every angle too, but that's nothing new. Those who speak up about abuse have always faced consequences themselves, including more harassment and often much worse. People will try to ruin your life if you speak up. However, the fault lines can and must be mapped in terms of power—starkly visible in the hierarchical and increasingly exploitative power structure of universities.

Outside the context of academia, and in the popular imagination of #MeToo and "getting canceled," I think of Monica Lewinsky, not of Harvey Weinstein. Throughout my early adolescence, kids were joking about Lewinsky's appearance, trashing the intimate details of her life that were being dragged through the media, and laughing about how she gave Bill Clinton blowjobs. I don't remember anyone wondering if she was OK, or whether she should be left alone—or whether Clinton owed her an apology. Now, as we know, she was deeply suicidal throughout that period. She survived, but spent a decade in a depressive hole, and re-emerged in 2014 to begin speaking publicly about a "culture of humiliation," and her own personal experience of being nearly "humiliated to death" on a global scale. In 2014 she broke her silence in a *Vanity Fair* essay, in which she detailed her experiences surviving this humiliation, as well as the ways in which Hillary Clinton's presidential campaigns perpetuated her silence. Throughout her account of trying to find jobs, I hear echoes of those who speak of what's "bad for the left." In what she thought to be a "promising job interview" soon before the 2008 primary season, she recounts how the "conversation took an interesting turn":

> "So here's the thing, Monica," the interviewer said. "You're clearly a bright young woman and affable, but for us— and probably any other organization that relies on grants and other government funding—it's risky. We would first need a Letter of Indemnification from the Clintons. After all, there is a 25 percent chance that Mrs. Clinton will be the next president. I gave a fake smile and said, "I understand."[32]

This is how the joke works.

32 Monica Lewinsky, "Exclusive: Monica Lewinsky on the Culture of Humiliation," *Vanity Fair*, May 28, 2014, https://www.vanityfair.com/style/society/2014/06/monica-lewinsky-humiliation-culture.

What ultimately motivated Lewinsky to come out of hiding was Tyler Clementi's suicide in 2010. Clementi was a gay Rutgers University student who jumped off the George Washington Bridge after his roommate filmed him having sex with his boyfriend without consent and posted it to Twitter in 2010. Suicide is the second leading cause of death for youth in the United States, and recent studies show that LGBTQ youth are four times more likely to consider, plan, or attempt suicide.[33] Transgender youth and adults are especially at risk of suicide. All this lurks in the background of *The Closer*, Dave Chappelle's 2021 comedy special, in which the comedian doubles down on the antitrans tirade of his previous special. Since the release of that special in 2019—entitled *Sticks and Stones*, as in: "words will never hurt me"—the trans woman Chappelle mentions in some of the material, Daphne Dorman, killed herself. Chappelle and Dorman were friends, and she supported his comedy, as Chappelle's publicity team frequently explains. At the same time, as Aja Romano suggests, Chappelle "seems to be at pains to use his offstage support of trans people to justify his overtly transphobic onstage comedy."[34] In *The Closer*, Chappelle recounts his relationship with Dorman, who was an aspiring comedian, and how she defended him in a tweet after *Sticks and Stones* was released and then "the trans community dragged that bitch all over Twitter." After explaining to his audience that, since then, Dorman killed herself, he insists "It wasn't the jokes . . . I don't know if it was them dragging on her . . . but I'll bet dragging on her didn't help." Without taking a beat, he proceeds:

> I felt like Daphne lied to me. She always said that she iden-
> tified as a woman, and then one day she goes up to the roof
> of her building and jumps off and kills herself. Clearly . . .
> only a man would do some gangster shit like that.

While relinquishing his own responsibility—"it wasn't the jokes," he says with certainty—Chappelle consistently implies that the "trans community" should be blamed for her suicide, concluding "I don't know what the trans community did for her, but I don't care because I feel like she wasn't

33 "Estimate of How Often LGBTQ Youth Attempt Suicide in the U.S.," *The Trevor Project*, accessed January 1, 2022, https://www.thetrevorproject.org/research-briefs/estimate-of-how-often-lgbtq-youth-attempt-suicide-in-the-u-s/.
34 Aja Romano, "Dave Chappelle vs. Trans People vs. Netflix," *Vox*, October 14, 2021, https://www.vox.com/22722357/dave-chappelle-the-closer-netflix-backlash-controversy-transphobic.

their tribe, she was mine. She was a comedian in her soul." For "comedian," read "jokester."

"It wasn't the jokes," he tells us. This is how the joke works.

"I have never had a problem with transgender people," Chappelle asserts, "if you listen to me, my problem has always been with white people. I have been arguing with whites my entire career."[35] This latter claim is undeniable—and indeed, the reason why so many people are coming to Chappelle's defense. But as Danielle Fuentes Morgan suggests in her book about the politics of Black satire, these conversations often overlook a reactionary turn in Chappelle's career. Just like the fact of his friendship with Dorman, his early work simply cannot justify the more recent choices he's made in stand-up material. By the late 2010s, "Chappelle is no holds barred" with women and LGBTQ communities, Fuentes Morgan writes, "not only is his tone in the jokes themselves vastly different, but the potential trauma they create is likewise unequal." Here, she identifies a certain betrayal in Chappelle's politics, once he returned from a partial hiatus from comedy between 2005–2013:

> [It may be] that Chappelle is leaning into the argument of his current supporters that his comedy is "just jokes." This shift from public responsibility is difficult to reconcile not only because prior to his departure, Chappelle indicated at every level his belief that these are not just jokes—indeed, his initial departure from comedy was in view of his concerns that his jokes were misinterpreted and enacting harm.

Precisely because Chappelle's "platform was built on his ability to reconcile the comedic and the socio-politically progressive, his deep consideration of the cause and effects of the social realm," as Fuentes Morgan explains, this more recent refusal to consider impact "outside of that which immediately impacts himself is incredibly disheartening."[36] Distinguishing between Chappelle's earlier, antiracist satire, Fuentes Morgan raises crucial questions about the comedian's frequent insistence that he never "punches down." These questions hang over the end of *The Closer*: before dropping his mic, Chappelle addresses

---

35 Stan Lathan, *Dave Chappelle: The Closer* (Netflix, 2021).
36 Danielle Fuentes Morgan, *Laughing to Keep from Dying: African American Satire in the Twenty-First Century* (Urbana: University of Illinois Press, 2020), 159–60.

the "LGBTQ-LMNOP-QIZ" community: "It is over. I'm done talking about it," he claims, "All I ask from your community, with all humility, will you please stop punching down on my people." Here and elsewhere, Chappelle rests on the assumption that he can speak of "my people," and be interpreted as meaning Black people. Earlier into his career, this would have been hardly debatable. By now, however, part of this assumption is not just that Chappelle is speaking on behalf of Black people but making the case that by "trans" he means exclusively white people.

Chappelle "was such a groundbreaking comedian particularly in the early aughts and now he's going out like this," Imani Gandy wrote soon after *The Closer* was released, "also can somebody please tell [Dave Chappelle] that there are Black people who are LGBTQ? Like what the fuck man."[37] Black trans comedian Dahlia Belle begins her powerful open letter to Chappelle by emulating his language from the special: "Dear Dave," she writes, "We're both comedians. I guess that makes me a member of your tribe. I'm sure you've never heard of me, though, and I can think of at least three reasons for that: I'm Black; I'm a woman; I'm transgender (ie 'a trans')." She continues, referring to some of *The Closer*'s material:

> On behalf of the trans community, I'll go ahead and address your weakest defenses. How much do you have to participate in my self-image? Not at all. I just want you to shut up. You said: "You shouldn't discuss this in front of Black people." Why, Dave? Why shouldn't you discuss this in front of Black people? Did you once again imagine all trans people are white, or do you assume there is some inherent danger awaiting us among the larger Black community? And why might that be? Regardless, neither explanation sits well with me.[38]

Throughout Belle's letter, she considers how this has done particular harm to her and Black trans people she knows:

37 Imani Gandy, "Also Can Somebody Please Tell Dave Chappelle That There Are Black People Who Are LGBTQ?," *Twitter*, October 6, 2021, https://twitter.com/AngryBlackLady/status/1445787263783215107.
38 Dahlia Belle, "Dear Dave Chappelle, Transgender Comedians Can Take a Joke, but Why Are Yours so Unfunny?," *The Guardian*, October 9, 2021, https://www.theguardian.com/stage/2021/oct/09/dave-chappelle-letter-trans-comedian-netflix.

Dave, some of us are Black, and when I was growing up in the midwest, there was never a shortage of racist white dudes to tell me about their Black friend, who gave them permission to say ['n****']. I hear you, Dave. I hear you holding up our fellow comedian Daphne Dorman as the Good Tranny, who never made Dave feel bad for being transphobic. Daphne Dorman, your "friend," who you describe as a terrible comedian, and didn't know she had a child until reading her obituary.

Pointing to Chappelle's tokenization of Dorman, Belle also troubles the ways in which Chappelle relies, continually, on claims to innocence. "Every transgender person I know has lost someone by suicide," she explains, "the marginalization, mockery, dehumanization, and violence many of us face everyday of most of our lives is what fuels our despair."

In *The Closer*, after reminding his audience (and perhaps himself) that his "problem has always been with white people," he proceeds to defend J.K. Rowling. "I'm team TERF. I agree. Gender is a fact," he declares.[39] Then he turns to Caitlin Jenner as another "Good Tranny," which Belle traces as a persistent strategy in Chappelle's comedy: "Caitlin Jenner— whom I've met, wonderful person—was voted *woman of the year*, her first year as a woman," Chappelle says with outrage, "I'd be mad as shit if I was a woman." Sure, there are lots of reasons to be mad about Jenner, who hoped to run for Governor on a political platform that included a wide range of antitrans policies such as a ban on transgender youth from playing sports, being lauded as "woman of the year," or as a representative of trans people. But when Chappelle ends the special with the request "please stop punching down on my people," who does he really mean by this? In the closing credits of his special, after this address to the implicitly all-white trans community, there's a slide show—set eerily to Gloria Gaynor's "I Will Survive," an anthem of Black women's and LGBTQ survival and solidarity if there ever was one—with photographs featuring Chappelle with his close friends, such as Kanye West, David Letterman, Chance the Rapper, The Foo Fighters, Bill Burr, Bill Murray, Morgan Freeman, Jon Stewart, John Mulaney, John Mayer, Quincy Jones,

---

39 However consciously or unconsciously, Chappelle's use of "gender" is of course fundamentally wrong—gender is a fiction for how power is organized—and also conflates gender with sex, presuming a biological "truth" which has been thoroughly disproven. My purpose here is obviously not to debate the science of his comedy, but its ideology. Still, the point should be raised.

Bradley Cooper, Jerry Seinfeld, Kevin Hart, Mick Jagger, Joe Rogan, and of course, Netflix CEO, Ted Sarandos.

According to leaked documents from Netflix, the company paid Chappelle $24.1 million for *The Closer*. Within days of its release, Sarandos began issuing public statements about the special, defending Chappelle against criticism from Netflix subscribers and workers alike. "Some people find the art of stand-up to be mean-spirited but our members enjoy it, and it's an important part of our content offering," Sarandos explains in an internal email at the company, responding to concerns raised by Netflix workers about hate speech and an inch away from just saying "that's entertainment." Addressing his employees, the CEO writes that "several of you have also asked where we draw the line on hate. We don't allow titles on Netflix that are designed to incite hate or violence, and we don't believe *The Closer* crosses that line." He adds: "Externally, particularly in stand-up comedy, artistic freedom is obviously a very different standard of speech than we allow internally as the goals are different: entertaining people versus maintaining a respectful, productive workplace."[40]

Alongside the email, Sarandos made it perfectly clear to his employees what it means to oversee a "respectful, productive workplace."[41] On October 6, 2021, the day after *The Closer* premiered, Terra Field, a software engineer at Netflix, spoke publicly about the special's "attacks [on] the trans community, and the very validity of transness."[42] The next day, Field and two other trans employees at Netflix were suspended from the company. While they were all reinstated within 24 hours, probably from the buzz of media attention, Netflix's trans resource group began organizing a walkout to protest the company's handling of the Chappelle special, and primarily Sarandos's public responses. The target wasn't Chappelle and his artistic freedom, but the company and its treatment of workers. A few days before the planned walkout, one of the organizers, a Black, transgender, and pregnant employee named B. Pagels-Minor, was fired. A Netflix spokesperson confirmed the news, explaining "We understand this employee may have been motivated by disappointment and hurt with Netflix, but maintaining a culture of trust and transparency is core to our

40 Zoe Schiffer, "Netflix Suspends Trans Employee Who Tweeted about Dave Chappelle Special," *The Verge*, October 11, 2021, https://www.theverge.com/2021/10/11/22720724/netflix-suspends-trans-employee-tweeted-dave-chappelle-the-closer.
41 Schiffer, "Netflix Suspends Trans Employee."
42 Schiffer, "Netflix Suspends Trans Employee."

company."[43] As another former Netflix employee remarked at the time in an interview, "the only person who gets fired [read: canceled] is [a] Black person," adding that it "just further shows that Black trans people are the ones being targeted in this conversation."[44] The company claimed that Pagels-Minor leaked sensitive information. Pagels-Minor categorically denies these claims and has spoken out about the dismissive way in which workers' concerns were treated in Sarandos's company memos: "The tone of the message was basically like: You employees can't possibly understand the nuance of comedy, and that's why you're [upset]," they explained to a reporter from *The New York Times*, the day before the walkout. "That's not the point. It's not that we don't understand comedy. It's that this comedy has tones of hatred. And what are we going to do to mitigate that?"[45]

During all of this, the "antiwoke" sector of social democrats and democratic socialists found in Chappelle the perfect alibi: a way to deflect the familiar charges of racism and anti-Blackness, which still enacted an antitrans and anti-Black agenda. The "leftist" publisher Zer0 Books took to Twitter with the following commentary: "Chappelle's latest special is legitimately moving. People who are angry at him about transphobia clearly HAVE NOT watched the show."[46] Then, in a comment, the publisher promoted one of their latest books—Ben Burgis's *Canceling Comedians While the World Burns*.

The central claim of Burgis's book is that "we" need a more *strategic* left, citing the "failure of the contemporary left to think strategically instead of turning politics into a moral performance."[47] The "we" he speaks for are presumably comprises those whose relationship to racism, sexual violence, trans hatred, and ableism, can seem merely a matter of "performance" getting in the way of "unity": "The more we present ourselves as moralistic hall monitors," Burgis warns "us," "the harder it is for us to win over the masses of ordinary people we need to convince in order for us to

43   Zoe Schiffer, "Netflix Just Fired the Organizer of the Trans Employee Walkout," *The Verge*, October 15, 2021, https://www.theverge.com/2021/10/15/22728337/netflix-fires-organizer-trans-employee-walkout-dave-chappelle.
44   Schiffer, Netflix Just Fired the Organizer of the Trans Employee Walkout."
45   John Koblin and Nicole Sperling, "Netflix Employees Walk out to Protest Dave Chappelle's Special.," *The New York Times*, October 20, 2021, https://www.nytimes.com/2021/10/20/business/media/netflix-protest-dave-chappelle.html.
46   Zer0 Books, "Chappelle's Latest Special Is Legitimately Moving. People Who Are Angry at Him about Transphobia Clearly HAVE NOT Watched the Show," https://twitter.com/Zer0Books/status/1446596174148890625.
47   Burgis, *Canceling Comedians While the World Burns*, 33.

have any change of doing much of anything[.]"[48] Here, I think of a friend, who had been active in a political group until someone in the group sexually assaulted her. After the assault, she didn't say anything in the group, she just left. She didn't want to be retraumatized, she just wanted out. While people in the group speculated that she just wasn't that political, she found other ways, even though she lived in a small town. There are so many people with this kind of story. These kinds of disappearing acts happen throughout the left, along with stories of "passing the abuser"—kicking someone out of a group or a town after they've harassed or assaulted, only for them to presumably do this again somewhere else. But these are matters of "moral performance," as Burgis suggests, not things getting in the way of winning over the masses. From Burgis's vantage of doing what it takes "to win," the defense of a rapist in a political organization may appear simply beside the point. Premised on this uneasy analogy between the left and the world of comedy, Burgis's book continually insists that there are bigger priorities than canceling comedians—which is to say, playing "moralistic hall monitors" to the left. The world is burning, as Burgis keeps reminding us.

Likewise, there are bigger priorities than *defending* comedians as the world burns—and, by extension, whatever leftist pathologies Burgis seeks to uphold by analogy. To the "representative example of cluster of left pathologies," what Burgis caricatures throughout his book is the correspondent figure of the antiwoke paranoiac, for whom the jokester (and jokesterism) represents heroism and bravery. For this paranoiac figure, the threat of cancelation looms everywhere. Much of the time, this is a fear of consequences—of being criticized—which the paranoiac catastrophizes. The paranoid structure develops "in a pseudological unity of themes of grandeur, persecution, and revenge," as Michel Foucault suggests, against the background of a "systematized, coherent delusion, without hallucination[.]"[49] In this sense, the paranoiac simultaneously amplifies the victimization of those who have been "canceled"—a claim that, for many, actually cultivates solidarity—while delegitimating the possibility of any other forms of trauma in its midst. Positioned as "the autonomous rational individual to which modernity aspires," Kenneth Paradis explains, the paranoiac strikes "an uncanny reflection that foregrounds the potential

---

48 Burgis, *Canceling Comedians*, 97.
49 Michel Foucault, *Madness: The Invention of an Idea*, prev. published as *Mental Illness and Psychology* (New York: Harper & Row, 1954), 8.

for violence in that subject's capacity for intellectual self-deception and moral self-justification."[50] It's by this logic that Burgis's argument against "turning politics into a moral performance" itself works as a moral performance, condemning condemnational politics, and projecting guilt onto that which supposedly propagates guilt but little else.

Just as disturbing as this fairly conventional set of moral judgments at work in Burgis's plea for the left "to be smarter,"[51] however, is the book's starkly anti-utopian understanding of comedy. "Comedy is a form of entertainment that, when executed with enough skill and vision to have a deeper effect than just eliciting a quick laugh in the moment, becomes art," he asserts in this rather strict definition. "What it isn't," he continues, "is *a way of changing the world*."[52] But what if it could be? What if comedy wasn't just stand-up specials and "entertainment," but a way of relating to each other and thinking about and caring for this world that's burning all around us? What if comedy was a way of taking that world seriously—not as "just a joke"?

In defense of jokesterism, a fascistic reactionism is currently building throughout different sectors of the left. This is not "class reductionism," as Burgis describes as a charge he'd grown accustomed to—often implying the exclusion of race and gender from political analysis. At the heart of this "leftist" authoritarian brand of jokesterism is a familiar, and predictable, non-recognition of contradictions that should be plainly clear. While these jokesters expound lectures about a "strategic left," they align themselves with a millionaire celebrity and a CEO against workers. While they talk the talk about "worker solidarity," they scoff at a walkout and demands for a better workplace. This isn't a joke.

50 Kenneth Paradis, *Sex, Paranoia, and Modern Masculinity* (Albany: State University of New York Press, 2007), 23.
51 Burgis, *Canceling Comedians While the World Burns*, 120.
52 Burgis, *Canceling Comedians*, 24.

CHAPTER SIX

Ode to Killjoys

> "It seems I knew you long before our common ties—of
> conscious choice
> Threw under single skies, those like us
> Who, fused by our mold
> Became their targets, as of old ...
>
> Anti ... Anti-Fascistas!
> That was your name ...
>
> I saw you in the passion-flower
> In roses full of flame ...
>
> O anti-fascist sister—you whose eye turn to stars still
> I've learned your wondrous secret—source of spirit and of
> will
> I've learned that what sustains your heart—mind and peace
> of soul
> Is knowledge that their just—can never reach its goal"
>
> —Claudia Jones, "For Consuela—Anti-Fascista"[1]

In what is by now a notorious incident in recent comedy history, stand-up
Daniel Tosh made a series of jokes about rape during a set at the Laugh
Factory one night in July 2012. When he proclaimed that rape is *always*
funny, a woman yelled from the audience "actually, rape jokes are never
funny!" Then Tosh replied with another "joke": "wouldn't it be funny if

---

1 Carole Boyce Davies, *Left of Karl Marx: The Political Life of Black Communist Claudia Jones* (Durham: Duke University Press, 2007).

that girl got raped by like, five guys right now? Like right now? What if a bunch of guys just raped her ..."[2] A few days later, Tosh crafted a weak public apology for social media, while other comedians took to Twitter to voice their support of his freedom to rape-joke: "Some attention-seeking woman heckled a comedian, so if anything, she owes him an apology for being a rude brat," Jim Norton wrote;[3] Dane Cook chimed in, "If you journey through this life easily offended by other people's words I think it's best for everyone if you just kill yourself";[4] and then there was Anthony Jeselnik, who remarked, "This Daniel Tosh rape joke controversy really has me second guessing some of my rapes."[5] "Comedians and feminists [are] natural enemies,"[6] Louis C.K. snarked on *The Daily Show* later that week. It was just another episode of an ongoing war.

Over the last decade, the stakes of these debates have certainly changed, especially since #MeToo, while the perception of this "natural" enmity continues to control the narrative. Key to this familiar dynamic is the figure of the killjoy, the jokester's hysterical antithesis. The killjoy conjures a vision of feminists, Sara Ahmed writes, as "those who refuse to laugh at the right points; those who are unwilling to be seated at the table of happiness." Killjoys are "willful women, unwilling to get along, unwilling to preserve an idea of happiness,"[7] she explains. Accused of overthinking, reading too far into things, taking it all too seriously, the killjoy is determined to raise problems where problems are seemingly off-limits, reducing feminism to a way of "making your life harder than it needs to be."[8]

Feminist critiques of comedy have historically been deflected by the familiar claim and jokester logic that a rape joke is "just a joke." Used as a tactic to reflexively disavow what one has just said, it's a double attack:

2   See Amanda Holpuch, "Daniel Tosh Apologises for Rape Joke as Fellow Comedians Defend Topic," *The Guardian*, July 11, 2012, https://www.theguardian.com/culture/us-news-blog/2012/jul/11/daniel-tosh-apologises-rape-joke.

3   Jim Norton, "Some Attention-Seeking Woman Heckled a Comedian, so If Anything, She Owes Him an Apology for Being a Rude Brat.," *Twitter*, July 11, 2012, https://twitter.com/JimNorton/status/223119997881434113.

4   Dane Cook, "If You Journey through This Life Easily Offended by Other Peoples Words I Think It's Best for Everyone If You Just Kill Yourself.," *Twitter*, July 11, 2012, https://twitter.com/danecook/status/223115169394470912.

5   Anthony Jeselnik, "This Daniel Tosh Rape Joke Controversy Really Has Me Second Guessing Some of My Rapes.," *Twitter*, July 11, 2012, https://twitter.com/anthonyjeselnik/status/223172033347981312.

6   "Louis C.K.," *The Daily Show with Jon Stewart* (Comedy Central, July 16, 2012).

7   Sara Ahmed, *Willful Subjects* (Durham: Duke University Press, 2014), 4–5.

8   Sara Ahmed, *Living a Feminist Life* (Durham: Duke University Press, 2017), 246.

first the assault, then the gaslight. If the trouble with feminism and comedy is that feminism takes what is supposedly "just a joke" as an object of critique and interpretation, then what does that imply about comedy and its perceived critical and artistic capacity otherwise? Why is it that "feminists" are scorned for taking comedy "too seriously," while "authentic" stand-ups like George Carlin are held up as philosophers of their time and prophets of ours? You can't have it both ways. But that is the attempt.

This still quite pervasive conception of feminism as the enemy of comedy has little to do with comedy or feminism, and everything to do with antifeminism, far beyond the demarcated "free speech zone" of the stand-up industry. For decades, the price of admission for women in comedy was not only the capacity to endure shockingly sexist and abusive work environments, but an active and explicit dissociation from feminism. In the early seventies, Phyllis Diller complained "the young girls are into women's lib . . . I don't want a message on stage. I may offend them. I know I have offended some. But I can't let that affect my work." [9] Elayne Boosler, who came up in that era, explained "when asked if I'm a feminist, I've always said that I'm just a human being trapped in a woman's body." [10] These assumptions remain widespread throughout the industry. In 2018, Hannah Gadsby began her special *Nanette* by wondering if she should quit comedy, no longer willing to work under the constant pressure to "lighten up . . . Stop taking everything so seriously! Fucking learn to take a joke."[11]

The myth of "female humourlessness" is put hilariously (and pathetically) on display in Christopher Hitchens's chauvinist diatribe "Why Women Aren't Funny," an unfortunate *Vanity Fair* essay published in 2007. Attributing the "humor gap" between men and women to some sort of natural order, Hitchens spews: "Men have to pretend, to themselves as well as to women, that they are not the servants and the supplicants. Women, cunning minxes that they are, have to affect not to be the potentates."[12] Note the way in which this sexism is packaged strategically in defensive posturing, and feigned inferiority, carefully maintaining the conventions of wounded white masculinity. Through this posturing,

9   Susan Horowitz, *Queens of Comedy: Lucille Ball, Phyllis Diller, Carol Burnett, Joan Rivers, and the New Generation of Funny Women* (Amsterdam: Gordon and Breach, 1997), 49.

10   Horowitz, *Queens of Comedy,* 51.

11   Madeleine Parry, *Hannah Gadsby: Nanette,* Stand-up Special (Netflix, 2018).

12   Christopher Hitchens, "Why Women Aren't Funny," *Vanity Fair,* January 1, 2007, https://www.vanityfair.com/culture/2007/01/hitchens200701.

Hitchens enacts a certain reversal, vital to what Sally Robinson describes of this wounded subjectivity: "the marking of white men as victimizers can easily produce its opposite: an understanding of white men as victims of that feminist critique."[13] At the height of the comedienne boom of the 2000s, Hitchens stirred up hilarious outrage, and became the ultimate strawman for the likes of Tina Fey, Amy Poehler, Sarah Silverman, and many more. Not surprisingly, Hitchens had a hard time taking the jokes.

The thing is, most killjoys are hilarious. Some of the funniest nights of my life have been spent watching movies with feminists, no matter the genre, picking apart every problem, pulling to the surface the contradictions like pus from a wound. There's a healing that comes with these moments. The concern is hardly ever, if at all, over realism. There are no pure or perfect representations to the killjoy, only the pleasure of reading critically, and together. I think back on the most seemingly benign sitcoms of my youth, and the incredible violence which they reproduced—all the shows that, in every way possible, almost reached out of the screen, grabbing me by the shoulders, and told me and every adolescent girl I knew that we should learn to starve ourselves—and I remember what it felt like to make fun of that garbage with my best friend, and how that made all the difference. We loved to laugh at this world of false promises. To laugh at it was an act of solidarity; it was pedagogical, as in we were teaching each other how to survive. It was as if we could cut through everything that told us to suffer and refuse the joylessness of what we were told was joy.

Killing joy, as Ahmed suggests, is a project of world-making: "we make a world out of the shattered pieces even when we shatter the pieces or even when we are the shattered pieces."[14] This practice might also be understood as having an erotic function, as in Audre Lorde's account of "the open and fearless underlining of my capacity for joy" in erotic connection.[15] Cynthia Willett takes this up as a libidinal politics of comedy: through collective practices of interpreting, re-articulating, and negating configurations of power, there are "glimpses into richly subversive forms of negative freedom." Willett understands this capacity of comedy as an antidote to philosophical doctrines of continental rationalism and liberal individualism: "Comic insights into our libidinal desires and social relationships," she writes, open up "political thought beyond

---

13 Sally Robinson, *Marked Men: White Masculinity in Crisis* (New York: Columbia University Press, 2000), 130.
14 Ahmed, *Living a Feminist Life*, 261.
15 Audre Lorde, *Sister Outsider: Essays and Speeches* (Berkeley: Crossing Press, 1984), 44.

liberalism's narrow focus on the claims of the abstract individual."[16] The killjoy demands a theory of comedy based in this drive to de-individuate, through shared joy and active world-making—and not in the individual freedom to tell rape jokes.

§

As the frequent target of hate jokes, many trans comedians have mused over what we might call a killjoy work ethic. "I am quite an offensive comic from time to time," explains comedian Jordan Raskopoulos. "But the people I offend, I intend to offend … politicians, religious fundamentalists, trans exclusionary radical feminists, and nazis."[17] As a trans woman, Raskopoulos is constantly harassed by audiences and fellow comedians. Fighting back with comedy is a matter of strategy and precision, demanding an ethical framework for joking. Of her first few years performing stand-up, Alice Rose recounts the everyday struggle to continue working in comedy as a trans woman: "I routinely had to follow transphobic or homophobic acts, or worse, have a comedian take the stage after me only to target me specifically in their tasteless jokes," she recalls, "I have been on gender-balanced shows with comedians complaining about 'male comics transitioning to female' for more stage time" (as if that's how it works), and "[having] hosts joke about sexually or physically assaulting me, and have even been groped onstage on more than one occasion." Despite these ongoing struggles, Rose insists, "I not only found a way to claim the stage, but to use standup as a way to find acceptance and self-love; now, it's time to make room for more trans comedians to do the same."[18]

Killjoy comedy both interrogates jokes and does the work of joking, based on an understanding of the joke not only through its potential to inflict harm but through its power to enact care as well. Some of the most fascinating killjoy comedy of recent years has focused, in some way, on collective healing. Cameron Esposito's 2018 stand-up special, *Rape Jokes*, makes such an attempt. Rather than impose a limit on what comedy is

---

16   Cynthia Willett, *Irony in the Age of Empire: Comic Perspectives on Democracy and Freedom*, American Philosophy (Bloomington: Indiana University Press, 2008), 125.

17   Hallie Lieberman, "'It Gets to You': Trans Comedians on Transphobia and Cancel Culture," *The Guardian*, January 23, 2021, https://www.theguardian.com/culture/2021/jan/23/trans-comedians-transphobia-cancel-culture.

18   Alice Rose, "Standup Helped Me Embrace Myself. It's Time to Make Space for Other Trans Comedians to Do the Same," *CBC*, accessed January 1, 2022, https://www.cbc.ca/arts/standup-helped-me-embrace-myself-it-s-time-to-make-space-for-other-trans-comedians-to-do-the-same-1.5699659.

and isn't—the kind of genre-policing at the core of jokesterism—*Rape Jokes* meditates on the possibilities of killjoy comedy: "There are a lot of folks in my field," Esposito remarks of stand-up comedians, "[who'll] say things like 'oooh, how can I tell jokes? How can I tell jokes without those words?' And I will just say, if there are any particular words that you need in order to do this job, I am a better stand-up comic than you."[19] After leaving *Saturday Night Live* and years of doing voice-over work, Sasheer Zamata came out with her first special, *Pizza Mind*, in 2017, filled with observations about casualized racism, in and out of the comedy world. In "Racist Radio," produced by UCB Comedy, Zamata parodies the kind of discussions she often has with casting directors, who ask her things like "'could you make that a little more . . . urban. Like more . . . *ethnic*?' She stretches out this awkwardness: ". . . more, uh, *ghetto*. Or like um . . . *blacker*. Can you be *blacker* about it? Do you know what I mean when I say *blacker*? Like a, like a *colored person*, like a *negro* . . . like a *mammy*. You got something like a mammy for me? ... like a *bush woman*?"[20] Like the best parody, Zamata's killjoy comedy exaggerates, but only slightly. It gives voice to an experience shared by many, which remains mostly unspeakable.

The question of what it means to joke might be better asked through poetry. I hear aspects of a killjoy comedy emerge, for instance, throughout Patricia Lockwood's poem "Rape Joke," detailing an experience of sexual violence, and messing with the idea of joking. The poem begins with the speaker mocking her rapist: "Imagine the rape joke looking in the mirror, perfectly reflecting back itself, and grooming itself to look more like a rape joke. 'Ahhhh,' it thinks. 'Yes. A goatee.'"[21] The speaker then moves in and out of the joke, at times inducing fear:

> The rape joke is that he carried a knife, and would show it to you, and would turn it over and over in his hands as if it were a book.
>
> He wasn't threatening you, you understood. He just really liked his knife.

What's remarkable about these passages is the way Lockwood so meticulously troubles the joke through poetry. "It gets funnier[,]" the speaker continues, "The rape joke is that *come on*, you should have seen it coming.

---

19   Cameron Esposito, *Rape Jokes*, stand-up special, 2018, www.cameronesposito.com.
20   Sasheer Zamata, "Racist Radio," May 23, 2014, https://ucbcomedy.com/media/1187.
21   Patricia Lockwood, "Rape Joke," *The Awl*, July 25, 2013, https://www.theawl.com/2013/07/patricia-lockwood-rape-joke/.

This rape joke is practically writing itself." Questions of form are everywhere throughout "Rape Joke": "Can any part of the rape joke be funny. The part where it ends—haha, just kidding!" Here, to be funny cannot be reduced to a matter of technical proficiency in the craft of joke-telling—the joke can be told, and the joke will not be funny.

Of Medusa—the snaky-haired monster, beheaded by Perseus—Hélène Cixous contends that "you only have to look [straight on] to see her. And she's not deadly. She's beautiful and she's laughing."[22] Rejecting Freud's interpretation, fixated on castration, she looks to Medusa as a figure of women's self-hatred to be rigorously redefined. Cixous links this to a broader vision of écriture feminine, the possibilities of what she conceived as feminine modes of writing, which extend to a killjoy ethics of comedy. Her call to reimagine Medusa presents a foundation for this killjoy ethics, as a way to question the terms of self-hatred, and to "decide for yourself on your position in the arena of contradictions," as she writes, "where pleasure and reality embrace."[23]

§

The series *Feel Good*, starring and created by stand-up comedian Mae Martin, explores some of what a killjoy utopianism in comedy might be, in its semi-autobiographical portrait of Mae, an up-and-coming comedian and Canadian based in London, who struggles with gender dysphoria, addiction, and severe anxiety. By the end of the series, Mae comes out as nonbinary, begins using they/them pronouns, relapses and gets sober, falls in love, and confronts their rapist, all while trying to make it in the troubled world of comedy. At no point does the show romanticize stand-up as the art of truth-telling, as many of today's "brave" stand-up comedians will have it. In fact, in one of the most pivotal scenes, Mae indulgently and hurtfully insults their partner George (Charlotte Ritchie) and kills on stage, unaware that George is in the audience.[24] The contrast between the laughter in the crowd and the look on George's face brings out ethical questions about Mae's approach to comedy, which I wish were even further explored. But crucial to these questions is the bigger problem of the show: what are the ethics of feeling good? What does this look like

---

22 Hélène Cixous, "The Laugh of the Medusa," trans. Keith Cohen and Paula Cohen, *Signs: Journal of Women in Culture and Society* 1, no. 4 (Summer 1976): 875–893, https://doi.org/10.1086/493306. 885.

23 Cixous, "The Laugh of the Medusa," 891.

24 Ally Pankiw, "1.5," *Feel Good* (Channel 4 and Netflix, March 18, 2020).

in everyday life? Throughout the series, Mae asks these questions more directly in terms of drugs and romantic relationships—but the same could be asked of their stand-up, which at times illuminates dimensions of care that draw out a different kind of laughter, based in killjoy solidarity.

Some of the more compelling insights about comedy in *Feel Good* transpire off-stage, in behind-the-scenes moments of the comedy club circuit Mae works in. The show focuses primarily on two different clubs, one in London and another in Toronto. At one point in London, Mae is sexually harassed by Arnie Rivers, a stand-up has-been who's attempting post-cancelation redemption and looking for an opening act for his upcoming tour. Almost in the same breath as asking Mae to be his opener, he asks them to touch his penis. By now this kind of scene probably seems fairly typical to anyone who's followed the #MeToo controversies in stand-up, many of which detail casualized and ongoing sexual harassment both on and off stage in comedy clubs. But what follows is not as typical. Soon after Rivers pulls out his penis, Mae goes to Nick (Tobi Bamtefa), the club booker, and relays what happened. Without hesitation, Nick kicks Arnie out. Mae's friendship with Nick overrides Arnie's attempts to manipulate his minor power in the industry, and exemplifies the comradeship that often emerges in struggles against these conditions. These are killjoy bonds which are not taken for granted, or made to seem incredibly effective at addressing the broader problems in the comedy industry, but which come up in everyday interactions among workers in comedy and elsewhere.

Initially skeptical of Arnie, especially with the knowledge that George finds him attractive, Mae in time becomes quite taken with him—that is, before he pulls out his penis. Leading up to that interaction, Arnie is charming, and even ostensibly up for critique as well. He laughs and nods as Mae calls him on his schtick—the kind of hyper-masculine "authenticity" I describe earlier on. Then Arnie challenges Mae to take the stage "as honestly as possible," leading to the angry rant about George that nearly ruins their relationship. When Nick tells Mae that George was in the crowd that night, Mae rushes home and finds themselves deploying an eerily familiar rhetoric: "those were just jokes," they insist, "that was just joking."[25]

Like any drug, comedy lets Mae *feel good*—but just for a little while. The series captures the adrenaline rush of stand-up performance, and in many ways, the perpetual risk of bombing sets the narrative pace, along

---

25 Ally Pankiw, "1.5."

with Mae's vacillation between healing, self-harm, and toxic behaviors. There are moments when Mae's relationship to comedy is a highly reflexive ethical practice. As when they come out on stage as nonbinary, Mae's stand-up accentuates some of the possibilities of killjoy comedy, which chooses its targets with care, and frames its problems with the hope of not only feeling good but thinking and being together. The more Mae critically engages with these possibilities of stand-up, the clearer the utopian dimensions of the show's conception of comedy becomes.

The critique of the comedy industry builds towards the end of *Feel Good*, as Mae begins to unpack their complex relationship with Scott, a character Martin based on multiple comedians who were problematic mentor figures from their early years in comedy in Toronto. Scott is an older comedian and fellow recovering junkie. He brought Mae into the comedy scene when Mae was a teenager. And during that time, they were also in a sexual relationship. Gently, yet precisely, *Feel Good* confronts this relationship—gradually exploring how its power dynamic was ambiguous to Mae at the time but discernable with hindsight (and through the recognition of trauma), but not without asking how the relationship was possible in the first place. Mae sits with the messiness of this for a while, until they learn that they are not alone, and that Scott had other relationships with a transparent pattern of sexual coercion, emotional grooming, and, crucially, comedic mentorship.

Eventually, Mae goes to the comedy club in Toronto, where Scott still holds court. As Mae approaches Scott, surrounded by sycophantic comedians, it's clear what this visit is about. When Scott tells everyone to give them some privacy, Mae contests. "Why?" they ask, "They can stay . . . they knew . . . everybody knew." As Mae says this, everyone walks away. "You gonna get me canceled?" Scott immediately asks. Mae rolls their eyes. They want to have a conversation. "Listen, I've apologized over and over again," Scott explains, "I'm a piece of shit and I wish I was dead. I don't know what you want me to say. You can tell yourself that I'm the root cause of all your problems if that's easier for you but when I met you, you were fucked up." He continues with this performative self-loathing, the stuff of so many "canceled" comedians' comeback tours. As he does this, he avoids Mae's questions, moving the conversation towards what will happen to him. "Fuck you Scott," Mae says. Then they hug. "I don't want to see you or talk to you ever again,"[26] Mae explains, and then leaves. A few minutes later, they throw up. Mae

---

26   Luke Snellin, "2.6," *Feel Good* (Channel 4 and Netflix, June 4, 2021).

throws up because this shit is toxic. Before that, Mae hugs Scott because this shit is complicated.

Perhaps the most clarifying moments of killjoy utopianism arise from the series' depictions of Mae's relationship to George. George, at the outset, could be characterized as a heteropessimist—what Asa Seresin theorizes as an "anesthetic feeling" and an effect "especially seductive because it dissociates women from the very traits . . . for which straight culture is determined to make us ashamed."[27] Disgusted by straight culture, George does not yet imagine herself as queer, but when she discovers Mae at her local comedy club, she becomes infatuated. When they finally get a drink together in the first episode, George has already seen a number of Mae's performances, always seated in the front. Whether or not George is willing to come out for the sake of her relationship with Mae is one of the mobilizing tensions of the narrative. Part of this process is a troubling of her heteropessimist sensibilities. Before becoming involved with Mae, George was not in a relationship for many years. Not wanting to ever get married or have children, she found herself increasingly marginalized among her peers. "Quite often framed as an anticapitalist position," Seresin explains, "heteropessimism could be read as a refusal of the 'good life' of marital consumption and property ownership that capitalism once mandated . . . yet this good life, which was always withheld from marginalized populations, is now untenable for almost everyone." Part of what George discovers with Mae is that pessimism is not the only way of living with this critique of the straight world. These insights come through with faint glimmers of mutual care and shared joy between George and Mae, as in the final moments of the series, when Mae turns to George, looking at a leaf, and asks "so . . . what is photosynthesis?"[28]

Killjoy comradeship is regenerative, as *Feel Good* seems to ultimately suggest. It doesn't look like monogamy, marriage, or property ownership, but it does consist of laughter.

§

"Laughter is a good weapon, a weapon they have been using against us," Anca Parvulescu writes, posing the question, echoing Hélène Cixous, "Who will have the last laugh now?" [29] A killjoy comedy is not just

27 Asa Seresin, "On Heteropessimism," *The New Inquiry*, October 9, 2019, https://thenewinquiry.com/on-heteropessimism/.
28 Snellin, "2.6."
29 Parvulescu, *Laughter*, 112.

possible, it is already in our midst. But as Parvulescu stresses, "We need to start from laughter, rather than from the joke. And then we will be able to see that we do not need to stifle our laughter because the joke is a sexist one."[30] "When we can laugh at mistakes, laugh even in the midst of our tears …" writes bell hooks, "shared laughter helps create the context for feelings of mutuality to emerge."[31] In laughing, and finding ways to laugh together, we bump against and even push at what is possible.

As a mode of collective care and shared imagining, killjoy comedy refuses the weaponization of jokes as hatred, but not without demanding a distinction between hatred and anger. As Audre Lorde insists, "hatred is the fury of those who do not share our goals, and its object is death and destruction." Whereas Lorde conceives of hatred through destruction, she articulates anger as having a shared purpose with humor, in survival: "I have suckled the wolf's lip of anger," she writes, "and I have used it for illumination, laughter, protection, fire in places where there was no light, no food, no sisters."[32]

Interrogating hatred through anger, killjoy comedy plays with the ethics of revenge. What does it mean to have the last laugh? This question has been explored quite prolifically in recent years, in films like *Promising Young Woman* (2020), the story of Cassie (that is: Cassandra), who targets men who attempt to rape her. While taking the premise of a feminist, post-#MeToo retort to *American Psycho*'s misogynist serial killer, it remains ambiguous whether Cassie murders anyone. The film teases at our assumptions up to the end, as Cassie avenges her best friend Nina, who was raped while they were in medical school, going after all the individuals who, in Cassie's mind, denied Nina justice. This includes violence against women and children, all for the sake of revenge. Although the film messes with the fringes of black comedy in some noteworthy ways, it also eventually depends on the deeply misogynist trope of inevitable tragedy, invoked with the myth of Cassandra—who was raped by Apollo, and cursed to the life of a prophet who's never believed. Ultimately the film is an admonition against revenge, far more than an articulation of revenge as a mode of feminist comedy.

To this day one of the most generative attempts to think through the political possibilities of feminist revenge and comedy is Lizzie Borden's

---

30 Parvulescu, *Laughter,* 118.
31 bell hooks, *Writing Beyond Race: Living Theory and Practice* (New York: Routledge, 2013), 148.
32 Lorde, *Sister Outsider,* 129.

1983 film *Born in Flames*.[33] As it explores a speculative socialist future set in New York City, the film approaches feminist revenge and killjoy comedy as crucial elements of social revolution. One of the central characters, Honey, hosts a pirate radio show, and imparts revolutionary feminist interventions to the current social order, packed with its own problems: "We are here ready to deal with every lie that holds women responsible for rape and prostitution," she proclaims, "The lies that hold our sisters of the street responsible for the harassment of all women on the street. The lies that push women into the street as quickly as they force us out of the workplace." Perhaps dealing with lies is another way of thinking about revenge, and the task of killjoy comedy as well—breaking apart lies and making thinkable other possibilities. Honey's feminist comrade Isabel elaborates this as a process of revolutionary questioning: "It is all of our responsibilities as individuals and together to examine and to re-examine everything, leaving no stones unturned. Every word that we utter, every action and every thought," she insists, "We are all . . . the prophets of this new age."[34] This complete upturning is the making world into joke, a social transformation beginning with the minutiae of daily life, oriented toward collective care.

More than a utopian future, *Born in Flames* is a confrontation between dystopia and utopia, staged comedically, and in revolutionary feminist terms. At the film's center, this confrontation sheds light on the contradictions of the new regime, and all the ways in which this regime could not eradicate forms of capitalist suffering; while it also moves the narrative towards the full potentiality of this break from the social order. Through the course of *Born in Flames*, we begin to imagine this restructuring of the everyday as an estranging of capitalism, and a constant process of taking revenge on the systems of violence in capitalist life through collective power. Rather than perfect, this world is utopian in the sense of being transformational. When a woman is assaulted on the street, a brigade of women on bikes (with whistles) forms to interject and protect her. Scenes like this are hilarious, but also powerful, consistently pointing us to revolution as the greatest revenge we might hope for.

---

33 I must thank my killjoy comrade Jo for first introducing me to this film, and highly recommend some of her writings on it. See Johanna Isaacson, "Hollywood Kills Feminism: The Work of Lizzie Borden," *Blind Field: A Journal of Cultural Inquiry*, August 14, 2019, https://blindfieldjournal.com/2019/08/14/hollywood-kills-feminism-the-work-of-lizzie-borden/.
34 Lizzie Borden, *Born in Flames*, 1983.

Part Three

Comedy and Care Crisis

CHAPTER SEVEN

Comedy Under Lockdown: Housework and Utopian Longing

During the initial months of the pandemic, comedy workers who'd relied on comedy clubs and touring for their wages began to look for ways to perform comedy from home under lockdown. Specialized video messages on Cameo, happy hours and live shows on Zoom, and finding company sponsorships on social media were among some of the basic options available. Many comedians explored more creative ways to reflect on the situation of life under lockdown. Sydnee Washington started a weekly cooking show on Instagram live called *Syd Can Cook*, featuring various comedians as guests. Soon after that, she launched a podcast *Hobby Hunter*, in which she interviews guests about their hobbies. Taylor Tomlinson and Sam Morril, stand-ups who had just started dating, devised a podcast called *New Couple Gets Quarantined*, documenting their day-to-day co-habiting experiences. Comedian and flagrantly racist ventriloquist Jeff Dunham began a web series called *LIVE! (and Self-Isolated)* about living alone. Iliza Schlesinger started livestreaming a cooking show, *Don't Panic Pantry*, which she co-hosted with her husband every night at 8PM. The premise of the show was cooking under lockdown, based on limited ingredients.

More and more, the world of comedy seemed to mimic, in both form and content, the social totality of housework, just as the conditions of the pandemic made the problem with housework impossible to ignore. Comedy functioned as a way to commiserate, but also, to endure the loneliness. While suddenly, everyone was trying to bake sourdough bread, or just acquiring basic cooking skills, the comedian stepped in as an intermediary to the traditional cooking show, as in the at-home cooking show that Amy Schumer and her husband, chef Chris Fischer, launched on the Food Network in May 2020. Throughout *Amy Schumer*

Learns to Cook, Schumer sneaks drinks and cracks jokes, as Fischer provides helpful tips about fairly simple recipes. This is precisely the formula *The Great British Baking Show* has had all along, featuring friendly and lovable comedians as hosts to offset the expertise of judges (and the general awfulness of Paul Hollywood), and helping viewers to identify and relate with individual bakers. The appeal for this kind of programming, like housework, was nothing new to the early months of lockdown. But it was more generalized, adapting more clearly to the formal conditions of housework.

What happened to housework in 2020 cannot be forgotten. But to forget will be the pressure: to sweep it under the rug, to iron it out, or tidy it up—there's no shortage of housework metaphors for this erasure of work that is, nevertheless, never done but always happening. Over the course of the pandemic, housework increased exponentially. For some this came from the household's sudden transformation under lockdown into makeshift workplace, daycare, school, or healthcare facility. For far too many this was the work of living houseless, or struggling with housing insecurity, at its worst a non-stop process of finding shelter and resources, in the midst of mass evictions, layoffs, and widespread disease. For too many as well, this was the work of securing a home, and managing the unknowable health risks of what was termed "essential work," situated outside the household. The totality of housework, at this time, seemed both perceivable and perceivably political. This question of political perception comes to us always through a prism of class, and it was largely those forms of housework which are performed by those of us privileged enough to be able to "shelter-in-place" which gained visibility in 2020. And yet the problem with housework became even more acute—quickly into shutdown, there was a rise in domestic violence, self-harm and suicide, and substance abuse. The problem was everywhere and nowhere to be seen.

While the tasks, responsibilities, stakes, and contingencies of housework have only intensified since the pandemic, by the spring of 2021, the dominant narratives churning about our work-lives took focus on the distractedness and unproductivity of "pandemic brain," a fog and implicit laziness standing in the way of a return to normalcy (not to be confused with symptoms of long COVID). About a decade earlier, I remember reading articles of this sort, as I came to recognize that I was suffering from postpartum depression. While sleeping less than ever, doing more laundry and dishes than ever, physically healing from the birth, changing diapers, producing around 30 ounces of breastmilk a day,

I was also studying for my PhD qualifying exams and over and over again being bombarded with think-pieces about "mommy brain" from the very resources I relied on to learn a long list of new skills ranging from swaddling to burping, nasal degunking, sleep training, potty training methods, and beyond. I thought of this time throughout the 2020–21 school year, while there was much talk of the "learning deficit" to be anticipated among K–12 students. A friend of mine complained about this threat of a "learning deficit" reaching her kid's classroom, as a means of pressuring students to study more in the midst of preparing for a standardized exam. The message to the children was that they were failing to keep up, and that it was up to them to work harder to make up for the time they had lost to the pandemic. Her kid, like mine, had spent the year alongside a remote worker parent constantly reading, listening to audiobooks, and developing new interests like cooking, caring for pets, using tools, along with much else that might be otherwise conceived as "learning," but which did not constitute homework, merely housework.

Soon into the pandemic, comedy was instrumental to disrupting some of the dominant narratives of work life under lockdown. Against the perception of laziness and unproductivity, some comedies brought this explosion of housework to the foreground in different ways. In the re-mixed opening sequence of *SNL: At Home*, the brief series of episodes at the beginning of the pandemic, *SNL* cast members can be seen cooking, trying to cook, taking out the garbage, loading the laundry, doing the dishes, watering houseplants, getting the mail, all while playing with their kids, cuddling with and talking to their cats, wearing pajamas, eating cereal, pouring themselves glasses of wine, and on and on. Whether in the homemade aesthetic, or segments like "Let Kids Drink"—the musical sketch and mock public service announcement celebrating alcohol as a "babysitter on the cheap"—housework seeped into every aspect of the comedy. This was not the comedic turn of post-9/11, haunted by "the sincerity of trauma . . . with the ironies of the everyday," as Ted Gournelos describes it.[1] Instead it was a moment in comedy history infused with a strong sense of antiwork longing, proliferating on a broad scale, explicitly based in a critique of housework. In the months to come, on TikTok, Instagram, Twitter, Facebook, and all the rest, people everywhere were documenting, making fun of, and over housework. Comedy vocalized our shared problem.

---

1 Ted Gournelos and Viveca Greene, eds., *A Decade of Dark Humor: How Comedy, Irony, and Satire Shaped Post-9/11 America* (Jackson: University Press of Mississippi, 2011), 94.

The Problem with Housework

The problem with housework is not new because it is the very fabric of capitalist life. Capitalism transformed housework "into a natural attribute rather than [a] social contract because from the beginning of capital's scheme for women this work was destined to be unwaged," as Silvia Federici writes. Capitalism "had to convince us that [housework] is a natural, unavoidable, and even fulfilling activity to make us accept our unwaged work."[2] In putting forth a theory of reproductive labor, the International Wages for Housework movement that formed in the seventies conceived of housework not outside of capitalist production but at the center of it, comprising all activities involved in taking care of the waged worker as well as the future workforce—everything from mending socks and making meals to breastfeeding and blowjobs.

During the pandemic, even though this work became more difficult to ignore than ever before, it was still rarely included under the rubric of "essential" work, which was reserved for work taking place outside the home—despite the fact that housework is socially necessary, the work that makes possible the waged labor we agree to recognize as "work."

Wages for Housework has been a crucial demand to not only recognize and de-naturalize this work but, obviously, to pay for it as well. So long as we live in a world of wages, housework should be waged. At the same time, as a political rallying cry, Wages for Housework tends to generalize the predicament of the unwaged white housewife, and diminish the struggles of waged yet precarious houseworkers—not to mention all the other nuances involved in thinking about housework in more expansionary terms. As Angela Davis noted in her response to the Wages for Housework movement building in the United States, this strictly unwaged conception of housework only further invisibilizes the labor of Black women and women of color, whose "condition is more miserable than any other group of workers under capitalism."[3] This is a misery even more complex, more bound up in contradictions between what is socially necessary and what is socially valued, between the omnipresence and the invisibility of housework, and between labor and love. Any revolutionary project, as Davis asserts, must include "the abolition of housework as the private responsibility of individual women" and the consequent socialization of housework.

---

2 Silvia Federici, *Revolution at Point Zero: Housework, Reproduction, and Feminist Struggle* (Oakland: PM Press; Brooklyn: Common Notions; Brooklyn: Autonomedia, 2012), 16.
3 Angela Y. Davis, *Women, Race & Class* (New York: Vintage, 1983), 222.

These critiques of housework emerged from Women's Liberation in the seventies and early eighties, against the subsumption of "feminism" under the demand for equal pay and inclusion in the workforce. These demands have been the focus of liberal feminism in the years since, and in many ways, women have made up the difference through housework. By the late eighties, the problem with housework had moved into a paradigm of what Arlie Hochschild called the "second shift"—the unwaged, additional work done disproportionately by women in addition to the "on the clock" hours at a job. This concept of the "second shift" must be contrasted with what Claudia Jones conceived as the "triple oppression" of Black women. After spending a day, as Jones writes, "cleaning and scrubbing . . . caring for the children, laundering, cooking, etc., and all at the lowest pay . . . many a domestic worker, on returning to her own household, must begin housework anew to keep her own family together."[4] Predominantly non-white women picked up the housework for many white professional women in the era of the "second shift," but this predicament became more generalized with the dissolution of the family wage in this time. As an ideal based on the income of a male head of the household, adequate to support children and a wife and mother performing unwaged housework, the family wage "held greater sway among whites than among Blacks, and was at variance with actual practice for all of the poor and the working class," as Nancy Fraser clarifies, requiring "both employed and non-employed wives [to] perform work once considered crucial to a family economy."[5] The family wage's ideological and economic dissolution resulted in what Hochschild dubs a "family speed up": "[As] masses of women have moved into the economy, families have been hit by a 'speed up' in work and family life," she wrote in 1989. "There is no more time in the day than there was when wives stayed home, but there is twice as much to do. It is mainly women who absorb this 'speed up.'"[6]

Fundamental to this shift in the eighties was a transition in the popular imaginary of the housewife from the implicitly white, dimwitted, Quaalude-popping *non*-worker to the idealized managerial figure, epitomized by Margaret Thatcher, who quipped in 1988 that "it's taken a

4 Claudia Jones, "An End to the Neglect of the Problems of the Negro Woman!," in *Words of Fire: An Anthology of African-American Feminist Thought*, ed. Beverly Guy-Sheftall (New York: New Press, 1995), 115.
5 Nancy Fraser, *Fortunes of Feminism: From State-Managed Capitalism to Neoliberal Crisis* (New York: Verso Books, 2020), 93.
6 Arlie Russell Hochschild and Anne Machung, *The Second Shift* (New York: Avon, 1990), 8.

government headed by a housewife with experience of running a family to balance the books for the first time in 20 years—with a little left over for a rainy day."[7] The revised idealization of the housewife in this time came hand-in-hand with the outsourcing of housework to migrant workers, an integral dynamic of capitalist crisis. This process of "housewifization," as Maria Mies puts it, is the other side of what is sometimes described as the "feminization" of labor, marking a change in the gender composition of workforces as well as the more fundamental character of work alongside de-industrialization. However we might nominalize it, these periodizations characterize a multiplicity of historical processes between gendered labor and the gendering of labor—the rise of the service economy, the decrease in full-time employment and increase of part-time and temporary employment, and the loss of benefits and other resources—which tell us a certain story about the present. Today, so much of work and work life has come to simulate the logic of housework, the naturalization and never-endingness of what was once "women's work," reassembled as promises of flexibility and self-management under ever-worsening precarity.

The COVID-era of work-life has intensified what has long been underway, not unique to this period but accelerated by it. As Marx once wrote of the worker, "[he] feels himself only when he is not working, and not at home when he is working."[8] This account of the waged worker's alienation doesn't account for the household as a site of work, or, conversely (and more generously), it can be a basis for describing the condition of being never-at-home fundamental to housework. Today, by extension, we cannot be "at home," even under lockdown. In this sense, 2020 seemed to culminate the transition into an era of 24/7 multi-tasking. This is a juncture defined by the outmoding of jeans with sweatpants and leggings, the wine that many of us have filled our coffee mugs with before zoom sessions, and the broader casualization (aesthetically inasmuch as contractually) of work life—but it is also defined by the perception of non-stop availability, flexibility, and never-not-working. The increase in leisure wear of course has little to do with leisure, and everything to do with the changing conditions of work.

7   Margaret Thatcher, "Speech to Conservative Women's Conference," Margaret Thatcher Foundation, accessed January 1, 2022, https://www.margaretthatcher.org/document/107248.
8   Karl Marx, *Early Writings*, ed. Rodney Livingstone and Gregor Benton (London: Penguin, 1992), 359.

Rebooting, Netflixing, and Comedy as On-Demand Care

Throughout the pandemic there were various one-time special events in comedy, like cast reunions for popular sit-coms or one-time performances of classic scripts. In late April 2020, six weeks into lockdown, a *Parks and Recreation* special episode was released, five years after the show's conclusion. Then the *Friends* cast reunited for an HBO special. Another HBO special featured a *Fresh Prince of Bel Air* reunion. The high demand for these reunions is just one of many aspects of reboot culture.

In the years before the pandemic, reboot culture was on the ascendant, galvanized by Donald Trump's assumption of the presidency. Broadcast networks began packaging sit-com reboots as Trump-era social commentary: the day after ABC's *Roseanne* reboot premiered, Trump claimed that the show was "about us" at a rally in Ohio; NBC's *Will & Grace* reboot was launched by popular demand after the co-stars reunited for a Clinton campaign video in 2016; and on the evening of rapist judge Brett Kavanaugh's Senate Judiciary Committee hearing, 7.4 million distraught viewers tuned in for the return of *Murphy Brown* on CBS, featuring a surprise cameo by Clinton. These reboots, with varied success, cut through the experience of historical change with the comforts of familiarity. While white supremacists took to the streets, and later, to the Capitol building, reboots brought with them the promise that things wouldn't be so different after all—even instilling a sense that it had always been this way. If there was a substance at all to Biden's campaign, it was perhaps as much that Biden seemed most perceptible as an anti-Trump, as he and Kamala Harris campaigned as a reboot of the Obama years. At the heart of reboot culture is a turning to the past as an erasure of history, producing an amnesia effect that is at once a coping mechanism and a wishing away of the crises of the present.

The demand for rebooted sit-coms grew out of the phenomenon of "nostalgia binging" on streaming platforms, by now crucial to Netflix's business model. The company paid Warner Brothers nearly $80 million to keep *Friends* as part of its streaming platform through 2019, as the series was voraciously consumed by a variety of audiences, including a new generation watching it all for the first time, without ever having the experience of waiting a week—much less an entire summer—for the next episode. Aggregating nostalgia into different types of programming, Netflix has applied the reboot formula to sit-com sequels, adaptations, and period-based original series.

"In order to create nostalgia, a revival should come after a time gap and involve a historical rupture, a fracture," Giulia Taurino explains of this formula. "A cross-historical displacement is required, giving the viewer a perception of distance."[9] Pandemic viewing accentuated this sense of distance, as nostalgia-binging reached new peaks. Netflix's programming strategy resulted in the immense popularity of *The Crown*, for instance, which broke records for highest single-week streaming rankings between November 16–22, 2020.[10] More user accounts actually watched *The Crown*'s depiction of the royal wedding of Prince Charles and Princess Diana that week than had watched the live broadcast of the actual wedding in 1981.[11] That affective experience of mass simultaneous experience was integral to the nostalgia conjured by *The Crown*—the ongoing discourse on Twitter, the royal history clickbait and relentless chatter across media outlets, synchronized with the tabloid frenzy over Prince Harry and Megan Markle's exile from the royal family, and later their Oprah interview.

While simulating the "live" experience and imagined community of broadcast television for which many have nostalgia, Netflix's sit-com reboots combine this affective quality with the temporal rhythms of on-demand immediacy. Serialized "watch instantly" content offers "episodic intrapersonal and emotional regulation," as Daniel Beal and John Trougakos suggest of the temporalities of care work.[12] It's in this sense that netflixing has become an approximation of care, during a period of accelerated care crisis. With the privatization of healthcare and increasing commodification of care services, as Evelyn Nakano Glenn writes, come "multifarious forms of coercion, ranging from personal moral persuasion to the force of impersonal legal doctrines, from the internalized feelings

9 Giulia Taurino, "Crossing Eras: Exploring Nostalgic Reconfigurations in Media Franchises," in *Netflix Nostalgia: Streaming the Past on Demand*, ed. Kathryn Pallister (Lanham: Lexington Books, 2019), 13.

10 See Rick Porter, "'The Crown' Sets Single-Week Record in Nielsen Streaming Rankings," *The Hollywood Reporter*, December 17, 2020, https://www.hollywoodreporter.com/tv/tv-news/the-crown-sets-single-week-record-in-nielsen-streaming-rankings-4106891/.

11 See Joanna Crawley, "The Crown Had More Viewers in Its First Week than Royal Wedding," *Mail Online*, November 26, 2020, https://www.dailymail.co.uk/tvshowbiz/article-8989331/The-Crown-series-four-viewers-week-Charles-Dianas-real-wedding.html.

12 Daniel Beal and John Trougakos, "Episodic Intrapersonal and Emotional Regulation: Or, Dealing with Life as It Happens," in *Emotional Labor in the 21st Century: Diverse Perspectives on the Psychology of Emotion Regulation at Work*, ed. Alicia Grandey, James M. Diefendorff, and Deborah E. Rupp (New York: Routledge, 2017).

of obligation to external constraints of the labor market."[13] Netflixing, likewise, simulates the caregiver's working conditions in its consumer experience: always readily available, highly adaptable, formally flexible.

"Care reveals to us how our lives are not reducible to bare functionality or mere necessity," writes Emma Dowling in her book *The Care Crisis*, published a year into the pandemic. Dowling elaborates:

> There is a difference between bathing and clothing an elderly person so that they can survive, and the act of doing so carefully, which means taking time, acting attentively, with affection and concern. The latter makes life worth living, but it may also very well prolong the cared-for person's life.[14]

This distinction is vital to the hoped-for-care of netflixing, and the ways in which care is sought. In its on-demand format, netflixing mimics the intimacies of what Dowling uncovers as the most "fragile dimensions of care—love, concern, regard, attention, affection[.]"[15]

The experience of on-demand care becomes a narrative strategy in rebooted sit-coms like *One Day at a Time*, Netflix's adaptation of the 1975–84 series, produced by original creator Norman Lear. The show follows the everyday struggles of a Cuban immigrant family in Los Angeles, centered around Penelope (Justina Machado), a single mother raising two kids and caring for her mother Lydia (Rita Moreno) on a nurse's paycheck. As a Netflix series, *One Day at a Time* is of course designed to be consumed more than one episode at a time. Yet at a formal level, the series does much to emulate the experience of a more traditional, multi-camera broadcast sit-com, complete with a studio audience and laugh track. When Penelope is feeling lonely, isolated, and overwhelmed, the sounds of audience reaction (laughter, but also sighs, claps, gasps) become sources of comfort and relief, bringing Penelope as well as the viewer into this sense of collective experience. In its traditional conception, the laugh track "presents the audience as a mass, whose responses are unambiguous and who signal a collective understanding of what is and isn't funny," Brett Mills explains, describing a "pleasure to be had in going along with the

---

13 Evelyn Nakano Glenn, *Forced to Care: Coercion and Caregiving in America* (Cambridge: Harvard University Press, 2010), 11.
14 Emma Dowling, *The Care Crisis: What Caused It and How Can We End It?* (New York: Verso, 2021), 45–46.
15 Dowling, *The Care Crisis*, 46.

rest of the crowd."[16] Whereas the traditional sit-com relies on the laugh track for a predictable tempo, delivering laughs as a "measure and control system of the comic effect," as Antonio Savorelli writes, sit-com reboots like *One Day at a Time* use the laugh track to move through a more complex set of affective registers, meeting a more varied set of emotional demands.[17] Through the course of the day there's laughter, crying, frustration, confusion, fear. And scene-by-scene, the series delivers a steady stream of feeling not alone in all of this.

Longing for Simultaneity

What is promised but never delivered from the on-demand care of net-flixing is an experience of simultaneous co-existence that became even more scarce under lockdown. Early into the pandemic, the 2019 Netflix comedy-dystopia *Russian Doll* seemed to prefigure the monotonies and insularities of sheltering in place. *Russian Doll* is about a woman's attempt to escape a temporal loop in which she endlessly relives her 36th birthday, dying over and over again only to be reborn in the bathroom of her friend's apartment over and over as well. Nadia (Natasha Lyonne) begins in a state of perpetual personal, professional, and psychological crisis. Once she becomes trapped in her birthday, things start to get even worse. Rock bottom keeps getting lower and lower, as the day continues to reoccur. Throughout, the show induces claustrophobia in its repetitions of the day, and reworkings of the same scenario, all the while resonating with what many bemoaned as drudgeries of life under lockdown.

Eventually *Russian Doll* complicates this repetition. Nadia begins to approach the redundancies and predictability of each day as opportunities to revise her behavior, playing with outcomes but also, making her life better. She befriends a man, Charlie (Alan Barnett), who is magically in the same predicament of constantly re-experiencing the same day. But the closer they become, the more time gets scrambled between them, as they begin to chase each other through different temporalities in which they co-exist but never simultaneously.

While the plot of *Russian Doll* becomes oriented towards Nadia and Charlie coming together as a couple, the series is most compelling for its dodging the narrative logic of the romantic comedy. Feeling trapped,

---

16 Brett Mills, *The Sitcom* (Edinburgh: Edinburgh University Press, 2009), 103.
17 Antonio Savorelli, *Beyond Sitcom: New Directions in American Television Comedy* (Jefferson, NC: McFarland, 2010), 30.

Nadia and Charlie contemplate suicide, in their separate temporalities, just as they try to find each other in other temporalities. These planes of existence finally merge when, under a bridge, they join in a parade beneath a bridge, led by houseless people and punks, costumed and carrying banners and puppets. As they unite, Nadia crosses paths with two other Nadias, walking through and away from the crowd of people. She grabs a lantern from another person marching, and becomes, in that moment, a part of something bigger than her. While not a direct citation, the parade evokes the Tompkins Square Park Riots of 1988, when hundreds of people protested a 1AM curfew imposed on the East Village Park, targeting its homeless encampment. In some ways nostalgic for this past struggle and its punk legacy, this moment of closure in *Russian Doll* is also a point of continuation. The spell finally breaks not with the coupledom of Nadia and Charlie, or with their healing as individuals, but with this simultaneous, shared experience, and political solidarity. This dream of collectivity and de-individuation, so beautifully rendered by *Russian Doll*, captures two things at once, split between a dystopian portrait of our irrevocably atomized social world and a utopian dive into what is not quite envisioned yet certainly longed for.

Welcome (Back) to the Working Week

Back in 2016, Apple announced that it would begin producing and distributing original content, competing with Netflix, Hulu, Amazon, and other streaming services. In late 2019, Apple TV launched original programming across several genres. What was distinct about Apple's programming was its decelerating of binge consumption. For each of its initial series, Apple dropped the first three episodes and then rolled them out once a week for the remaining seven episodes. Through the run of its first season from November 1–December 20, 2019, Apple's blockbuster hit *The Morning Show* (starring Jennifer Aniston, Reese Witherspoon, and Steve Carell) meditates on this slow-down, as a black comedy portrait of a daily cable news show fighting off its own extinction, trying to stay relevant in the news cycle speed-up of the Trump era. In the time of "nostalgia binging," for which *Friends* and *The Office* alumni Aniston and Carell are certainly emblematic figures, *The Morning Show*'s tremendous success perhaps indicates another kind of longing for the past—a time before binging, before the supposed "post-network" era of TV, when you had to wait until next week.

Historically, weekly "primetime" programming has been structured by the working week, a predictable routine of half-hour sit-coms and one-hour dramas. For more than six decades, our history with television "has been very much defined by its schedule and particular patterns of use that developed in response," as med scholar Amanda Lotz explains, with specific air times throughout the day mimicking "patterns of work and leisure schedules."[18] NBC's "must-see TV" Thursdays, or ABC's "TGIF" were defining features in the traditional work week of the nineties, part of how the days could be told apart, always offering something to look forward to at the end of the day. All of this was of course based on the tempo of 9–5 working days, an assumption that always excluded many workers and now, in our era of flexibility, excludes many more.

For the streaming campaigns of Apple TV and Disney+, the slowed down pace of a weekly schedule enabled the platforms to continue integrating content, with the assurance that viewers would not watch all of the short list of series by the end of the first week. How else could the company compete with Netflix's vast catalog? Instead, Apple and Disney offered something that Netflix couldn't. This wasn't just delayed gratification; it was a nostalgia induced not by content, but by the formal and temporal experience of watching TV again.

While appealing to this nostalgia in some of its formal features, this new era of weekly-streaming programming was a whole new landscape in terms of genre. In the place of half-hour sit-coms and one-hour dramas, there's an expansive array of hybridized genres, with varying runtimes (everywhere from 25 minutes to 70 minutes). This is not the flattened world of procedurals or dramedies, but a generically pluralistic world of sci-fi, mysteries, musicals, psychological horror, sports drama, workplace satire—a world where comedy has diffused into nearly everything. Apple's most popular shows all blend or move between generic registers, sometimes with a wink and a nod, as in the musical-comedy *Schmigadoon!*, in which a married couple wanders into an alternate reality (à la *Brigadoon*) where everyone sings and dances in extremely well-choreographed musical numbers. *Mr. Corman*, similarly, moves between a dark and satirical portrait of the often-depressing life of a public school teacher in the San Fernando Valley, intercut with song and dance routines. *Ted Lasso* and *The Shrink Next Door* both take major comedic actors (Jason Sudeikis, Will Ferrell, Paul Rudd) and put them in dramatic

---

18 Amanda D. Lotz, "Introduction," in *Beyond Prime Time: Television Programming in the Post-Network Era*, ed. Amanda D. Lotz (New York: Routledge, 2009), 1–2.

situations. Even one of the darkest shows on the platform, *The Mosquito Coast*, can easily be read as a wicked satire.

The integration of comedy into all narrative worlds is vital to the managerial quality of this new period of binge-regulation and slowed down, weekly programming. Comedy takes the edge off of anything too dramatic or horrifying, counterbalancing the ongoing risks of trauma, depression, or the feeling of having to work. It is what so many of us have relied on, to varying extents, during the pandemic, as a way to get through the day.

When COVID vaccines became accessible, and many of the workforces that had suddenly gone remote in spring 2020 steadily transitioned back to in-person in the summer and fall of 2021, Netflix started experimenting with how it released content, following the trends of these new platforms. In September 2021, the company began to offer episodes of some of its programming week by week. Part of this, as Josef Adalian suggests, is Netflix's "endless quest to end scrolling" and the need to conquer "decision fatigue."[19] Another part, however, goes hand-in-hand with the shifting regime of work.

Just like the world of work today, the world of infinite streaming content demands self-management—keeping track of different series, platforms, release dates, and more. On a piece of paper in one of my desk drawers, I have a list of platforms, usernames, and passwords from my best friend, grandma, mother-in-law, co-worker, former housemate, and friend of a friend. For a while I was accessing Hulu through the account of a friend's dissertation advisor. Most people I know have their own systems for this kind of juggling already. More and more, these platforms have to find ways for us to keep them in circulation, creating routines to break up the day-to-day sludge, things to look forward to every Monday, Tuesday, Wednesday night, and so on. The demand of these platforms is not just to give us more content, but to give us our lives back, beginning with our experience of time.

The Comedy of Crisis Management

In the initial weeks of sheltering in place in spring 2020, late night talk shows regained some currency as they reinforced the temporal flow of the daily and weekly schedule. These shows provided a shared sense of time,

19   Josef Adalian, "Inside Netflix's Quest to End Scrolling," *Vulture*, April 28, 2021, https://www.vulture.com/article/netflix-play-something-decision-fatigue.html.

but little else. Especially in the beginning of the pandemic, part of the appeal of these shows was their low-fi awkwardness—essentially these were Zoom meetings being broadcast from Stephen Colbert's converted storage room, Seth Meyers's attic, and James Corden's garage. There was a group chat energy, with members of the band and writing staff providing laughter and clapping, with occasional back-and-forths.

While millions still tune in to watch late night talk shows broadcast on television (and ratings generally increased during the initial months of the pandemic), most of the viewers watch this content in disjointed clips on YouTube. It's something to do with morning coffee or late-night ice cream, or between shifts at work. Like so many of today's workers, it's flexible and adapts to your schedule; and unlike the world of work, it feels safe and predictable. The sense of duty and responsibility which late night hosts expressed about continuing to show up for viewers, being themselves good workers with grit and perseverance, reveals so much about why they were turned to in this time. These hosts provided enduring emotional support to their viewers—each day, offering a bit more to laugh at or commiserate over, a sense of company if not solidarity to dull the pain of isolation, the drudgery of housework, and so much more. Being funny was never the point. Nor was that ever really the expectation. Instead, comedy was there to make life feel more bearable under seemingly unlivable circumstances—for better or worse.

To the extent that we might find all this utopian, dystopia creeps. While there is something fundamentally beautiful about finding laughter in moments of suffering, there is also something profoundly terrifying about the ways comedy so often steps in to do this work of crisis management, on behalf of capitalism.

CHAPTER EIGHT

Quieting the World of Work

Years ago someone asked me, "do you listen to podcasts? Because I just don't get the appeal." It was the sort of question posed by a successful academic, packed with judgments. It was the sort of question that is not actually a question. As he asked, I tried to anticipate his critique—that is, the trap he was setting for me. *Why listen to a podcast when you could read a book?* Or something like that. I took a breath, answered "yes I do," and fumbled my way out of the conversation.

At this point, perhaps listening to podcasts is not so much a *guilty pleasure*, and more just a way of life. By now, most people I know listen to podcasts, with a few notable exceptions. Some people never seem to stop listening to podcasts—they're listening to them when they go to sleep, when they wake up, while they commute to work, as they make dinner, and in many cases, as they steal away moments from their jobs, or find ways to make their jobs more tolerable. A friend of mine spends the majority of the year growing and then processing marijuana in Mendocino County. For a part of the year, they're in the woods with a dog and no one else for miles. Their cell service is shoddy at best. I worry about them. When I asked about their podcasting habits, I got a long list of recommendations in comedy, true crime, history and news shows. "I absolutely listen to different content for various elements of my job," they told me, describing a set of listening routines that helped manage focus, but also loneliness. Throughout the day, podcasts (if downloaded in advance) are there for my friend.

In 2006, 22 percent of adults in the U.S. were even aware of podcasting at all, and only 11 percent ever listened to one,[1] while by 2021, 57 percent of adults reported listening to podcasts on an infrequent to

---

1 "Topic: Podcasting Industry," *Statista*, accessed January 1, 2022, https://www.statista.com/topics/3170/podcasting/.

daily basis—a number that's drastically changed with the pandemic. As COVID-19 took hold in early 2020, there were 850,000 active podcasts, and by the fall there were over 1,500,000.[2] By the next summer, estimates grew to over two million.[3]

Comedians laid claim to the world of podcasting over a decade before Michelle Obama, Hillary Clinton, Bill Gates, Bruce Springsteen, and many more A-list celebrities and public figures launched podcasts in 2020. Joe Rogan and Marc Maron both began podcasting in 2009. Rogan and Maron, along with Conan O'Brien, Dax Shepard and Bill Burr, are among the comedians[4] whose shows were high ranking in the top 50 podcasts in the U.S. in 2020 (with Rogan's as number one, right above The Daily podcast from *The New York Times*).[5] Through the course of those slow-burning weeks of 2020 under lockdown, it seemed that almost every prominent comedian or comedy actor either launched their own podcast or made frequent appearances on others, shows ranging from sketch and improv to cultural commentary and interviews, with several blockbuster hits. Less than a year after Will Arnett, Jason Bateman, and Sean Hayes started their podcast *SmartLess* in the summer of 2020, they signed a three-year contract with Amazon valued between $60–80 million.[6] Rogan, the king of podcasting as it were, signed a $100 million deal with Spotify. Spotify acquired Shepard's podcast with a multi-year contract as well. Fewer and fewer of the high-ranking podcasts at all resemble their scrappy origins, becoming increasingly bogged down with high-produced advertisements, and less of the weird stuff that happens when someone decides to record themselves in a garage or basement.

Just like the world of late-night talk shows, the top comedy podcasters are all white men, each with their own brand of commentary and interviewing, some explicitly political and others supposedly "apolitical" [read: liberal centrist]. What they have in common, however, is the promise of a

---

2 Ross Winn, "2021 Podcast Stats & Facts," *Podcast Insights*, December 28, 2021, https://www.podcastinsights.com/podcast-statistics/.

3 Jonathan Berr, "Amazon Signs Multi-Million Dollar Deal For 'SmartLess' Podcast," *Forbes*, June 30, 2021, https://www.forbes.com/sites/jonathanberr/2021/06/30/amazon-signs-multi-million-dollar-deal-for-smartless-podcast/.

4 Not that I believe you have to be funny to be a comedian (in which case I would discount Burr and Rogan as well), but I want to clarify that I include Shepard in this list because he began in improv at The Groundlings, and is at least comedy-adjacent.

5 Edison Research, "The Top 50 Most Listened to U.S. Podcasts of 2020," *Edison Research*, February 9, 2021, https://www.edisonresearch.com/the-top-50-most-listened-to-u-s-podcasts-of-2020/.

6 Berr, "Amazon Signs Multi-Million Dollar Deal For 'SmartLess' Podcast."

hang-out. The host is going to be there, anywhere between one and four hours, once or twice a week. As the host goes through his opening monologue or dialogue with his assistants and producers, and then moves onto a new guest each time, he speaks to you, the listener, as someone he's close to. Unlike the guest, you've been there before. And the more you hang out, the more you'll be in on the inside jokes and the ongoing schticks. But this is also a private world, one that no one else has to know about.

This insularity is perfect for workers stealthily wearing an earbud on the job, but it's also ideal for incels ("involuntary celibates"), who dwell in online hate forums in relative stealth themselves. This seems to be the appeal of Rogan's brand of macho "free-thinking"—or some of the other high-ranking podcasts in the U.S., like *The Ben Shapiro Show*. These podcasts respond to an insatiable demand for friendship and companionship, during a time of historic loneliness—in fact, O'Brien makes the "friendship deficit" of middle-aged men in the U.S. into the gimmick of his show, titled "Conan O'Brien Needs a Friend." Standing in for something like friendship, these shows also model and facilitate divergent ways of relating to the world after #MeToo and Black Lives Matter, during what Donald Trump called "a very scary time for young men" [read: young white men].[7] For Bill Burr, who releases a weekly show called "Bill's Monday Morning Podcast," this has meant trashing white women. He chest-thumped about this in his *SNL* monologue as well: "The nerve of you white women," he said, never forgetting to mention that he's married to a Black woman. "You guys stood by us toxic white males through centuries of our crimes against humanity. You rolled around in the blood money[.]"[8] While he proceeds to frame his criticism in terms of the history of false accusations of rape against Black men, some of which is on-point (but also in the service of neglecting the long history of sexual violence by white men), he fills his podcast rants with white male rage all the same, exhibiting rhetorical tactics for his listeners which assert that misogyny is still ok, so long as it's a particular kind of misogyny. By contrast, O'Brien makes use of his already well-developed strategy of self-deprecation. As he caricatures himself as a villain and perpetual bully with his co-hosts Sona Movsesian

7 Jeremy Diamond, "Trump Says It's 'a Very Scary Time for Young Men in America,'" *CNN*, October 2, 2018, https://www.cnn.com/2018/10/02/politics/trump-scary-time-for-young-men-metoo/index.html.
8 Lexy Perez, "Bill Burr's Controversial 'Saturday Night Live' Monologue Draws Mixed Reactions," *The Hollywood Reporter*, October 11, 2020, https://www.hollywoodreporter.com/tv/tv-news/bill-burrs-controversial-saturday-night-live-monologue-draws-mixed-reactions-4075205/.

and Matt Gourley, he positions himself as the old, out of touch celebrity, mocking himself relentlessly and often stating his own sense of ignorance, rather than preaching against the "woke police" and the threat of cancel culture, as many of his contemporaries spew nonstop. Each in their own way, these top comedy podcasts explore competing versions of masculinity—however reactive or reflexive.

The early years of Marc Maron's podcast *WTF* were a mix of toxic rants and interviews with fellow comedians. But after more than a thousand episodes, Maron evolved into a much more thoughtful interviewer. Now over a decade into his podcast, Maron has never missed a show, releasing two new episodes every week. When any previous guest dies, Maron re-releases the interview from the show's archives, along with a special message. May 18th, 2020 was different, though—his memorial episode was for Lynn Shelton, his girlfriend, who had died unexpectedly two days before. "I imagine most of you know at this point that [...] Lynn Shelton died," he tells his listeners through tears, "She was my partner, she was my girlfriend. She was my friend and I loved her. I loved her a lot. And she loved me and I knew that." He continues to cry, taking deep breaths as he attempts to get through an introduction to their interview from 2015. "I was getting used to love in the way of being able to accept it and show it ... I was so comfortable with this person, with Lynn Shelton. And I'm not really that comfortable emotionally or otherwise. But I was," he remembers, "I was able to exist in a state of self-acceptance because of her love for me."[9] Though Shelton didn't die of COVID (she died of previously undiagnosed acute myeloid leukemia), the suddenness and mysteriousness of her death struck a chord with many listeners, at the outset of the pandemic. As Maron mourned her, his podcast listeners wrote in letters, relating to their own experiences, and chatted with each other during the livestreaming sessions he began hosting most mornings on Instagram.

While manifesting conditions of social and political atomization, these podcasts bring to the surface (or keep repressed) a much broader set of desires—fantasies of collectivity, explored through a medium that adapts easily to isolation, but which also cultivates it. With a podcast, one not only has a constant companion, but a contained soundscape in which to escape from one's co-existence with others—the sounds of housemates having sex, neighbors having an argument, construction down the street, a coworker loudly snacking in a nearby cubicle, and so on. As my good

---

9 "Remembering Lynn Shelton, May 16, 2020," *WTF with Marc Maron*, May 18, 2020, http://www.wtfpod.com/podcast/in-memoriam-remembering-lynn-shelton.

friend likes to joke, podcasts are good for quieting all the other voices in our heads.

Perhaps podcasts project a dark future, in which we're all in our own little sound worlds, experiencing simulated friendships; but they also reveal so much of what we wish could feel more possible, longings that are indistinct yet visceral.

§

It began as something to accompany my evening routine of washing the dishes. Silent, headphone-based activities had quickly become most of my life while caring for an infant. I moved through hour after hour of minimal contact with anyone but the baby and my cats, once my housemates and partner had gone to work for the day. I started to put T in a front-pack and walk a lot, through downtown Santa Cruz and into the surrounding redwood forest, listening to audiobooks on headphones much of the time. I was preparing for my PhD qualifying exams, trying to make it through a list of hundreds of books on utopian theory and literature, but finding myself suddenly unable to sit down for long periods to read. If I was moving around, away from my kitchen, with both my hands free to rock the baby, change diapers, wipe spit-up, breastfeed, I had a better chance of getting through some of the books with my headphones. Critical theory was a different matter—that I had to sit down and read, ideally while my partner was home to do care work—but the eighteenth and nineteenth century novels were plot-driven and welcome companions during that time: Daniel Defoe's *Robinson Crusoe*, Voltaire's *Candide*, Samuel Butler's *Erewhon*, Edward Bellamy's *Looking Backward*, William Morris's *News from Nowhere*, were all texts I encountered first as a listener, or more specifically, as a listening-reader and worker.

When I wasn't listening to audiobooks, however, I was finding other ways to quiet the stream of anxious thoughts about the impending week of written and oral exams. While I think back on that time as my "maternity leave," it wasn't, of course. As a graduate student worker and teaching assistant, I could get only six weeks out of a ten-week quarter to recover from childbirth, and historically such arrangements just exacerbated the workload of another TA in the course. So instead I did what other parent-workers advised me to do: I filed for medical leave and took out student loans. Thanks to a recent victory from the graduate student union, I had an excellent healthcare package. But the whole time, I found myself panicking more and more about falling behind. Audiobooks helped me continue working and feeling "on track" with what the graduate division charmingly termed "normative time," a running clock set on dissertation completion, instituted as part of the wave of budget cuts that swept the UC system following the financial crisis. "Normative time" restricted graduate students to 18 quarters of teaching for the university. This was a deadline imposed on us as workers, not as students. It sets a funding clock on everyone, ticking in the background at all times, unless it can be drowned out. It was only years later that I realized how much this pressure to do the work and do it on time had increased when I became a parent. I felt like I was forever in a hurry, always catching up. Now it brings great pain to my heart—what I lost to that ticking clock, as my kid's childhood flashed before my eyes.

§

Roland Barthes conceived of numerous ways of listening, beginning with a form of "alert" listening shared with animals (e.g., the prey listens for the sounds of predators). Where the human begins, Barthes claims, is with another form of listening, what he calls "deciphering." "[F]or centuries listening could be defined as an intentional act," he wrote in 1976. "Today it is granted the power (and virtually the function) of playing over unknown spaces."[10] From this disintegration of intentional listening, Barthes marks the emergence of "panic listening." He describes a freedom of listening, for which "what is listened to here and there" is the "shimmering of signifiers, ceaselessly restored to a listening which ceaselessly produces new ones from them without ever arresting meaning." In this sense, listening is externalized, compelling the subject "to renounce his 'inwardness'."[11]

To renounce one's inwardness seems to be at least some of what we're doing when we listen to interviews, a significant subset of the top podcasts in comedy. Interviews also carry with them an illusion of eavesdropping, vital to this question of why and how we listen. As an act of interpretation, eavesdropping "dramatizes our sense-making urge: the human craving for meaning," writes Ann Gaylin.[12] Taking up eavesdropping as an often-overlooked form of connectivity, Gaylin suggests that in this process of sense-making, "eavesdropping often reveals those secrets about

---

10   Roland Barthes, *The Responsibility of Forms: Critical Essays on Music, Art, and Representation*, trans. Richard Howard (New York: Hill and Wang, 1985), 258.
11   Barthes, *The Responsibility of Forms*, 259.
12   Ann Elizabeth Gaylin, *Eavesdropping in the Novel from Austen to Proust* (Cambridge: Cambridge University Press, 2002), 9.

ourselves that we may not wish to know or to acknowledge."[13] By contrast, there's nothing covert about listening to a podcast interview. There's no misconception of privacy within the conversation itself. And yet much of the time the experience of listening feels much closer to eavesdropping than to being a part of that conversation whatsoever.

I think of this literary trope of eavesdropping often as I listen to podcast interviews, washing or putting away dishes, doing laundry, making dinner, packing up lunch for my kid, cleaning the litter box, taking out the trash, sweeping, decluttering, and all the rest. So often in nineteenth and early twentieth century literature, eavesdropping displayed a particular class dynamic—the domestic worker overhearing matters of the private life of their employers. Sometimes it feels this way, listening to a celebrity interview. At times it's just morbid curiosity; at other points it's admiration or respect for someone's work, or interest in their perspective; and then there's the infrequent but noteworthy frustration-fueled-listening. A certain kind of care becomes available to the listener, however inadequate and indirect, in listening to a conversation between rich people detailing the ways that they still struggle with mental health issues, despite the fact that they've managed to somehow "find success"—the false promise of happiness from work gets disrupted, though often not at a conscious level in the conversation. There is likewise an enjoyment, perverse as it might be, in listening to celebrities who epitomize the capitalist work ethic turn out to be just boring, if not miserable (this is basically the fascination with *Succession*, right?)

While my literary associations with eavesdropping may come from Balzac, Dickens, Austen or Proust, my lived experiences of eavesdropping bring with them a certain nostalgia for train rides. Back when I lived in Chicago, I would ride the Ls to school and work, back and forth from Logan Square to Hyde Park and a few spots in-between. I quickly learned it was impossible for me to do my reading for class on the train. Instead, I looked out the window, watched different neighborhoods go by, and overheard the conversations of strangers in the background. I heard and couldn't help but listen to mundane conversations between housemates or lovers on their way to work, making plans for the evening. But there were more dramatic scenes that still feel like recent memories fifteen years later. Experiences like this still happen but they are increasingly rare because of what we're listening to instead—often in our own separate worlds. Train cars today are not just a sea of headphones, but masked faces.

---

13 Gaylin, *Eavesdropping*, 12.

For all the "radical novelty" of this headphoned atomization, as Kate Lacey writes, new sound media must be understood within a longer history of cultural practices, for which "the relatively recent possibility of listening to sounds mediated across time and distance did not just change the experience of listening, but reconfigured the experience of public life."[14] As soundscapes have been privatized with new technologies, our ability, or willingness, to listen to each other has steadily eroded as well. Like train conversations, podcast interviews obscure the boundaries of eavesdropping, as conversations that share the conventions of a private interaction, but that take place in public, practically inviting us to listen. This desire to listen remains a utopian drive in everyday life.

§

In an interview with Maria Bamford, Andy Richter joked about the premise of his comedy podcast, *Three Questions with Andy Richter*, pulling back the curtain: "this whole three questions thing is bullshit," he confesses, "I just wanted to trick people into having a therapy session." Bamford laughs, "I love being tricked! . . . ooooooh, *the reveal*."[15] Taking his guests through these questions—Where do you come from? What have you learned? Where are you going?—Richter often delves into his own issues as well. He started the podcast just a few months after announcing the end of his twenty-five-year marriage, and he discusses his life as a recent divorcee with candor, along with his struggles with depression, family trauma, and more.

The hope for secret therapy can be traced throughout comedy podcasting—away from the masculinist shock-jockeying of Joe Rogan and his top competitors, and toward variations on queer and feminist "self-help." With a few exceptions (like Richter), this niche of the comedy podcasting world is for the most part comedienne- and queer-centered. Take Cameron Esposito's *Queery*, which states as its mission to promote self-acceptance and community conversations. "There may be times when folks use identifying words or phrases that don't feel right to you. That's part of what we're exploring here," Esposito explains in the very sincere opening of each episode, "Please listen with an open heart and as always, I welcome your polite, engaged feedback. And I encourage you to continue

---

14 Kate Lacey, ed., *Listening Publics: The Politics and Experience of Listening in the Media Age* (Cambridge, UK: Polity Press, 2013), 22.
15 Andy Richter, "Maria Bamford," *Three Questions with Andy Richter*, n.d.

the conversation in your own life, and with your own community."[16] As Esposito interviews queer public figures and fellow comedians about their experiences and struggles, it's hard for me not to imagine what it would be like to hear these stories as a trans teenager, closeted and afraid in a bigoted family or community, struggling with suicidal ideation. One of the most poignant episodes of *Queery* that I've heard was an interview with Larkin Christie, a nonbinary teenager and activist who wrote in to see if Esposito would be willing to include younger guests on the podcast to talk about issues facing queer youth.

While Esposito's podcast focuses on queer life and struggles, Jameela Jamil's podcast *I Weigh* revolves around issues of body dysmorphia and eating disorders, and Busy Philips's podcast *Busy Philips is Doing Her Best* grazes on questions about parenting trans and nonbinary youth, what it means to be a white "ally," and more. Some of these self-help-tinged comedy podcasts have the distinct feeling of being invited to a boozy brunch or slumber party—*2 Dope Queens, Cuddle Club, Las Culturistas with Matt Rogers and Bowen Yang, How Was Your Week? with Julie Klausner, Best Friends with Nicole Byer and Sasheer Zamata, The Deep Dive* with Jessica St. Clair and June Diane Raphael, *Wheel of Misfortune* with Alison Spittle and Fern Brady, are among some of the enduring and interesting examples of these friendly and friendship-oriented shows. Other sectors of self-help comedy are more explicit: comedian hosts act as AA sponsors, guidance counselors, relationship experts, and more. In her podcast *Doing Great*, comedian and drag queen Vicky Vox does tarot card readings. In his show *In Your Dreams*, Chris Gethard performs dream interpretations.

Nicole Byer satirizes this self-help formula of so many comedy podcasts in *Why Won't You Date Me?*, in which she seeks dating advice from her guests, mostly comedians and drag queens. Part of the joke, on many of these shows, and to varying degrees *as* a joke, is the comedian's conceptualization as expert. Byer plays with this as a schtick. But on other shows, this expertise is more heartfelt and sincere. Sarah Silverman dedicates a large part of her weekly podcast to responding to voice messages from her listeners, which range from silly to full of despair. "You do not deserve to be treated this way, and the only person who can get you out of this situation is you," Silverman tells a listener calling in about experiences of emotional abuse in their relationship. "Life's too short to be scared all the time."[17] Anna Farris's podcast *Unqualified* leans further into

---

16 Cameron Esposito, *Queery*, n.d., https://www.earwolf.com/show/queery/.
17 Sarah Silverman, "I Will Disappoint You," *The Sarah Silverman Podcast*, n.d.

this role of amateur advice-giver, beginning with somewhat customary celebrity interviews that include some "secret therapy" maneuvering, and closing with interviews with relationship counselors, behavioral psychologists, OBGYNs, self-help gurus, and more. On *Don't Ask Tig*, Tig Notaro invites guests (with a wide range including Roxane Gay, Stephen Colbert, Molly Ringwald, Seth Rogan, LeVar Burton, Cyndi Lauper) who provide advice for fans writing into the show looking for help. In characteristic dry form, Notaro tells her audience in each episode that, despite all her attempts to discourage them, people keep writing in.

For many of these shows, the secret therapy is not so secret—not in the slightest. About a week after the initial orders to shelter in place following the first COVID outbreak in California, Whitney Cummings put out a bonus episode of her podcast *Good For You* featuring a recorded session with her therapist. Cummings opens the episode explaining that she has been getting a lot of messages from listeners "saying they are consumed with anxiety, fear, stress."[18] She reads some of the questions sent in for her therapist to respond to over the course of nearly two hours. While this is not a therapy session, it's a not-quite-therapy session, in which Cummings—specifically, as a comedian—conceives of herself in distinction from the expertise of her therapist, and as a resource of care for her listeners.

Although these podcasts and livestreams are not therapy, therapy, of some sort, is clearly their appeal. In 2020, the top advertiser in comedy podcasts was BetterHelp.com, an online counseling platform that many comedians promote alongside sincere accounts of their own mental health struggles.[19] In addition to BetterHelp.com and other therapy resources, comedy podcast sponsors include meal kit delivery services like Hello Fresh and Blue Apron, online course companies like Lynda, and wellness subscription services like FabFitFun. Between monologue and interview segments, comedian-hosts package these advertisements with a personal touch. They talk about their own issues and offer intimate details about their everyday lives—how they eat, sleep, think, parent, stay sober, etc. The comedian is yet again cast as an intermediary figure, in this case setting the listener at ease by making therapy relatable, familiar, and funny.

---

18 Whitney Cummings, "Bonus: Whitney's Therapist," *Good For You*, n.d., https://goodforyouwhitney.libsyn.com/bonus-whitneys-therapist-0.
19 "Top 15 Podcast Advertisers - September 2020," accessed January 1, 2022, https://www.magellan.ai/pages/archive/2020/top-15-podcast-advertisers-september-2020.

On average there are 130 suicides per day in the U.S., with an estimated 1.38 million suicide attempts per year.[20] The rate of workplace suicides (including murder-suicides) has risen consistently since the Bureau of Labor Statistics began tracking it in 1992, reaching a total of 304 deaths in 2018.[21] Work-related suicides are almost impossible to estimate. According to the CDC, the suicide rate has increased by 40 percent in the last twenty years.[22] In this already ongoing crisis, we seem to be turning more and more to comedians for help. Whether consciously, unconsciously, satirically, or in earnest, many of these self-help comedy shows are premised on an imaginary of the comedian not as an expert, but as a co-patient of sorts. In many ways, the comedian symbolizes the possibility of being mentally ill and still successful in capitalist life—a horizon of hope for listeners which also reflects the impossible entanglement of today's mental health epidemic with the demands of our working lives.

There are numerous popular podcasts which explore this link between mental illness and comedy in interviews with comedians and comedy writers. In *The Hilarious World of Depression*, Paul F. Tompkins processes childhood trauma, Margaret Cho discusses depression as a driving force of her stand-up, Angelina Spicer talks about post-partum depression. Dispersed among these interviews are episodes about how to get help if you're struggling, playlists based on listener suggestions designed to cheer you up, and interviews with therapists and specialists. One of the more explicitly antiwork in this niche of comedy podcasts is called *Entry Level*, in which host Brooks Wheelan interviews mostly comedy workers about the worst jobs they ever had. *Entry Level* is mostly uninterested in success stories, and how to make it even though you're crazy, which is more or less the focus of *The Mental Illness Happy Hour*, another popular podcast, hosted by Paul Gilmartin. At points *Entry Level* is just about commiserating, which I find more honest.

Whether they're about jobs, PTSD from sexual or racist violence, intergenerational conflicts, depression or suicide, these conversations generate what television scholar Bernard Timberg describes as *talk worlds*: "a point of intersection or site in which a small group talks to itself while

20 "Suicide Statistics," American Foundation for Suicide Prevention, November 15, 2019, https://afsp.org/suicide-statistics/.

21 "Workplace Suicides Reach Historic High in 2018," U.S. Bureau of Labor Statistics, accessed January 1, 2022, https://www.bls.gov/opub/ted/2020/workplace-suicides-reach-historic-high-in-2018.htm.

22 Cora Peterson et al., "Suicide Rates by Industry and Occupation," *Morbidity and Mortality Weekly Report* 69 (2020), https://doi.org/10.15585/mmwr.mm6903a1.

simultaneously addressing an invisible but clearly defined collective audience."[23] A dual consciousness "characterizes all talk worlds of private conversations made public," as Timberg explains, which must be completed by its last participant, the decoder: "In the case of written accounts of talk worlds, that decoder may read a written description of spoken words at a distance of centuries and through various filters of translation and narrative framing," he writes, "The last decoder—the reader or listener— imaginatively re-frames or 'hears' the words that are spoken *as if they are being spoken in the present tense.*"[24] The act of decoding, however indirectly, emulates a therapeutic experience. We might call this a listening cure, as a divergence from the psychoanalytic talking cure, or perhaps just the hope of one, based in a practice of interpreting—of seeing one's life as a text to interpret, not one's self as the text awaiting interpretation.

To listen, in this most utopian sense, involves a process of narrative transaction and transference. "[T]he desire of narrating, the desire to tell," as Peter Brooks suggests, "has much to do with the need for an interlocutor, a listener who enters into the narrative exchange."[25] Decoding and re-narrating this exchange as listeners has the potential, at least, of extending to what Fredric Jameson defines as "collective or associative" modes of interpretation, at work in the political unconscious of narrative.[26] To listen in and ponder a stranger's story, while constructing a narrative of shared experience, in some ways collapses the process of interpretation as simply a matter of individual identification. By contrast, part of listening, and not just talking, is the possibility of upending the individualism so pervasive to our conceptions of healing and contemplating a more deeply collective set of desires.

Underlying so many of these talk worlds is a dream for our struggles to be not just ours, to be not unique, but systemic and shared. While capitalism pits us against each other, infusing us with the ambition to overcome all obstacles by working harder, no matter what, we long for collectivity, and common ground.

§

---

23 Bernard Timberg and Bob Erler, *Television Talk: A History of the TV Talk Show* (Austin: University of Texas Press, 2002), 15.

24 Timberg and Erler, *Television Talk,* 15.

25 Peter Brooks, *Reading for the Plot: Design and Intention in Narrative* (Cambridge: Harvard University Press, 1992), 216.

26 Fredric Jameson, *The Political Unconscious: Narrative as a Socially Symbolic Act* (Ithaca: Cornell University Press, 1994), 53.

In her book, *The Distance Cure*, Hannah Zeavin complicates these boundaries of therapy and not-quite-therapy, telling a history of teletherapy and teletherapeutic care long before such practices became normalized by COVID lockdowns.[27] By the end of 2020, remote therapy sessions no longer simply denoted a lesser, watered-down version of therapeutic care, but became more recognizable as a distinct therapeutic practice. As Zeavin argues, this was always the case. Teletherapy is an approach to therapy just like any other, demanding attention and care. In March 2020, Aetna, Anthem, Cigna, and Empire, the majority of the Big Five insurance companies, began covering teletherapy—including all out-of-pocket expenses. While many therapists and their patients adapted to Zoom or phone sessions, new patients were seeking care from a variety of circumstances that had, in the past, precluded therapy. It was time to take teletherapy more seriously. "Despair, loneliness, and alienation didn't start with heavy screen use or the pandemic and obviously haven't gone away," Zeavin writes; and yet, "the feeling structures associated with teletherapy, that extraordinary version of an ordinary communicative relationship, determine the possibilities for relating over distance, a distance that is currently everywhere."[28] Distance in therapy may be nothing new, but in the context of COVID-19, distance-based methods of therapy have gained huge potential for addressing disparities in mental health care and access to resources. The de-stigmatization of distance therapy is certainly a part of this. More broadly, however, it could include a variety of interpretations of what constitutes therapy at a distance.

To the extent that we seek "secret therapy" in many forms, including podcasts, perhaps we might consider this therapy at a distance as something that includes such practices of listening, involving the listener's active participation in the therapeutic process as an interpreter, rather than as the nearly passive vessel of unconscious drives who simply talks, laying themselves bare for interpretation. In this sense, I might think of my weekly phone calls with my therapist as an aspect of my therapy, but not all of it. I could also consider therapy the daily walks I take to clear my head, the baths I take instead of doing the dishes sometimes, the banana bread I made the other day with my kid, the time I spend petting (and yes, talking to) my dogs and cat, and sometimes my turtle. When we start to think about therapy as something more like a set of habits in everyday life, we catch glimpses of a life against work.

---

27 Hannah Zeavin, *The Distance Cure: A History of Teletherapy* (Cambridge: MIT Press, 2021), 220.
28 Zeavin, *The Distance Cure*, 232–33.

These glimpses are obscured by work, and though we might only understand the therapeutic function of these habits in relation to work, they are, at the very least, an attempt to wiggle through the crevices in our imagination that still retain some space for antiwork energy and curiosity, reaching toward something else. But at the same time, as everyone seems to insist, therapy only works if you do "the work." And so many of us, feeling ourselves already overworked, listen to comedy podcasts instead, thinking that perhaps it's possible to avoid that work—or at least, that the work can be kept a secret.

CHAPTER NINE

Care, Laughter, and the Constraints of Capitalist Life

> "The world is full of painful stories. Sometimes it seems as though there aren't any other kind and yet I found myself thinking how beautiful that glint of water was through the trees."
> —Octavia Butler, *Parable of the Sower*[1]

> "Nowadays, the only possible way of reproducing oneself or others, as individuals and not as commodities, is to dam this stream of capitalist 'love'—a 'love' which masks the macabre face of exploitation."
> —Leopoldina Fortunati, *The Arcane of Reproduction*[2]

While more and more comedy has come to resemble emotional crisis-management in the face of ever-worsening capitalist destruction, "care" is what stands for so many of the demands of capitalist work. Here I want to consider the possibilities of care in comedy—how, through comedy, we might deconstruct the work ethics implied by the "self-care" industry, and also enact forms of collective care based in antiwork critique and struggle. But before turning to this possibility, we should ask what care even means in capitalist life.

With the shift in the relative proportion of jobs to service work in the last few decades especially, however we might characterize this dramatic change, more kinds of work have blurred with care work, just as more workers find themselves neverendingly in conflict with "this vexed

---

1 Octavia E. Butler, *Parable of the Sower* (New York: Seven Stories, 2016), 263.
2 Leopoldina Fortunati, *The Arcane of Reproduction: Housework, Prostitution, Labor and Capital*, ed. Jim Fleming (Brooklyn: Autonomedia, 1995), 28.

emotion known as 'care,'" as Jasmine Gibson calls it. Projected outside the logic of work, often exceeding the idea of work with notions of love and responsibility, care describes the process by which capitalism takes what's beautiful and makes it dreadful and violent. Gibson asks what it means "to care when your labor power is being exploited, when you are susceptible to sexual, emotional, and mental violence on the job, or in conflict about the emotions you experience for the children you care for, feeling both compassion and resentment all at once?"[3] While care is the defining feature of the most exploitative and devalued kinds of work, care is also key to how we might approach our everyday activities as reaching beyond, if not undermining and sabotaging the logic of work. To the call of post-work imagining, care exposes this entanglement of dystopian constraints, and utopian desires.

For years I have vacillated between a few different feelings about care, and by now I'm certain that making up my mind isn't quite the point (though it may be for others). At times, I become captivated by a thought, feeling, or faint expression of something that may be in work's stranglehold but which still breathes a different air. In moments of caring for my kid, it's sometimes as if I'm not in this world of work, but another one entirely, that's just ours. Watching my friends show up for another friend, after her mother died, there is a certain quality to the light and sound, time slows down and we find ourselves caring for each other in a way that nevertheless quickly evaporates. And then there are times at my job which have this flavor to them as well. These are moments of making a difference in someone's life unquantifiably: supporting someone as they read Marx or Angela Davis for the first time; watching someone discover that Batman is actually fascist; getting to be there when someone figures out something essential about their childhood; even when helping someone understand the difference between parenthetical clauses and em dashes, this feeling is there lurking. There are times when I find myself chipping away at the world of work, with the hope of finding something else buried beneath it, the revolutionary drive that has merely been robbed from us and hidden away. But then I remember that this is part of the trap of work—that this is how so much of work works.

Even the "supposedly virtuous 'activities of life-making' carried out by professional women state employees such as teachers, nurses, and social workers," as Kirstin Munro argues, "perpetuate the antagonism and social

---

3 Jasmine Gibson, "The Fire This Time?" *Lies II: A Journal of Materialist Feminism*, 2015, 148–49.

misery inherent to capitalism."[4] This virtuosity is of course part of why these kinds of work, along with household labor and other forms of reproductive labor, are so precarious despite being so socially necessary. But it is often a visceral experience of these jobs, which demand workers to work with their hearts. Beyond minor acts of sabotage, there's little we can do for ourselves on an individual basis as workers in this trap. I know teachers from K-12 to college who have worked incredibly hard to develop approaches to grading that strive to be equitable, student-centered, and social justice oriented. We spend countless hours discussing ways that we can modify our individual philosophies of grading, without any hope of changing the system of grading we are all still beholden to—a system that reproduces inequalities, creates competition, and ultimately conveys to the student that everything they've experienced as a learner can be reduced to a letter (as a future worker). And the more we care, it would seem, the more we are trapped in these contradictions. We can do our best to approach these contradictions ethically, and that's of course important, but it hardly makes up for political transformations that remain urgent across education systems.

One of my friends is an ICU nurse in southern Oregon, whose days are devoted to the closest I could imagine as being truly virtuous work, but which are still mixed with intense political compromise and frustration. "When people ask me how work is going right now, it's beyond difficult to describe. The suffering and loss feel immense already," they explained in a social media post, "We are exhausted every day and spread thin. It is scary to think that it will continue to get worse, and to face a public who scoff at the reality of the pandemic." Outside the hospital where they work, there are anti-vax protestors every day, threatening workers along with patients and their family and friends. So much of this work of care is shaped by violence.

When I extend these questions of what happens to care under capitalism to my life—and work—as a parent, it often feels unbearable. What does it mean to be "life-making" in this world, as Munro asks, when this entails "[cultivating and sustaining] the desired human qualities and capacities that capitalism simply appropriates for profit"?[5] These questions

---

4 Kirstin Munro, "Unproductive Workers and State Repression," *Review of Radical Political Economics* 53, no. 4 (December 1, 2021): 623–30, https://doi.org/10.1177/04866134211043284.

5 Based on a forthcoming chapter, Kirstin Munro, "Unproductive Workers, 'Life-Making', and State Repression," in *The State Today: Politics, History, Law*, ed. Eva Nanopoulos et al. (Palgrave Macmillan, 2022).

are amplified by ongoing ecological crisis. With each wildfire that eviscerates the west coast, where I live with my kid in smoke for months out of the year, I am often overwhelmed with sadness about the future, and the world I brought this child into. To these unbearable moments, haunting motherhood, Jacqueline Rose asks: "what are mothers being asked to carry, what forms of failure and injustice are they made accountable for[?] . . . What are the fears we lay on mothers? . . . Why do we expect mothers to subdue the very fears we ourselves have laid at their door?"[6] Mothering, as I have learned, wrestles with these questions without end—there is no reconciliation. The only way to stop wrestling is to become subsumed. "Unless we recognise what we are asking mothers to perform in the world—and for the world," Rose writes, "we will continue to tear both the world and mothers to pieces."[7] Of course part of this can be tearing one's self apart. To be a "mother" often means to blame oneself for the world or trying to make up for it.

Care crystallizes the most dystopic, coercive aspects of capitalist life, distorting, it would seem inevitably, whatever we might be able to comprehend as love into a system of profit. And yet care also approximates our most utopian urges and catches insights into revolutionary practices with the sparks of antiwork critique. Care demands that we think about what it would take, individually and collectively, to live against work. How might we differentiate this from the "life-making" activities that are all the while reproducing capitalism? Where can we sever the possibilities of care from the realities of work?

These questions rush to my mind as I make stew. Over the pandemic, I cultivated a habit of making a stew or a soup about once a week, to spread across several meals for my partner and kid. It first occurred to me as an inexpensive way to make my work in the kitchen more efficient. Stew cuts down on nightly cooking tasks and the incessant dishes, as you just heat the stew up again every night with only bowls and spoons to rinse. But there is also the pleasure of hours melting away as I stand, part-daydreaming, tending to a pot of various ingredients, letting the heat and smells hit my face, almost taking me somewhere else, while keeping me there just the same. I have learned from the pleasure of watching, as a pot of water becomes broth with the addition of a few bones and onion peels, and from the techniques and questions asked in minding its flavor. I add to the pot what's around in my pantry, which is always a little bit different,

6 Jacqueline Rose, *Mothers: An Essay on Love and Cruelty* (New York: Farrar, Straus and Giroux, 2018), 37.
7 Rose, *Mothers*, 2.

and involves experimentation. Having studied Marxist-feminism for much of my adult life, I am certainly armored against romanticizing the kitchen, the setting of so much invisible labor, while I often wonder about this space and all that I do in it—what worlds it puts me into contact with, even faintly. With invisibility comes a different sense of what could be.

In fact much of this book has been written from my kitchen, mostly at a desk beside a window, but also from the kitchen counter, where I move between paragraphs and chopping vegetables on a butcher block beside the stove where I every so often dip my wooden spoon into a pot and stir. I have come to understand stew, much like this book, as both parts labor of love and housework strike, never one without the other.

One of my favorite concepts from the initial Wages for Housework movement is the tactic of instrumentalized invisibility which Nicole Cox and Silvia Federici call "counterplanning from the kitchen." While making the case that reproductive labor is fundamental to (rather than separate from) capitalist production, they invert the logic of their critics: according to the left, they write, "our problem, it seems, is that capital has failed to reach into and organize our kitchens and bedrooms," adding, daringly, that "obviously, if our kitchens are outside of capital, our struggle to destroy them will never succeed in causing capital to fall."[8]

What happens in kitchens, as the pandemic made quite clear, is absolutely essential to the survival of capitalism—and by extension, what happens in kitchens is absolutely essential to how we destroy capitalism. In a time when the most arbitrary work to serve the rich is labeled "essential work," there are meanwhile so many activities that must persist, such as childcare and eldercare, which remain unwaged, unappreciated, and taken for granted. These are activities from which withdrawal is not an option—which call for a more rigorous understanding of the refusal of work. This distinct quality of care work is part of why "no strike has ever been a general strike," as Mariarosa Dalla Costa would put, it "When half the working population is at home in the kitchens, while the others are on strike, it's not a general strike. We've never seen a general strike."[9] While Dalla Costa made this declaration in 1975, it remains a compelling challenge today. How do we enact the refusal of work in more powerful ways,

8   Silvia Federici and Nicole Cox, "Counterplanning from the Kitchen," in *Revolution at Point Zero: Housework, Reproduction, and Feminist Struggle* (Oakland: PM Press / Common Notions / Autonomedia, 2012), 29.
9   Mariarosa Dalla Costa, Harry Cleaver, and Camille Barbagallo, *Women and the Subversion of the Community: A Mariarosa Dalla Costa Reader* (Oakland: PM Press, 2019), 54.

through a variety of registers? What does the refusal of work look like, when we engage with the totality of work? Here I imagine not just a withdrawal from so many activities which are destroying us and destroying the planet unnecessarily, but an expansion of forms of collective care from the logic of capitalist work.

Writing of care as a form of protest in the pandemic, Carol Zou thinks through some of these questions, imagining reproductive labor as both a means of perpetuating and sabotaging the miseries of capitalist life. "Protest is reproductive labor insofar as it creates the conditions for those of us who were not meant to survive, to live another day," Zou argues, "Protest recognizes that white supremacist capitalism is a death cult and protest says let us rupture our reality so that we may live."[10] Along these lines, the Spanish feminist collective Precarias a la Deriva seeks to conceptualize the "care strike": "It seems a paradox, if, because the strike is always interruption and visibilization and care is the continuous and invisible line whose interruption would be devastating," the collective writes, "But all that is lacking is a change of perspective to see that there is no paradox: the care strike would be nothing other than the interruption of the order that is ineluctably produced in the moment in which we place the truth of care in the center and politicize it."[11] These are not visions of a post-capitalist world so much as attempts at reorienting ourselves and each other toward the problems of care in capitalist life.

As a site of counterplanning, the kitchen is at once a scene of exploitation and experimentation. While it symbolizes so many of the constraints of capitalist life, it also puts us in touch with the possibilities of some other kind of life, awakening in our senses an awareness of ourselves as part of a human history for which capitalism is not inevitable, but contingent, and for which care is a kind of reminiscence—a conjuring, not quite here, though never entirely elsewhere. However held captive by capitalism, care must be salvaged, uncertainties and all, if we are to struggle together for a better way of life.

---

10 Carol Zou, "9 Theses on Pandemic and Reproductive Labor," *A Blade of Grass*, accessed January 1, 2022, https://www.abladeofgrass.org/articles/9-theses-on-pandemic-and-reproductive-labor/.

11 Precarias a la Deriva, "A Very Careful Strike – Four Hypotheses," *Caring Labor: An Archive*, August 14, 2010, https://caringlabor.wordpress.com/2010/08/14/precarias-a-la-deriva-a-very-careful-strike-four-hypotheses/.

Care Against "Self-Care"

By now the idea of care has been thoroughly hijacked by the self-care industry. As a measurement of "self-care," care is reduced to a matter of *treating yourself because you're worth it,* and more specifically, *treating yourself because you worked for it.* In this Instagram-filtered imaginary, care is earned through work, but also un-imagined as work—just as care has become ever more commodified. Theorizing this as a terrain of care crisis, Emma Dowling writes that a "heightened emphasis on personal responsibility for care" is key to "the search for profitability through the further commodification of care."[12] This ideology of "self-care" corresponds with the expansion of service workforces, many premised in the promise of care. In 2014, "self-care" was a $10 billion industry; by 2021, a little more than a year into a global pandemic, it became a $450 billion one.[13] Under worsening conditions of care, "self-care" thrives as both a consumer ideology and the distinctive work ethic of capitalist care crisis.

In its ascendance, the self-care industry has drawn deeply from the cliché "laughter is the best medicine," especially in its literary output of self-help books.[14] *The Laughing Cure* (2016), by psychologist and comedian Brian King, conceives of laughter as a form of stress management, meditation, and exercise. *Laugh* by Lisa Sturge (2017), *Laughology* by Stephanie Davies (2013), *The Laughing Guide to Well-Being* by Oscar and Isaac Prilleltensky (2016), and *Laugh Your Way to Happiness* by Leslie Lyle (2014) are among the scores of laughter-themed self-help books written

---

12　Emma Dowling, *The Care Crisis: What Caused It and How Can We End It?* (New York: Verso, 2021), 12.

13　Lindsay Crouse, "Why I Stopped Running During the Pandemic (and How I Started Again)," *The New York Times*, March 7, 2021, https://www.nytimes.com/2021/03/07/opinion/pandemic-wall-fitness-running.html.

14　In 2020, among the more popular books published by comedians and comedy writers were Ali Wong's *Dear Girls: Intimate Tales, Untold Secrets & Advice for Living Your Best Life,* Cameron Esposito's *Save Yourself,* Desus and Mero's *God Level Knowledge Darts: Life Lessons from the Bronx,* D.L. Hughley's *Surrender, White People! Our Unconditional Terms for Peace,* Lindy West's *The Witches Are Coming,* Chloé Hillard's *F*ck Your Diet: And Other Things My Thighs Tell Me,* and Tara Schuster's *Buy Yourself the F*cking Lilies: And Other Rituals to Fix Your Life, from Someone Who's Been There. Recovery: Freedom from Our Addictions, Revelation: Connecting with the Sacred in Everyday Life, Mentors: How to Help and Be Helped, Revolution*—these are just *some* of the self-help books authored by Russell Brand alone, not to mention his memoirs. Switching between jokes and the "very special episode" voice of 90s sit-coms, comedians expound life lessons through confessions and insights, all while conceptualizing comedy not only as self-care, but as a form of spiritual enlightenment.

by behavioral psychologists and mental health practitioners in the last decade. These books typically package "everyday laughter" in terms of wellness practices, building resilience through mood regulation, and using comedy to achieve goals. In a symptomatic entry, *Humor, Seriously*, by Stanford business professors Jennifer Aaker and Naomi Bagdonas, outlines how one might deploy humor for career success, "climbing the ladder of levity."[15]

Central to this psychologizing of humor, and to self-help ideology at large, is an internalizing of capitalist crisis. Self-help books assure us that all the problems that arise from our social conditions under capitalism can be overcome through individual hard work, without ever resorting to collective action. A complimentary if implicit argument of these books is that if the self-help program doesn't result in your success, it isn't because of the program, or because of capitalism; instead, it's a matter of personal failure. But you can never succeed at this game—there's no career advice that will get you out of the racism, sexism, ableism and nepotism of the job market, just as there's no flash diet or "nutritional lifestyle" that will get you to the magical waist size that disappears the fatphobic world around you or the years of fat-shaming you've already suffered, and there's no secret philosophy of household organizing that will eradicate housework from your life forever. In the world of self-help, everything boils down to your personal accountability. While the fantasy of self-help is something like self-care, the narrative logic of self-help is undoubtedly self-blame. Despite the optimistic language about joy, happiness, and wellness with which it is littered, self-help literature terrorizes its readers, not only through mechanisms of self-blame, but with the constant assertions that the "self" at its center is devastatingly and inexorably alone. There is no way out, just ways to keep coping—laughing, smiling, and working harder, so as to keep the possibility of social transformation beyond the "self" out of mind by whatever means necessary. "Self-help" is the ultimate dystopia.

But all of this should be actively set apart from the vision of "self-care" that Audre Lorde began to develop decades ago, through a Black feminist, anticapitalist, and fundamentally collectivist framework. "Caring for myself," Lorde famously wrote in 1988, "is not self-indulgence, it is self-preservation, and that is an act of political warfare."[16] This notion of caring for oneself and each other as warfare gets at the utopian energy

---

15 Jennifer Lynn Aaker and Naomi Bagdonas, *Humor, Seriously* (New York: Currency, 2020), 44.
16 Audre Lorde, *A Burst of Light: And Other Essays* (Mineola, New York: Ixia Press, 2017), 130.

woven throughout this book, and applied to the question of antiwork comedy, as an imperfect yet illuminating expression of our shared desire to experience the care of a non-capitalist life, unimaginable as that might be.

It has become politically crucial to disentangle the "language that Lorde's name is marshaled to co-sign," as Nick Mitchell argues, in an era of political memes and thinkfluencers from the possibilities of what Lorde once called "self-care." "We're still learning to read Audre Lorde," Mitchell writes, "We're still learning to become the collectivity, the 'we,' that would make reading Audre Lorde possible."[17] Today, Lorde's conception of "self-care," Mitchell clarifies, needs to move toward a language of community care. Christina Sharpe has developed such a language as "wake work," a practice of living in the wake of slavery: "I want to think 'care' as a problem of thought,"[18] she explains, describing "an ethics of care (as in repair, maintenance, attention), an ethics of seeing, and of being in the wake as consciousness[.]"[19] As Sharpe suggests, this is an account of care as *shared risk*.

Quite powerfully, Jennifer Nash further complicates this question of how to imagine and enact care in refusal of "self-care," warning against the "allure of care" to "[emphatically interrogate] moments where care, love, and affection mask a pernicious possessiveness," and engaging with what she conceives as the "political pull of care" in order to "reanimate it, asking how we might display our care—our affection, our regard, our love, even[.]"[20] While moving critically within and in relation to an imaginary of self-care, as well as Black feminist thinking, Nash insists, in agreement with Sharpe, on the care of shared risk, echoing Lorde's notion of care as political warfare: "it is risky to view one's self as bound up with others and to fully accept the responsibility and potential peril," Nash explains, "but this is the visionary call of black feminist love-politics—a radical embrace of connectedness." [21]

This connectedness should be brought to the foreground of Lorde's idea of self-care, as it is mutilated into a consumerist regime and work ethic—a white liberal feminist imaginary for which care can only be envisioned at the level of the individual and in market-mediated terms. By contrast, in Lorde's account, care is slippery, escaping the constraints of

---

17   Nick Mitchell, "On Audre Lorde's Legacy and the 'Self' of Self-Care, Part 1 of 3," *low end theory*, accessed January 1, 2022, https://www.lowendtheory.org/post/43457761324/on-audre-lordes-legacy-and-the-self-of.

18   Christina Elizabeth Sharpe, *In the Wake: On Blackness and Being* (Durham: Duke University Press, 2016), 5.

19   Sharpe, *In the Wake*, 131.

20   Jennifer C. Nash, *Black Feminism Reimagined: After Intersectionality* (Durham: Duke University Press, 2019), 80.

21   Nash, *Black Feminism Reimagined*, 80.

power, enduringly, because there is a purpose to survival. Not away from, but beyond the "self," it orients toward care as always already collective.

On Revolutionary Laughter

What if we could know care not just as an impossibility of capitalist life, but as a revolutionary force—as bursts of anticapitalist energy, transitory and fluid, resistant toward commodification, unabsorbed by the logic of work? Rather than in acts of virtue, how might care be enacted through a collective practice of sabotage, and through an ethics of antiwork, instead of through capitalist work ethics?

The history of Black women's humor in the U.S. sheds light on some of these questions. Reflecting on this history, Daryl Cumber Dance describes the ways that humor "has helped us to survive the broken promises, lies, betrayals, contempt, humiliations, and dehumanization," functioning as a practice of mutual care but also self-protection: "We use our humor to speak the unspeakable, to mask the attack, to get a tricky subject on the table, to warn of lines not to be crossed, to strike out at enemies and the hateful acts of friends and family," she elaborates, "to camouflage sensitivity, to tease, to compliment, to berate, to brag, to flirt, to speculate, to gossip, to educate, to correct the lies people tell on us, to bring about change."[22] This is not a humor of coping, escaping, anesthetizing. This is a humor of surviving, not alone, for which there is a revolutionary drive in laughter, toward collective care. With a nod to Langston Hughes, Danielle Fuentes Morgan articulates this as "laughing to keep from dying." Satire has been especially important to the history of Black humor, as a collective practice "necessary for day-to-day survival," as Fuentes Morgan suggests, which "reinforces the humanity of both the satirist and their audience while secretly, simultaneously constructing an in-group positioned with more knowledge than their oppressor[.]" In practice, she writes, this "is an act of self-affirmation and imagining yourself otherwise[.]"[23] In constructing this in-group, satire forges collectivity—making shared experiences of suffering, exploitation, and brutality somehow more livable; but also, and just as crucially, making resistance and acts of sabotage, however minute, more possible, and thinkable in everyday life.

---

22   Daryl Cumber Dance, ed., *Honey, Hush!: An Anthology of African American Women's Humor* (New York: W.W. Norton, 1998), xxi–xxii.
23   Danielle Fuentes Morgan, "Introduction: Twenty-First-Century African American Satire," *Post45*, June 22, 2021, https://post45.org/2021/06/introduction-twenty-first-century-african-american-satire/.

The collectivity generated through inside jokes is an essential dynamic in the history of slavery in the U.S. Writing of the early records of slavery, Jelani Cobb frames the practice of inside jokes as a "Black humor out of necessity," remarking on the frequent accounts of paranoid slave masters, "who hear slaves laughing and believe they must be the subject of the joke." [24] The inside joke functions not only as a source of relief and solidarity-building, as Cobb argues, but as a powerful weapon to be used against the enemy. It models a version of collective care that is not just about getting by, but fighting back, by whatever means possible. The idea of a survival-based, necessary comedy represents a "wrested freedom" in Black history—"the freedom to laugh at that which was unjust and cruel in order to create distance from what would otherwise obliterate a sense of self and community," Glenda Carpio suggests. [25] It is a freedom based in conditions of unfreedom, but more specifically, a freedom to defy and disarticulate unfreedom.

Laughing to keep from dying, as Fuentes Morgan puts it, is a revolutionary practice. "How our ancestors resisted, and even that they resisted, is a necessary framework for understanding resistance today," she explains. "The satire undertaken in slavery was an active revolution, and it inspires the revolutionary laughter that keeps us alive in the twenty-first century." [26] This practice resonates with what Marquis Bey describes as an "obstinately fugitive Black feminism," compelled by the refusal "to concede to the categorical truth of things staying as they are, indeed of things staying as they are presumed to always have to be[.]" [27] Based on collective survival and shared risk, this vision of humor conceives of laughter as "living [as] a process of rebellion," and a "fugitive praxis of daring to exist." [28]

Revolutionary laughter unleashes the utopian onto the dystopian. It illuminates the possibilities of collective care but also the horrors and violence of capitalism and its history. We might also understand this fugitive Black feminism, and its revolutionary capacity, as a critical utopianism—a "utopianism within, against, beyond (and paradoxically for) the utopia in which they are set," as David Bell remarks, drawing from Tom Moylan's

24 Jelani Cobb, *The Devil & Dave Chappelle & Other Essays* (New York: Thunder's Mouth Press, 2007), 249.
25 Glenda Carpio, *Laughing Fit to Kill: Black Humor in the Fictions of Slavery* (Oxford: Oxford University Press, 2008), 4–5.
26 Fuentes Morgan, *Laughing to Keep from Dying*, 23.
27 Marquis Bey, *Them Goon Rules: Fugitive Essays on Radical Black Feminism* (Tucson: The University of Arizona Press, 2019), 153.
28 Bey, 119.

conception of "utopia as struggle."[29] This critical utopianism induces revolutionary laughter, separating the practice of "laughing to keep from dying" from mere survival, and amplifying the collective care of shared risk and dreaming. It is an orientation in the midst of dystopian despair, pointing to what could be, or what is not-quite, and inspiring different ways to care and be cared for.

Jayna Brown examines utopian expression as "acrobatic, rhythmic, melodic, full of sensation," in ways that could certainly extend to the possibilities of revolutionary laughter.[30] Brown looks to Black women mystics as figures of an ecstatic utopianism, for whom "the feeling self is not a stable, unified self" but rather a site of ongoing struggle. Laughter destabilizes the self, spilling out and among each other, accentuating "the utopian urge of felt experience," as Brown writes, and touching "a collective sense of self." She describes these experiences as "moments of melting,"[31] calling for "new paths to our survival," across differences of age, race, class, and gender. Contemplating the political possibilities of this utopian urge, Audre Lorde conjures this sensation of melting as well:

> We have chosen each other
> and the edge of each others battles
> the war is the same
> if we lose
> someday women's blood will congeal
> upon a dead planet
> if we win
> there is no telling
> we seek beyond history
> *for a new and more possible meeting.*[32]

It's in the Stew

Stirring another pot of stew, my thoughts whirl towards the etymology of "humour," rooted in the Latin for "liquid" or "fluid."[33] The ancient

---

29   David Bell, *Rethinking Utopia: Place, Power, Affect* (London: Routledge, 2017), 82.
30   Jayna Brown, *Black Utopias: Speculative Life and the Music of Other Worlds* (Durham: Duke University Press, 2021), 149.
31   Brown, *Black Utopias*, 25.
32   Audre Lorde, *Sister Outsider: Essays and Speeches* (Berkeley: Crossing Press, 1984), 114.
33   See Salvatore Attardo, ed., *Encyclopedia of Humor Studies* (Thousand Oaks, California: SAGE Publications, 2014), 350.

Greeks designated four humours to the body: blood, phlegm, and yellow and black bile. These humours flow through the body and must be balanced. Until the mid-nineteenth century, disease was conceptualized as an imbalance of humours, treated through draining, often bleeding out or through induced vomiting. Western humoral medicine idealized an equilibrium between these fluids, associated with different elements and qualities. Yellow bile was associated with fire and the liver; black bile, with earth and the spleen; phlegm, with water and the brain; and blood, with air and the heart.

Today humoralism seems antiquated as a medical practice, needless to say, but it endures as a powerful set of ideas that structure our imagination of health. The idea of a balanced temperament persists in contemporary rhetoric of health and wellness, by now often framed in terms of a "work-life" balance. Yet underlying these formulations of work-life is an inability to think life outside the terms of work. The purpose of striking a supposed balance between work and life is to conceptualize life as simply that which recharges us for more work. While subsumed by ideologies of work, this idea of balance takes as its counterpart a logic of excess, hence a particular fixation on the fantasy of cleansing.

Modern conceptions of humor, though estranged from this history of humoralism, continue to operate through the logic of excess and imbalance—imagined as the phlegm, bile, blood, vomit, and toxins that must be drained away.[34] In the contemporary melancholic subject, Carol Owens traces "desperate operations on the body," such as bulimia and cutting, as attempts "to bring about a drainage of an excess jouissance to restore the body to a point of being where living (in one's body) is for the moment once again minimally tolerable."[35] Humor is conceived as a kind of exorcism—a process of emptying out, and unburdening. This describes at once what is most caring and what is most violent about comedy.

In comedy we encounter the plurality of the pharmakon. As drug, the pharmakon has the dual potential, which Plato cautions against, between remedy and poison. What distinguishes between these possibilities is a matter of method. Depending on how it is used, the drug can heal or it can kill—and everything in-between. For Derrida, the pharmakon is "linked as much to the malady to its treatment," in that

---

34 Carol Owens, "Not in the Humor: Bulimic Dreams," in *Lacan, Psychoanalysis, and Comedy*, ed. Patricia Gherovici and Manya Steinkoler (New York: Cambridge University Press, 2016), 119.

35 Owens, "Not in the Humor: Bulimic Dreams," 118–19.

it "partakes of both good and ill, of the agreeable and the disagreeable," and specifically as "that which, always springing up from without, acting like the outside itself, will never have any definable virtue of its own."[36] By extension, comedy can be weaponized, enacting incredible harm. This is the slimy world of jokesterism, slithering between harassment and bullying and "just joking." But comedy is also a healing practice, whether we understand this to be a matter of merely coping, or perhaps we dare to approach it as a form of revolt.

In the history of medicine, much like the history of comedy, women have long been rendered witches. The witch-healer posed a threat up until the seventeenth century, against the medical paradigm of humoralism. In their history of nurses and midwives, Barbara Ehrenreich and Deirdre English claim that if anything "it was the male professionals who clung to untested doctrines and ritualistic practices—and it was the women healers who represented a more humane, empirical approach to healing." [37] The wise women, or witches, had "a host of remedies which had been tested in years of use," they explain, "Many of the herbal remedies developed by witches still have their place in modern pharmacology," including pain-killers, digestive aids, anti-inflammatory agents, and "ergot for the pain of labor at a time when the Church held that pain in labor was the Lord's just punishment for Eve's original sin."[38]

This history of witchcraft and healing extends to the possibilities of killjoy comedy today and helps to define killjoy comedy through a set of practices: the carefulness of interpretation, questioning, experimenting, re-imagining, cultivating. Witches were midwives, but also killjoys: "[rebel women] who talked back, argued, swore, and did not cry under torture," as Silvia Federici writes.[39] Against the charge of witchcraft, and throughout the bloody history of witch-hunts during which more than a hundred thousand women were killed between the mid-fifteenth and sixteenth centuries in Europe, women struggled to maintain methods of collective care, through medicinal healing practices as well as practices of collective interpretation and critical thinking. The history of witches, healers, and killjoys reveals the dangers of care, and the collective stakes of that danger.

---

36 Jacques Derrida, *Dissemination*, trans. Barbara Johnson (Chicago: University of Chicago Press, 1993), 99–102.

37 Barbara Ehrenreich and Deirdre English, *Witches, Midwives, and Nurses: A History of Women Healers*, 2nd ed. (New York: Feminist Press, 2010), 3.

38 Ehrenreich and English, *Witches, Midwives, and Nurses*, 13.

39 Federici, *Revolution at Point Zero*, 184.

Perhaps this is a cauldron that I'm stirring, as I think back on the *humors* of blood, phlegm, and bile, adding to this amniotic fluid. Sophie Lewis writes of an amniotechnic imaginary as a state of co-existence and de-individuation, based in our shared wateriness—an "amniotechnics" of "holding and caring even while being ripped into, at the same time as being held."[40] "Hydrofeminist" Astrida Neimanis theorizes water as that which "calls to us . . . from a realm of materiality that is also, simultaneously, more-than-human and beyond any kind of intentional grasp."[41] It is our wateriness that we share, but which also requires us to question the non-boundaries of collectivity.

I continue to wonder about this amniotic humor. Among other things, it gets at questions of regeneration—why and how we use humor to bring ourselves back to life in a world that is killing us, however slowly or quickly. But this only goes so far. Just as a drug can slip between remedy and poison, humor shifts between revolutionary and reactionary registers. It is not enough to save us in a sick world.

---

40 Sophie Lewis, *Full Surrogacy Now: Feminism against Family* (New York: Verso, 2019), 163.
41 Astrida Neimanis, *Bodies of Water: Posthuman Feminist Phenomenology* (London: Bloomsbury Academic, 2017), 22.

CONCLUSION

Antiwork Comedy as Utopian Method

> "The exercise of imagination is dangerous to those who profit from the way things are because it has the power to show that the way things are is not permanent, not universal, not necessary."
> —Ursula K Le Guin, "The Operating Instructions"[1]

> "The desire to live is a political decision."
> —Raoul Vaneigem, *The Revolution of Everyday Life*[2]

One of the miseries of capitalism is that, despite our greatest efforts, it's impossible to lead an anticapitalist life without a host of contradictions which we are bound to internalize, at least on some level. This is our lot, in the absence of revolution. These obstacles to anticapitalist life are too often perceived in consumer terms—what we buy or avoid buying, how and when we compromise our ethics in a world monopolized by corporations—but of course we face these contradictions primarily as workers. Every day, we reproduce this capitalist dystopia through work. Hardly anything can be disentangled from the idea and reality of work, making the very notion of a life beyond work seem futile, even foolish. And yet, as Kathi Weeks suggests, "life as an alternative to work does not pretend to be something more authentic and true, which we can find somewhere outside of work." Instead, a life against work "must be continually invented in the struggle to mark distinctions between fields of experience that nonetheless remain intertwined."[3]

---

1 Ursula K. Le Guin, *The Wave in the Mind: Talks and Essays on the Writer, the Reader, and the Imagination* (Boston: Shambhala, 2004), 219.
2 Raoul Vaneigem, *The Revolution of Everyday Life*, trans. Donald Nicholson-Smith (Oakland: PM Press, 2012), 4.
3 Weeks, *The Problem with Work*, 216.

All the same, we make contact with the possibilities of anticapitalist life all the time, through everyday practices which could help to make such a life more collectively imaginable as well. Here is where my thinking about comedy emerges from—and where I end this book with a cluster of utopian problems.

With each of these problems, I'll attempt to formulate a theory of antiwork comedy as a practice of everyday life. But to think through these problems demands a much fuller picture of what comedy could be and already is—far beyond the parameters of comedy club stages and the generic conventions of joking, and towards a conception of comedy as a utopian method. Throughout this book, I've tried to chip away at comedy as an exclusive art form, with the hope of uncovering it as a way of life instead. The further we move away from this understanding of comedy as liberal, individualist artistry, the closer we get to a shared revolutionary practice. Here are three brief attempts to push utopian problems in this direction:

I. Play

Since the mid-fifties, free play has nearly disappeared from childhood in the United States. Defining free play as intrinsically motivated, self-directed activity, child psychologist Peter Gray has argued of this continual decline that "adults have exerted ever-increasing control over children's activities outside of the world of labor."[4] While children's outdoor play has decreased most dramatically, research indicates that 89 percent of children still prefer outdoor play with friends to watching TV, and 86 percent prefer it to computer and video games. More than screen time, the threat to children's outdoor play is rooted in the fears of their caretakers.

These fears are complicated and entangled in the racism and sexism of everyday violence in capitalist life. Revisiting her experiences in childhood and the fears of her parents, Brianna Holt wrote a powerful essay a week into the George Floyd uprisings about growing up Black: "When I was a child, I thought my parents were extremely unreasonable," she explains, "I watched my white friends receive more privileges with age, while my parents' grip on me seemed to get tighter." Throughout her childhood, her parents' rules "felt annoying," but as she got older, she

---

4 Peter Gray, "The Decline of Play and the Rise of Psychopathology," *The American Journal of Play* 3, no. 4 (Spring 2011): 444.

remembers realizing that they were somehow necessary: "My parents had explicit conversations with me about how to behave with cops and about the racism I would face out in the world." As an adult, looking forward to becoming a parent, she writes, "I expect my parenting style will most likely mimic that of my parents. If it doesn't, it will be because we have created a safer world for my kids[.]"[5] These rules do not reflect the world that caretakers want for their children, but political compromises made under conditions of inescapable danger. Rather than ideals, these rules are expressions of impossibility, and the totalizing threat of white supremacy that is essential to the idea of "childhood." While many white parents may be afraid to tell white children about racism—a conversation which is sometimes described as a "loss of innocence"—Black mothers "are scared not of talk of race, but of the impact of racist oppression," writes Dani McClain, "We're scared because we have no choice." There is no option of hoping that the realities of racism will be learned through experience, as McClain explains, "Instead, we must act as a buffer and translator between them and the world, beginning from their earliest days."[6]

Children in immigrant families in the U.S. grow up with their own rules, double-standards, and survival tactics. Because immigrant children "typically come into contact with American culture sooner and, indeed more intensely, than their parents do," as Carola and Marcelo M. Suárez-Orozco explain, "parents may try to slow down the process by warning children not to act like other children in the new setting."[7] Children in undocumented families experience even greater pressure in managing risks often on behalf of adults in their life. Thinking back on her own experiences, Karla Cornejo Villavicencio describes the "twisted inversion" of such a childhood, that "at some point, your parents become your children, and your own personal American dream is making sure they age and die with dignity in a country that has never wanted them."[8]

5 Brianna Holt, "Now I Understand Why My Parents Were So Strict," *The Atlantic*, June 3, 2020, https://www.theatlantic.com/family/archive/2020/06/my-black-parents-had-be-strict/612610/.
6 Dani McClain, "As a Black Mother, My Parenting Is Always Political," *The Nation*, March 27, 2019, https://www.thenation.com/article/archive/black-motherhood-family-parenting-dani-mcclain/.
7 Carola Suárez-Orozco and Marcelo M. Suárez-Orozco, *Children of Immigration* (Cambridge: Harvard University Press, 2002), 73–74.
8 Karla Cornejo Villavicencio, "For the Child of Immigrants, the American Dream Can Be a Nightmare," *Vogue*, April 17, 2018, https://www.vogue.com/article/child-of-immigrants-daca-personal-essay. See also Karla Cornejo Villavicencio, *The Undocumented Americans* (New York: One World, 2020).

These different pressures faced by non-white children strike a harsh contrast with the fears dominating the white liberal parental imaginary, fixated instead on the "stranger danger" of child molesters, as well as crime and safety hazards. What get lost in such fears of danger outside the household, of course, are the dangers within households. The majority of child abuse happens either within or in relation to the family, either by family members or family friends. Only 7 percent of reported cases of child abuse actually involve strangers.[9]

While the outdoors conjures many different fears and parental anxieties, ranging from police violence to bullying to scraped knees, what's at stake in all of these conceptions of the outdoors is some notion of children's liberation. Children are as much figures of utopian possibility as dystopian dread. They must be taught about the world in order to survive in it; at the same time, they dream of other worlds in ways that "adults," supposedly, can't. In all of this, it is *adulthood* that is the problem—however much that problem is conceived in terms of children.

Another aspect of this disappearance of play is enforced by the education system. In elementary schools across the U.S., recess time has been steadily reduced over the last twenty years. Today only 16 percent of states require daily recess at elementary schools.[10] Even among vocal advocates of recess, demanding changes in state legislature and classroom management, recess is hardly articulated as a matter of children's free play. While emphasizing the need for "unstructured activities," these demands for increased recess in school systems are often instead framed in terms of adult surveillance, primarily to address concerns of bullying. Concurrent with this decline in recess time has been a pronounced increase in both standardized testing and homework. A 2015 study revealed that, on average, students in big-city public school systems across the U.S. take about 112 mandatory standardized tests by the end of 12th grade, with an average of eight a year beginning in prekindergarten.[11] While standardized testing was called into question during the pandemic in 2020, with some colleges announcing that they would no longer base admissions on SAT or ACT scores, the amount of homework sky-rocketed for many remote

---

9   "Children and Teens: Statistics," RAINN, accessed January 1, 2022, https://www.rainn.org/statistics/children-and-teens.

10   Society of Health and Physical Educators, "2016 Shape of the Nation Full Report," Shape of the Nation, n.d., https://www.shapeamerica.org/advocacy/son/.

11   This has come under crisis during the pandemic. See Valerie Strauss, "It Looks like the Beginning of the End of America's Obsession with Student Standardized Tests," *Washington Post*, June 21, 2020, https://www.washingtonpost.com/education/2020/06/21/it-looks-like-beginning-end-americas-obsession-with-student-standardized-tests/.

learning students. In a study affiliated with the Stanford Graduate School of Education published in early 2021, researchers surveyed over 75,000 high school students from 86 high schools across the country and found that about 56 percent of students reported that their stress about school had increased during fall 2020. 51 percent reported that they were spending more time on homework during the pandemic, with the average student reporting three hours of homework per weeknight, in addition to 5–7 hours of remote instruction during each weekday.[12] More and more of childhood has been taken over by these pressures, and this world of work.

To absorb the shock of decreased recess time, classrooms have adapted different ways of managing children's activities away from play. Rather than recess, children are provided with workstations, designed to heighten their productivity. North Carolina math teacher Bethany Lambeth, for instance, received much media attention and praise for the increase in her students' test scores after installing pedal desks in her middle school classroom. "[T]hey're sitting still all day long," she explains of her students in an interview, "they start to get restless and start tapping their desks and their feet . . . They're not doing it to be defiant—it's just about being able to move."[13] Individual changes that teachers make to classrooms all take place in a context of limited options. A survey of five school districts compiled by AFT (American Federation of Teachers) between 2014–2017 found that 100 percent of responding teachers agreed that recess is beneficial to their students. 97 percent believed that recess promotes health and wellness, 96 percent believed that recess promotes social development, and 77 percent believed that recess promotes students' autonomy or self-direction.[14] As workers, however, teachers are of course beholden to their administrators, facing their own pressures of state law and funding, to reduce students' time for play, compromising their pedagogy while making efforts to integrate aspects of play into the classroom workspace.

For many elementary schools' disciplinary policies, deprivation from play is a frequent form of punishment, integral to the school-to-prison pipeline in the U.S. Deprivation of play is among the earliest forms of

---

12 See Challenge Success, "Kids Under Pressure," 2021, https://challengesuccess.org/wp-content/uploads/2021/02/CS-NBC-Study-Kids-Under-Pressure-PUBLISHED.pdf.
13 Annie Flury, "Pedal Power Boosts N Carolina Pupils' Performance," *BBC News*, September 20, 2016, https://www.bbc.com/news/world-us-canada-37420834.
14 Catherine Ramstetter and Dale Borman Fink, "Ready for Recess?" American Federation of Teachers, accessed January 1, 2022, https://www.aft.org/ae/winter2018-2019/ramstetter_fink.

punishment that Black and Brown students experience in the school system. As many researchers suggest, this has not only led to a sense of inevitable criminality among youth most vulnerable to racial discrimination, but to an upturn in mental health struggles. In recent years, the largest surge in emergency psychiatric visits to the hospital occurred in the adolescent group, with a 53 percent increase among Black youth and 91 percent increase among Latino youth.[15]

In her recent book *Educational Trauma*, psychologist Lee-Anne Gray argues that the withholding of play constitutes an Adverse Childhood Experience (ACE), causing "traumatic stress to developing children" with long-term impacts, and also leading to the mis-diagnosis of learning disabilities and other forms of unnecessary pathologization.[16] This restriction of play, as Ann Arnett Ferguson has argued, is part of a broader, white supremacist process of disciplining Black masculinity as "bad boys" in the educational system. "School rules govern and regulate children's bodily, linguistic, and emotional expression," Ferguson explains, "They are an essential element of the sorting and ranking technologies of an educational system that is organized around the search for and establishment of a ranked difference among children."[17] The "zero tolerance" policies deployed by many underfunded public schools tend to punish non-white children at a much higher rate. Consequently, students who are suspended or expelled are less likely to complete high school, while becoming more than twice as likely to be arrested during forced leave from school.[18]

While classrooms are managed as work sites, systemically integrated into the prison industrial complex, the traditional workplace has undergone significant transformations over the last decade as well. As architect Florian Idenburg declares, "the office is no more": "We work anywhere, anytime. We don't even think we are working . . . work is everywhere

15   Luther G. Kalb et al., "Trends in Psychiatric Emergency Department Visits Among Youth and Young Adults in the US," *Pediatrics* 143, no. 4 (April 1, 2019), https://doi.org/10.1542/peds.2018-2192.

16   Lee-Anne Gray, *Educational Trauma: Examples from Testing to the School-to-Prison Pipeline* (Palgrave Macmillan, 2019), 78.

17   Ann Arnett Ferguson, *Bad Boys: Public Schools in the Making of Black Masculinity* (Ann Arbor: University of Michigan Press, 2001), 49–50.

18   Cheryl Healy, "Discipline and Punishment: How School Suspensions Impact the Likelihood of Juvenile Arrest," *Chicago Policy Review*, March 26, 2014, https://chicagopolicyreview.org/2014/03/26/discipline-and-punishment-how-school-suspensions-impact-the-likelihood-of-juvenile-arrest/.

but in the traditional office."[19] This new conception of the office space has involved "the increasing integration of informality, pleasure, and even play—notions often seen as the antithesis of work," architect and scholar Jeannette Kuo elaborates.[20] Silicon Valley has become emblematic of this regime of *playbour*, reinventing the workplace into an adult playground, with new ways of heightening and capturing worker productivity. These tech campuses have come to represent a "workplace utopia," as journalist Jade Chang suggests in her account of the Googleplex, where "the impulse is both beautiful and endlessly arrogant, an adolescent's willful dream."[21] The company headquarters are like Tom Hanks's apartment in *Big* turned into a more than 2 million square foot office complex, filled with toys, games, cafeterias, and colorful hang-out spaces. Part of what this has facilitated, as many workers attest, is an obliteration of the workday. Instead, there are more ways to stay at work, and not go home—everything from meal preparation to haircuts, all available in their office turned luxury cruise ship.

In this era of playbour offices and classroom workspaces, the idea of play is a point of intersection between the utopian, dystopian, and anti-utopian. Play is utopian in the sense that its absence is dystopian; but it is also anti-utopian in the sense that it is the false promise of more and more work. Moreover, play is at once the possibility, impossibility, and contradiction at stake in antiwork comedy. Play makes work into a *problem*—and it is as a problem that play demands utopian methods.

While more and more of comedy, just like everything else, has become unimaginable outside this problem of work, the possibility and desire to play are ever more crucial to how we might conceptualize, with the hope of enacting, an anticapitalist life. We are all caught in the same web. Instead of looking for straightforward examples of anticapitalist life, that is, we have to look for openings, ruptures, departures, and sites of utopian longing. With play as its possibility, whether or not fulfilled, comedy can generate such longings and dreaming, breaking apart the world and unraveling its miseries, helping us to un-imagine as part of the process of re-imagining.

---

19   Florian Idenburg, "The Office Is No More," in *A-Typical Plan: Projects and Essays on Identity, Flexibility, and Atmosphere in the Office Building*, ed. Jeannette Kuo (Zürich: Park Books, 2013), 117.
20   Jeannette Kuo, "Introduction," in *A-Typical Plan: Projects and Essays on Identity, Flexibility, and Atmosphere in the Office Building*, 19.
21   Jade Chang, "Behind the Glass Curtain: The Design Process for Google's New HQ," *Metropolis*, accessed January 1, 2022, https://metropolismag.com/projects/behind-the-glass-curtain-design-process-google-hq/.

II. Sleep

Far more than play, sleep is by now the closest approximation we have of anticapitalist activity in our daily lives. It is the last of what Marx called the "natural barriers" to capitalist totality. "Sleep is an uncompromising interruption of the theft of time from us by capitalism," as Jonathan Crary suggests: "Sleep is an irrational and intolerable affirmation that there might be limits to the compatibility of living beings with the allegedly irresistible forces of modernization."[22] The outmoding of sleep is the horizon of what Crary defines as "24/7 capitalism," colonizing the planet as a "non-stop work site or an always open shopping mall of infinite choices, tasks, selections, and digressions," for which sleeplessness is the state of "producing, consuming, and discarding [without] pause, hastening the exhaustion of life and the depletion of resources."[23] The pharmaceutical industry, the energy drink industry, the demands of "remote, asynchronous" work-life all point to this insomniac future of ceaseless production and consumption. In this world "work" no longer seems to exist, precisely because it has become everything. As Crary contends, looking toward such a future that is by now mostly already here, "the imaginings of a future without capitalism begin as dreams of sleep."[24]

The Nap Ministry was founded in 2016 by performance artist Tricia Hersey, with the sloganry "REST IS RESISTANCE." With strong influences of afrofuturism and Black liberation theology, the organization hosts workshops, lectures, and curates performance art and installations, such as collective naps and nap experiences. As Hersey explains in The Nap Ministry's mission statement:

> This work is a social justice movement and we have never
> identified ourselves as being a part of the wellness industry.
> We are deeply committed to dismantling white suprem-
> acy and capitalism by using rest as the foundation for this
> disruption ... I began experimenting with these ideals as a
> way to connect with my Ancestors, to receive a Word from
> them and to honor my body via rest for the rest they never

---

22 Jonathan Crary, *24/7: Late Capitalism and the Ends of Sleep* (London: Verso, 2014), 10–13.
23 Crary, *24/7*, 17.
24 Crary, *24/7*, 128.

were able to embody due to slavery and capitalism. This is about more than naps.[25]

Distancing this project from the wellness / self-care industry, The Nap Ministry also consistently disallows any fantasies of autonomy. Instead, quite powerfully, the emphasis is on refusal. In their conception of napping, The Nap Ministry provides a framework for antiwork dreaming. Their Instagram page is filled with ongoing attempts to articulate this framework. "Been seeing this narrative online of naps and rest being the new 'hustle,'" one post reads. "Ask yourself why you refuse to reject the idea of hustling. It needs to die too. We are not hustling. We are not grinding. We are not rushing."[26] "DIVEST FROM CAPITALISM," another reads, "LAY YO ASS DOWN."[27] And another: "We don't want a seat at the table. F#$k the table. The table is full of oppressors. We want a blanket and pillow down by the ocean. We want to rest."[28]

This dream of rest has been a key element of *The Amber Ruffin Show* since it began in September 2020. At the end of every half-hour episode, Ruffin closes with a new lullaby for her devoted audience. Sitting on top of her desk, she starts by explaining, "If you're like me you're up way past your bedtime, so here's a little lullaby to help get you to sleep tonight." "You were great today, you were a star today, you had a bunch of great ideas that you thought of alone," she sings, "and while you sleep tonight, you can rest assured, a man is passing those ideas off as his own."[29]

When Ruffin began her show, in a year of uprisings against police violence and racial injustice, she was the only Black woman hosting in late-night comedy, still almost entirely a world of white men (and multiple Jimmies). But as she jokes, hers is the "only late night show hosted by an adult woman who owns a My Little Pony."[30] While she might have taken a seat at this table, so to speak, she took the opportunity to reimagine the late-night talk show through a comedy of collective rest, shared exhaustion, and mutual care. Fully disinterested in the formula of monologues and celebrity interviews, Ruffin devised a format that's more like *The Carol Burnett Show* meets *The Chappelle Show*, a musical and sketch variety show with a social justice and anti-racist spin, which

---

25 Tricia Hersey, "About," *The Nap Ministry*, n.d., https://thenapministry.wordpress.com/.

26 @thenapministry, "Been Seeing This Narrative," *Instagram*, May 3, 2021.

27 @thenapministry, "LAY YO ASS DOWN," *Instagram*, February 12, 2021.

28 @thenapministry, "We Don't Want a Seat at the Table," *Instagram*, October 12, 2020.

29 "1.6," *The Amber Ruffin Show* (Peacock, November 6, 2020).

30 "1.35," *The Amber Ruffin Show* (Peacock, September 17, 2021).

she co-hosts with her close friend and performer Tarik Davis. In each episode, Ruffin tackles different aspects of systemic racism, ranging from standardized tests to credit scores and critical race theory, with anti-police segments like "Copaganda." In one episode, she makes a hilarious case for "White History Month," a time when we pick apart all the lies of white supremacy. As she explains the history of The United Daughters of the Confederacy, she tells her audience, "now you have to learn the real version from a fucking comedy show!"[31] Picking apart lies, through comedy, is a source of relief and even comfort in Ruffin's show, which often drifts away from punchline-driven humor, into a more ambient joy of collective rest and shared recognition.

In her lullabies and throughout her comedy, Ruffin plays at the boundaries of a killjoy ethics. "It's Ok to feel sad, it's Ok to feel blue, to just sit and stare at the walls," she sings, "And if a man on the street tells you to smile, it's Ok to kick him in the balls."[32] In another, she sings, "I hope you know you're special, I hope you know you're great, I hope you know that credit scores only exist in the United States."[33] Others lullabies are just silly—"Don't stress tonight, just lay back and sleep, don't let worry invade your dreams, and whatever you do, make sure that you never bend over while wearing low-rise jeans"[34]—but silly with the purpose of getting to relax. Rather than creating a dream world of escape, her joking lullabies take vengeance on the waking world through rest, play, and laughter.

"Napping wakes you up," The Nap Ministry insists, just as laughter can snap you out of a trance, if only for long enough to ask some questions. This joking exposes what is already a joke: that a sleepless world of non-stop work is a world that can never be truly awake. It is a world of insentience, knocked out and lifeless.

In the dystopia of 24/7 capitalism, antiwork comedy is instrumental to this anticapitalist dreaming. Comedy is not the purpose, but a mode of refusal—armoring our dreams against the nightmares.

III. Blob

One of my dearest friends used to come over for dinner on Friday nights. He'd usually be the one to cook, and I'd usually be the one to do the

---

31 "1.15," *The Amber Ruffin Show* (Peacock, February 5, 2021).

32 "1.26," *The Amber Ruffin Show* (Peacock, May 14, 2021).

33 "1.3," *The Amber Ruffin Show* (Peacock, October 9, 2020).

34 "2.6," *The Amber Ruffin Show* (Peacock, November 19, 2021).

dishes. Our dogs would play in the backyard, and my kid would sit on a kitchen stool beside him, or take a bath in the adjacent bathroom. It was a nice routine. Our other routine was going to the beach, all together, on Tuesday mornings. One Friday, we laughed together over dinner, and after putting my kid to bed, we sat outside. It was a warm night in early spring, with a big moon hanging over us. Perhaps I felt hopeful, but my friend seemed particularly grim as we began talking about the future. We were both trying to finish our dissertations, running out of time with university funding, struggling to imagine what might come next. He could see it clearly enough: an academic job market in which the prospects of tenure track security were running dry, of more and more adjunct positions with scarce benefits and short-term contracts, of endless applications and interviews if we were lucky. But that didn't seem so lucky after all. We commiserated and I probably made a pathetic attempt at emotionally problem-solving what was far beyond either of our reach. I remember putting my head on his shoulder, and how I wondered if I should give him a longer hug before he left. That next Tuesday, we didn't go to the beach, as he had killed himself on Monday night.

Chris's death was absolutely devastating to everyone who knew him—he was loved by many, hated by others, but such a vibrant, utopian thinker. He spent much of his time inhabiting an intellectual project that became psychologically exhausting, often putting him into contact with revolutionary desires that were so strong that they overwhelmed him, as he lived in a studio often going days without the company of anyone but his dog. It is painful work to continue insisting that a life against capitalism—or even, a life *after* capitalism—might be ours. For some it is too painful. How quickly the utopian bends toward dystopia. I've met few people as brilliant, and I can still hear his laugh—as any of his friends would. I can still see his Cheshire cat smile.

In my family and among friends, I had been this close and closer to suicide a few times before. Chris's death brought back all those deaths, and the complicated ways in which I had and hadn't fully grieved them. His death reminded me of my friend Alex, who killed himself a few months after we graduated from college. It was 2007, and he had just been released into the "adult" world under a pile of seemingly insurmountable student debt. In the years to come, deaths like this were happening everywhere, all the time. As the financial crisis would go on to obliterate so much that had been cast in the future, suicide rates spiked. While suicide rates were already steadily rising, the crisis years saw a dramatic increase—between 2008–2010, the suicide rate in the

U.S. grew four times faster than it did in the eight years leading up to the crisis.[35]

What made Chris's suicide so much more challenging for me to grieve than Alex's, or even that of my stepfather, was the experience of parenting through it. For a long time, it felt hopeless for me to keep in character, as a caretaker, as I was often fighting back tears and finding myself flooded with memories. What I wanted to do was crawl into bed and never get out. I wanted my time to be mine, so that I could heal from all this pain. But every morning I woke up to a three-and-a-half-year-old, needing me to be there. I had to build up emotional armor to get through the days. It took months before the crying spells and flashes of sadness and self-blame and anger slowed down, and life started to feel a bit more bearable. I began running in the woods with my dog, and almost every night, I would watch comedies.

One of my favorite comedies at the time (and for that matter, of all time) was Maria Bamford's 2012 special, *The Special Special Special!*, which I watched with a few of my friends on a regular basis. *The Special Special Special!* marked Bamford's first hour of material after an eighteen-month period of three hospitalizations in different psychiatric wards in Los Angeles.[36] The special was filmed in her house for an audience of two, her parents, almost a decade before COVID-19 would make these kinds of experiments much more commonplace. Throughout the special, Bamford pauses to serve her parents and the crew burnt cookies "fresh from the oven," administer her dog's eye medication, offer a pee break to her dad, answer the door for a pizza delivery, and go out to the breaker system when the lights go out; and she moves between recollections of her time in the psych ward, descriptions of her everyday experiences of anxiety, and her struggles with ongoing suicideation.

"If you stay alive for no reason at all, please, do it for spite," Bamford jokes. "People don't talk about mental illness the way they do about other illnesses," she explains, shifting into her Karen voice—a wealthy judgmental white woman who dips in and out of most routines— "*apparently Steve has cancer. It's like 'fuck off, we all have cancer, right?' I have cancer pretty bad right now but I go to chemotherapy, I get it taken care*

35 Benedict Carey, "Increase Seen in U.S. Suicide Rate Since Recession," *The New York Times*, November 5, 2012, https://www.nytimes.com/2012/11/05/health/us-suicide-rate-rose-during-recession-study-finds.html.

36 Sara Corbett, "The Weird, Scary and Ingenious Brain of Maria Bamford," *The New York Times*, July 17, 2014, https://www.nytimes.com/2014/07/20/magazine/the-weird-scary-and-ingenious-brain-of-maria-bamford.html.

of, I get back to work."[37] Then she pivots into the deep voice of a southern man:

> ...yeah I was dating this chick. All this time apparently, she let me know she's been wearing contact lenses. I said wow, you know, do what you need to do but I don't believe in all that western medicine shit. You know if you want to see like other people, it's all about attitude, you've gotta want it.

Much of Bamford's comedy targets these tropes of mental health stigmatization, and specifically, perceptions of mental health struggles as simply a matter of poor work ethic or lack of ambition. While reducing mental illness to something you just have to work harder to overcome, this perception also erases the never-ending work, often unseen if not hidden, that so many of us in this world have grown accustomed to as a matter of everyday survival.

Always speaking to her audience as fellow crazies and weirdos, Bamford offers practical (and funny) tips for how to get through the day, as in a "homeopathic remedy for depression, if you're ever feeling terrible and you don't have insurance," which she describes with step-by-step instructions: "Here's what you do. You take a blue or a black pen, you draw a rabbit's face atop your own face, make some rabbit ears out of paper plates, cotton balls—I don't know what you have," she explains, and then "You make some fudge, which is very easy to make from what I have read, you go out on your front porch, you open up your window, and you start yelling at people." She recommends saying "*hi, how you doin'? want some . . . fudge?*" because "it gets you out and about in your community and it shows everyone that you need help." What's remarkable about moments like this is how Bamford engages with comedy itself as a part of her mental health treatment. More than that, she conceives of comedy as a way to get out of the ideology of work which promises sanity, happiness, and fulfillment through more and more work. Hers is a comedy staunchly against work—it is a comedy of survival.

The first time I saw Bamford perform it was the summer of 2016, a little over a year after Chris's death, and a few months after I filed my dissertation. I was still a mess with grief and entering a whole new kind of turmoil, post-graduate school. When I found out that Bamford was

---

37   The special was originally a Chill production, later released on Netflix. See Jordan Brady, *Maria Bamford: The Special Special Special!*, stand-up special (Netflix, 2014).

going on tour, I got tickets for myself and two close friends. We'd all been through a lot in that time, and we all loved Bamford. It was something I looked forward to for months. Much of the show was material we hadn't heard before, more about mental health struggles. At some point in the show, I remember she talked about how healing feels better than hopelessness, and that while the laughter continued, I reached over to my friend and realized that she was crying. We held hands. I began to cry too. And we also kept laughing.

After the show, Bamford stayed for well over an hour in the theater lobby, speaking to fans one by one, as they waited in line to meet her. Standing in that line with my friends, I was struck by the way her comedy had brought this group of people together, in this dingy community theater in Campbell, California where I imagined decades of productions of *A Christmas Carol* and *The Nutcracker* had transpired. There were teenagers, elderly, people wearing anything from pajamas to expensive ensembles, people smelling like weed and BO and people smelling like perfume. As we got closer to Bamford in the line, I began eavesdropping on her interactions with fans. When one woman opened her arms for a hug and told Bamford, "you saved my life," I wondered how many others in the line she was speaking for.

I felt this energy again the next time I saw Bamford perform, long before she walked on stage. The crowd was similarly varied, but this time it was even more clearly a gathering of the weirdos who'd survived. Perhaps the feeling was so pronounced just because I expected it. By the end of the show, I had a name for this feeling—blob.

"This is the scariest part of the show," Bamford tells her audience, as she conducts this strange experiment as the closer for her 2017 special *Old Baby*. "This is more one-woman show territory . . . apologies, apologies," she mutters. "I'm trying to believe in something. You know something more, more bigger, than myself. And I just can't, I can't think of anything. But then I remembered there was this game we used to play when we were kids, and it's called One Big Blob . . . I'm it, you run away from me frightened, afraid. I begin running after you while chanting 'One Big Blob. One Big Blob. One Big Blob.'" Eventually, the blob "[ends up] catching one of you, and it's going to be you," she says, reaching out for the hand of someone in her audience, telling them quite sweetly, "I got you, come on!" The person laughs as they hold hands, and she continues: "And now we both have to begin chanting. 'One Big Blob. One Big Blob!' And now you catch the person next to you. 'One Big Blob!' And then we start catching each other . . . 'One Big Blob! One Big

Blob!'"[38] As Bamford chants this into the microphone, members of the audience slowly come together, grasping hands, and joining in the chant. Bamford keeps telling them, "I'm going to wait!" and "I know it's weird! You can do it!" as she hangs on until everyone has become part of the blob—at which point she tells them, "This is great. Isn't it uncomfortable to be in the blob? It's so awful, your hands are sweaty, but you have to do it and we have to stay together . . . and everyone must let themselves be caught because otherwise the game will never end and it is a *shit* game." Everyone laughs, still holding hands, looking at each other. "Anyways, if we could just blob it, on a few things, I could hang a religion on that," she explains, before letting go of the blob.

After the show, I tried to describe what it was like to be in the blob to several people, always feeling myself short of words, never quite getting at the thing. The blob stayed with me, though. It kept coming back. It felt awkward, and sweaty, but also warm, soft, and even caring.

The blob returned to me with intensity in April 2021, when I most recently saw Bamford perform. This time it was from my kitchen, under lockdown, and I was unsure of what I was in for. The show was not just a show, it was what Bamford had been promoting as a "slumber party." The night began with material from guest comedians, and then Bamford took the stage of a desk in her living room and performed about an hour of material. Like the other remote comedy performances I'd attended during the pandemic, this one felt stilted and at times uncomfortable. But Bamford has always put the awkward up front, and somehow seemed more at ease than during the live shows I'd attended. After delivering her set, she stayed briefly to answer some questions from the audience, and then promised everyone that she would be back to answer more questions at 6AM. She turned the camera to a pull-out sofa, arranged with dozens of stuffed animals, and she got under the blankets and spent some time reading. Then she went to sleep for about seven hours. At this point my partner went to bed, and I stayed up. In the chat room people were sharing their stories, telling each other about what their lives were like during COVID-19. Quite a lot of people lived alone, or for other reasons, experienced loneliness. When Bamford woke up the next morning, she opened up a Diet Coke, took her medications, and ate a spoonful of peanut butter. She spent a little time with those of us who were awake, whether because we had stayed up all night with each other, or like me, set at alarm for 5:55 to catch her goodbye. We laughed a bit more and

---

38 Jessica Yu, *Maria Bamford: Old Baby*, stand-up special (Netflix, 2017).

then she left, and so did everyone else.

If we could just blob it, I keep thinking . . .

A Laugh Beyond Work

When we laugh we come together as blob. Laughter, as we all know, is contagious. We know this intuitively, but it's also scientifically proven. Statistically we are far more likely to laugh around others, though of course some of us—the lucky of us, certainly—can laugh on our own too.[39] "When we laugh with people we are hardly ever actually laughing at jokes," cognitive neuroscientist (and stand-up comedian) Sophie Scott explains, but communicating with each other.[40] Laughter is a behavioral phenomenon, something which we primarily do with our friends. Being a blob, then, is about feeling this sense of belonging together, of friendship established by laughter. At the same time, laughter can be a mode of exclusion. Laughing on one's own is sometimes perceived as a sign of insanity, while psychopaths are supposedly immune to laughter. We don't just laugh together, but at each other. For the same reasons that laughter can be revolutionary, it can be fascistic as well. Laughter can be healing, it can be harmful, it can be so many things depending on how it's put into practice.

For these reasons there are countless managerial philosophies based on humor in the workplace, in which promoting laughter also promotes productivity, collaboration, and team morale. Cultivating humor in the workplace is framed as a method of disciplining workers, keeping them focused and managing their attention, as well as investing them in the workplace and aspiring to greater collective productivity. Likewise, each year there are more and more self-help books that theorize humor and laughter as crucial tools for careerism. Making people laugh is packaged as a networking and interpersonal skill, integral to all forms of success in life, ranging from business to parenting. Implicitly, laughter is envisioned as a means of controlling people—for instance, a way "to meet and attract high-quality women," as Andrew Ferebee promises in *The Dating Playbook For Men*,[41] one of so many

---

39 Andrew Anthony, "Sophie Scott: 'Laughter Works as a Behaviourally Contagious Phenomenon,'" *The Guardian*, December 24, 2017, https://www.theguardian.com/science/2017/dec/24/sophie-scott-agenda-q-and-a-royal-institution-christmas-lectures-neuroscience-standup.

40 Sophie Scott, "Why Is Laughter Contagious?," *NPR*, March 4, 2016, https://www.npr.org/2016/03/04/468877928/why-is-laughter-contagious.

41 Andrew Ferebee, *The Dating Playbook For Men: A Proven 7 Step System To Go From Single To The Woman Of Your Dreams* (Andrew Ferebee, 2015), 137.

poaching manuals of this sort. Ferebee's ideal reader is the incel "Men's Rights Activist," fuming with misogynist rage, preoccupied with fantasies of domination.

The laughter of crowds in Trump rallies continues to strike horror in our dystopian times, now years after the jokester-in-chief lost the election in 2020. In his time Trump has been described as the most successful stand-up comedian ever,[42] and the first stand-up president—in Trevor Noah's version of the joke, *The Daily Show* host explains "He goes out, he practices his jokes, he works on his material. You can see him trying it out! . . . He's like 'Who's going to pay? Mexico?' And the crowd sort of says, 'Yeah, yeah, new joke, we get it.'"[43] Like Mussolini, Trump cultivated his political persona through joking behavior and comic asides. He laughs strategically, as a sign of power. In turn, he invokes laughter, whether in agreement or out of disgust, to maintain power. Hatred fuels this laughter. His comedy preys on fury and perpetuates it.

But there are so many ways to laugh, and so many kinds of laughter. Laughing together, at and against capitalism, we not only find ways to survive, but come to understand, with each other, what it means to be a blob. Walter Benjamin claimed that "there is no better trigger for thinking than laughter . . . thought usually has a better chance when one is shaken by laughter than when one's mind is shaken and upset."[44] For Benjamin, laughter is at once catalyst and "shattered articulation,"[45] a jolt of energy or a flight of images through shock, and the most revolutionary emotion of the masses.[46] Laughter comes in waves, rippling through us, and disarticulating the world as both a "preemptive and healing outbreak of mass psychosis."[47]

42   See Scott Adams, "#BidenRiots, Vitamin D Saves the World, Celebrities Attack Me, UnAmerican Airlines, Polls," *Real Coffee with Scott Adams*, n.d., https://podcasts.apple.com/us/podcast/real-coffee-with-scott-adams/id1494763610.

43   Jay Willis, "Trevor Noah: Here's Why Donald Trump Is Like a Stand-Up Comic—or a Penis-Shaped Asteroid," *GQ*, September 7, 2017, https://www.gq.com/story/trevor-noah-donald-trump-stand-up-comic.

44   Walter Benjamin, *Selected Writings: 1927–1934*, vol. 2 (Cambridge: Belknap Press of Harvard University Press, 1996), 779.

45   Walter Benjamin, *The Arcades Project*, ed. Howard Eiland and Kevin MacLaughlin (Cambridge: Belknap Press of Harvard University Press, 2002), 325.

46   Walter Benjamin, "Chaplin in Retrospect," in *The Work of Art in the Age of Its Technological Reproducibility, and Other Writings on Media*, ed. Michael W. Jennings, Brigid Doherty, and Thomas Y. Levin, trans. Edmund Jephcott, Rodney Livingstone, Howard Eiland and Others (Cambridge: Belknap Press of Harvard University Press, 2008), 337.

47   Benjamin, "The Work of Art in the Age of Its Technological Reproducibility, Second Version," in *The Work of Art in the Age of Its Technological Reproducibility, and Other Writings on Media*, 39.

In laughter, if only we might try for it, we share "an affective state [with] the potential to open up the subject by temporarily dissolving its boundaries."[48] This is how Jackie Wang reconceptualizes what Freud called the 'oceanic feeling,' as the "illumination of an already-existing communalism and the direct experience of our embeddedness in the world." Of the political possibilities at stake, Wang asks what it would mean to "socialize (or communize) oceanic feeling? Could the oceanic act as a feeling-in-common that serves as the experiential basis for the co-construction of new worlds?" This oceanic feeling "has the capacity to denaturalize the individual and undo the fiction of the bounded subject," as Wang suggests, just as we might feel, through laughter, this communist horizon as well.

When we laugh with each other, we plunge into these possibilities.

---

48   Jackie Wang, "Oceanic Feeling and Communist Affect of Contemporary Art," RIGA International Biennial, accessed January 1, 2022, https://www.rigabiennial.com/en/riboca-2/programme/event-dreams-jackie-wang.

BIBLIOGRAPHY

"1.3." *The Amber Ruffin Show*. Peacock, October 9, 2020.

"1.6." *The Amber Ruffin Show*. Peacock, November 6, 2020.

"1.15." *The Amber Ruffin Show*. Peacock, February 5, 2021.

"1.26." *The Amber Ruffin Show*. Peacock, May 14, 2021.

"1.35." *The Amber Ruffin Show*. Peacock, September 17, 2021.

"2.6." *The Amber Ruffin Show*. Peacock, November 19, 2021.

Aaker, Jennifer Lynn, and Naomi Bagdonas. *Humor, Seriously*. New York: Currency, 2020.

Abad-Santos, Alex. "SNL's 2008 'Bitches Get Stuff Done' Sketch Foreshadowed Trump Calling Clinton a 'Nasty Woman.'" *Vox*, October 20, 2016, https://www.vox.com/2016/10/20/13346106/hillary-clinton-nasty-woman.

Abrahams, Daniel. "Winning Over the Audience: Trust and Humor in Stand-Up Comedy." *The Journal of Aesthetics and Art Criticism* 78, no. 4 (2020): 491–500. https://doi.org/10.1111/jaac.12760.

Abrams, Rachel, and Catrin Einhorn. "The Tipping Equation." *The New York Times*, March 11, 2018, https://www.nytimes.com/interactive/2018/03/11/business/tipping-sexual-harassment.html.

Adalian, Josef. "Inside Netflix's Quest to End Scrolling." *Vulture*, April 28, 2021, https://www.vulture.com/article/netflix-play-something-decision-fatigue.html.

Adams, Scott. "#BidenRiots, Vitamin D Saves the World, Celebrities Attack Me, UnAmerican Airlines, Polls." *Real Coffee with Scott Adams*, n.d. https://podcasts.apple.com/us/podcast/real-coffee-with-scott-adams/id1494763610.

Affleck, Casey. *I'm Still Here*. Mockumentary. Netflix, 2010.

Ahmed, Sara. *Living a Feminist Life*. Durham: Duke University Press, 2017.

———. *On Being Included: Racism and Diversity in Institutional Life*. Durham: Duke University Press, 2012.

———. *Willful Subjects*, Durham: Duke University Press, 2014.

Als, Hilton. "A Pryor Love." *The New Yorker*, September 13, 1999. https://www.newyorker.com/magazine/1999/09/13/a-pryor-love.

Alter, Robert. *The Rogue's Progress: Studies in the Picaresque Novel*. Cambridge: Harvard University Press, 1964.

Ando, Victoria, Gordon Claridge, and Ken Clark. "Psychotic Traits in Comedians." *British Journal of Psychiatry* 204, no. 5 (May 2014): 341–45. https://doi.org/10.1192/bjp.bp.113.134569.

Andy Kaufman Performance at the Improv, 1977. https://www.youtube.com/watch?v=fzKbqbjEjEE.

American Foundation for Suicide Prevention. "Suicide Statistics," November 15, 2019. https://afsp.org/suicide-statistics/.

Anthony, Andrew. "Sophie Scott: 'Laughter Works as a Behaviourally Contagious Phenomenon.'" *The Guardian*, December 24, 2017, https://www.theguardian.com/science/2017/dec/24/sophie-scott-agenda-q-and-a-royal-institution-christmas-lectures-neuroscience-standup.

Attardo, Salvatore, ed. *Encyclopedia of Humor Studies*. Thousand Oaks, California: SAGE Publications, 2014.

Auslander, Philip. "Postmodernism and Performance." In *The Cambridge Companion to Postmodernism*, edited by Steven Connor. Cambridge: Cambridge University Press, 2004.

Baccolini, Raffaella, and Tom Moylan. "Introduction: Dystopia and Histories." In *Dark Horizons: Science Fiction and the Dystopian Imagination*, edited by Raffaella Baccolini and Tom Moylan. New York: Routledge, 2003.

Barthes, Roland. *Image, Music, Text*. Translated by Stephen Heath. New York: Hill and Wang, 2009.

———. *The Responsibility of Forms: Critical Essays on Music, Art, and Representation*. Translated by Richard Howard. New York: Hill and Wang, 1985.

Baruch, Elaine. *Women, Love, and Power: Literary and Psychoanalytic Perspectives* New York: NYU Press, 1991.

Bassil-Morozow, Helena Victor. *The Trickster in Contemporary Film*. New York: Routledge, 2012.

Bataille, Georges. *The Unfinished System of Nonknowledge*. Edited by Stuart Kendall. Translated by Michelle Kendall and Stuart Kendall. Minneapolis: University of Minnesota Press, 2001.

Beal, Daniel, and John Trougakos. "Episodic Intrapersonal and Emotional Regulation: Or, Dealing with Life as It Happens." In *Emotional Labor in the 21st Century: Diverse Perspectives on the Psychology of Emotion Regulation at Work*, edited by Alicia Grandey, James M. Diefendorff, and Deborah E. Rupp. New York: Routledge, 2017.

Bell, David. *Rethinking Utopia: Place, Power, Affect*. London: Routledge, 2017.

Bellace, Matt. *A Better High: Laugh, Help, Run, Love ... and Other Ways to Get Naturally High!* Deadwood, OR: Wyatt-MacKenzie Publishing, 2012.

Belle, Dahlia. "Dear Dave Chappelle, Transgender Comedians Can Take a Joke, but Why Are Yours so Unfunny?" *The Guardian*, October 9, 2021, https://www.theguardian.com/stage/2021/oct/09/dave-chappelle-letter-trans-comedian-netflix.

Benjamin, Walter. "Chaplin in Retrospect." In *The Work of Art in the Age of Its Technological Reproducibility, and Other Writings on Media*, edited by Michael W. Jennings, Brigid Doherty, and Thomas Y. Levin, translated by Edmund Jephcott, Rodney Livingstone, Howard Eiland, and Others. Cambridge: Belknap Press of Harvard University Press, 2008..

———. *Illuminations: Essays and Reflections*. Edited by Hannah Arendt. Translated by Harry Zohn. New York: Mariner Books: 2019.

———. *The Arcades Project*. Edited by Howard Eiland and Kevin MacLaughlin. Cambridge: Belknap Press of Harvard University Press, 2002.

———. "The Work of Art in the Age of Its Technological Reproducibility, Second Version." *The Work of Art in the Age of Its Technological Reproducibility, and Other Writings on Media*.

———. *Selected Writings: 1927–1934*. Vol. 2. Cambridge: Belknap Press of Harvard University Press, 1996.

Berg, Heather. *Porn Work: Sex, Labor, and Late Capitalism*. Chapel Hill: The University of North Carolina Press, 2021.

Berlant, Lauren. "Nearly Utopian, Nearly Normal: Post-Fordist Affect in *La Promesse* and *Rosetta*." *Public Culture* 19, no. 2 (May 1, 2007): 273–301. https://doi.org/10.1215/08992363-2006-036.

———. "The Predator and the Jokester." *The New Inquiry*, December 13, 2017. https://thenew-inquiry.com/the-predator-and-the-jokester/.

———. "The Traumic: On BoJack Horseman's 'Good Damage.'" *Post45*, November 22, 2020. https://post45.org/2020/11/the-traumic-on-bojack-horsemans-good-damage/.

Berlant, Lauren, and Sianne Ngai. "Comedy Has Issues." *Critical Inquiry* 43, no. 2 (Winter 2017): 223–49.

Berr, Jonathan. "Amazon Signs Multi-Million Dollar Deal For 'SmartLess' Podcast." *Forbes*, June 30, 2021, https://www.forbes.com/sites/jonathanberr/2021/06/30/amazon-signs-multi-million-dollar-deal-for-smartless-podcast/.

Bey, Marquis. *Them Goon Rules: Fugitive Essays on Radical Black Feminism*. Tucson: The University of Arizona Press, 2019.

Bhattacharya, Tithi. "How Not to Skip Class." In *Social Reproduction Theory: Remapping Class, Recentering Oppression*, edited by Tithi Bhattacharya. London: Pluto Press, 2017.

Bhattarai, Abha. "Side Hustles Are the New Norm. Here's How Much They Really Pay." *Washington Post*, July 3, 2021, https://www.washingtonpost.com/news/business/wp/2017/07/03/side-hustles-are-the-new-norm-heres-how-much-they-really-pay/.

Binder, Mike. "The Comedy Store." Showtime, October 11, 2020. https://www.sho.com/the-comedy-store.

———. "The Comedy Store." Showtime, November 1, 2020. https://www.sho.com/the-comedy-store.

Blitz, Jeffrey. "Stress Relief." *The Office*. NBC, February 1, 2009.

Bolonik, Kera. "Nora Dunn: 'SNL Is a Traumatic Experience. It's Something You Have to Survive.'" *Salon*, April 8, 2015. https://www.salon.com/2015/04/07/nora_dunn_snl_is_a_traumatic_experience_it%e2%80%99s_something_you_have_to_survive/.

Boltanski, Luc, and Eve Chiapello. *The New Spirit of Capitalism*. New York: Verso, 2005.

Bonfiglio, Michael. "Tina Fey." *My Next Guest Needs No Introduction with David Letterman*. Netflix, n.d.

Borden, Lizzie. *Born in Flames*, 1983.

Boyce Davies, Carole. *Left of Karl Marx: The Political Life of Black Communist Claudia Jones*. Durham: Duke University Press, 2007.

Brady, Jordan. *Maria Bamford: The Special Special Special!* Stand-up special. Netflix, 2014.

Breslin, Mark. "Breslin: Why I Brought Louis C.K. Back from the Dead." *The Canadian Jewish News*, November 8, 2019. https://thecjn.ca/arts/breslin-why-i-brought-louis-c-k-back-from-the-dead/.

Brinkmann, Svend. *Diagnostic Cultures: A Cultural Approach to the Pathologization of Modern Life*. New York: Routledge, 2016.

Brooks, Peter. *Reading for the Plot: Design and Intention in Narrative*. Cambridge: Harvard University Press, 1992.

Brouillette, Sarah. "Creative Labor." *Mediations: Journal of the Marxist Literary Group* 24, no. 2 (Spring 2009). https://mediationsjournal.org/articles/creative-labor.

———. *Literature and the Creative Economy*. Stanford: Stanford University Press, 2014.

Brown, Jayna. *Black Utopias: Speculative Life and the Music of Other Worlds*. Durham: Duke University Press, 2021.

Brown, Stephanie. "Open Mic? The Gendered Gatekeeping of Authenticity in Spaces of Live Stand-Up Comedy." *Feminist Media Histories* 6, no. 4 (October 20, 2020): 42–67. https://doi.org/10.1525/fmh.2020.6.4.42.

Brownstein, Ronald. "The Unbearable Summer." *The Atlantic*, August 26, 2021. https://www.theatlantic.com/politics/archive/2021/08/summer-2021-climate-change-records/619887/.

Bruestle, Martin. "Do Not Resuscitate." *The Sopranos*. HBO, January 23, 2000.

Burgis, Ben. *Canceling Comedians While the World Burns*. Ridgefield: Zero Books, 2021.

Butler, Octavia E. *Parable of the Sower*. New York: Seven Stories, 2016.

"Capitalism Seen Doing 'More Harm than Good' in Global Survey." *Reuters*, January 20, 2020, https://www.reuters.com/article/us-davos-meeting-trust-idUSKBN1ZJ0CW.

Carey, Benedict. "Increase Seen in U.S. Suicide Rate Since Recession." *The New York Times*, November 5, 2012, https://www.nytimes.com/2012/11/05/health/us-suicide-rate-rose-during-recession-study-finds.html.

Carpio, Glenda. *Laughing Fit to Kill: Black Humor in the Fictions of Slavery*. Oxford: Oxford University Press, 2008.

Challenge Success. "Kids Under Pressure," 2021. https://challengesuccess.org/wp-content/uploads/2021/02/CS-NBC-Study-Kids-Under-Pressure-PUBLISHED.pdf.

Chang, Jade. "Behind the Glass Curtain: The Design Process for Google's New HQ." *Metropolis*. Accessed January 1, 2022. https://metropolismag.com/projects/behind-the-glass-curtain-design-process-google-hq/.

Charger, Jesse. "Negging Women—10 Awesome Negs That Work." *Seduction Science*, 2010. https://www.seductionscience.com/2010/negging-women/.

Cheng, William. "Taking Back the Laugh: Comedic Alibis, Funny Fails." *Critical Inquiry* 43, no. 2 (Winter 2017): 528–49.

Chibbaro Jr, Lou. "Meet the Legendary Queer Comedian 'Moms' Mabley." *LGBTQ Nation*, August 8, 2017. https://www.lgbtqnation.com/2017/08/meet-legendary-queer-comedian-moms-mabley/.

Child, Ben. "Casey Affleck Settles Sexual Harassment Lawsuits." *The Guardian*, September 15, 2010, https://www.theguardian.com/film/2010/sep/15/casey-affleck-settles-harassment-lawsuits.

"Children and Teens: Statistics" RAINN. Accessed January 1, 2022. https://www.rainn.org/statistics/children-and-teens.

Cixous, Hélène. "The Laugh of the Medusa." Translated by Keith Cohen and Paula Cohen. *Signs: Journal of Women in Culture and Society* 1, no. 4 (July 1, 1976): 875–93.

C.K., Louis. *Louis C.K. 2017*. Stand-up special. Netflix, 2017.

———. *Louis C.K.: Live at the Comedy Store*. Stand-up special. Netflix, 2015.

Cobb, Jelani. *The Devil & Dave Chappelle & Other Essays*. New York: Thunder's Mouth Press, 2007.

Cook, Dane. "If You Journey through This Life Easily Offended by Other Peoples Words I Think It's Best for Everyone If You Just Kill Yourself." *Twitter*, July 11, 2012. https://twitter.com/danecook/status/223115169394470912.

Corbett, Sara. "The Weird, Scary and Ingenious Brain of Maria Bamford." *The New York Times Magazine*, July 17, 2014, https://www.nytimes.com/2014/07/20/magazine/the-weird-scary-and-ingenious-brain-of-maria-bamford.html.

Cornejo Villavicencio, Karla. *The Undocumented Americans*. New York: One World, 2020.

———. "For the Child of Immigrants, the American Dream Can Be a Nightmare." *Vogue*, April 17, 2018, https://www.vogue.com/article/child-of-immigrants-daca-personal-essay.

Corry, Rebecca. "Louis C.K. Put Me in a Lose-Lose Situation." *Vulture*, May 24, 2018. https://www.vulture.com/2018/05/louis-c-k-put-me-in-a-lose-lose-situation.html.

———. "To Be Real Clear ..." Tweet. *Twitter*, October 22, 2018. https://twitter.com/HippoloverCorry/status/1054471083967959040.

Couch, Aaron. "Civil Rights Group to Lorne Michaels: Why Doesn't 'SNL' Cast Black Women?" *The Hollywood Reporter*, November 1, 2013. https://www.hollywoodreporter.com/tv/tv-news/snl-lorne-michaels-asked-by-652441/.

Coulter, Allen. "The Test Dream." *The Sopranos*. HBO, May 16, 2004.

Crary, Jonathan. *24/7: Late Capitalism and the Ends of Sleep*. London: Verso, 2014.

Crawley, Joanna. "The Crown Had More Viewers in Its First Week than Royal Wedding." *Mail Online*, November 26, 2020. https://www.dailymail.co.uk/tvshowbiz/article-8989331/The-Crown-series-four-viewers-week-Charles-Dianas-real-wedding.html.

Critchley, Simon. *On Humour*. New York: Routledge, 2002.

Crouse, Lindsay. "Why I Stopped Running During the Pandemic (and How I Started Again)." *The New York Times*, March 7, 2021, https://www.nytimes.com/2021/03/07/opinion/pandemic-wall-fitness-running.html.

Cummings, Whitney. "Bonus: Whitney's Therapist." Good For You, n.d. https://goodforyouwhitney.libsyn.com/bonus-whitneys-therapist-0.

Dalla Costa, Mariarosa, Harry Cleaver, and Camille Barbagallo. *Women and the Subversion of the Community: A Mariarosa Dalla Costa Reader*. Oakland: PM, Press, 2019.

Dance, Daryl Cumber, ed. *Honey, Hush!: An Anthology of African American Women's Humor*. New York: W.W. Norton, 1998.

Das, Lina. "I Felt Raped by Brando." *Mail Online*. Accessed December 31, 2021. https://www.dailymail.co.uk/tvshowbiz/article-469646/I-felt-raped-Brando.html.

Davidson, Donald. *Plato's Philebus*. London: Routledge, 2013.

Davis, Angela Y. *Women, Race & Class*. New York: Vintage Books, 1983.

De'Ath, Amy. "Reproduction." In *Bloomsbury Companion to Marx*, edited by Andrew Pendakis, Jeff Diamanti, and Imre Szeman. London: Bloomsbury Academic, 2021.

Dederer, Claire. "What Do We Do with the Art of Monstrous Men?" *The Paris Review*, November 20, 2017. https://www.theparisreview.org/blog/2017/11/20/art-monstrous-men/.

Derrida, Jacques. *Dissemination*. Translated by Barbara Johnson. Chicago: University of Chicago Press, 1993.

DeVega, Chauncey. "'Joker': A Harsh Indictment of Neoliberalism and Gangster Capitalism." *Salon*, October 9, 2019. https://www.salon.com/2019/10/09/joker-todd-phillips-indictment-neoliberalism-violence/.

Diamond, Jeremy. "Trump Says It's 'a Very Scary Time for Young Men in America,'" *CNN*, October 2, 2018. https://www.cnn.com/2018/10/02/politics/trump-scary-time-for-young-men-metoo/index.html.

Dowling, Emma. *The Care Crisis: What Caused It and How Can We End It?* New York: Verso, 2021.

Doyle, Andrew. "Ricky Gervais: Why I'll Never Apologise for My Jokes," *The Spectator*, Accessed January 1, 2022. https://www.spectator.co.uk/article/ricky-gervais-why-i-ll-never-apologise-for-my-jokes.

Dykstra, Chloe. "Rose-Colored Glasses: A Confession." *Medium*, July 7, 2018. https://medium. com/@skydart/rose-colored-glasses-6be0594970ca.

Eagleton, Terry. *The Illusions of Postmodernism*. Oxford: Blackwell Publishers, 1997.

Edgerton, Gary R. *The Columbia History of American Television*. New York: Columbia University Press, 2007.

Ehrenreich, Barbara, and Deirdre English. *Witches, Midwives, and Nurses: A History of Women Healers*. 2nd ed. New York: Feminist Press, 2010.

Enelow, Shonni. *Method Acting and Its Discontents: On American Psycho-Drama*. Evanston, Illinois: Northwestern University Press, 2015.

Engler, Michael. "Rosemary's Baby." *30 Rock*. NBC, October 25, 2007.

Esposito, Cameron. *Rape Jokes*. Stand-up special, 2018. www.cameronesposito.com.

———. Queery, n.d. https://www.earwolf.com/show/queery/.

The Trevor Project. "Estimate of How Often LGBTQ Youth Attempt Suicide in the U.S." Accessed January 1, 2022. https://www.thetrevorproject.org/research-briefs/ estimate-of-how-often-lgbtq-youth-attempt-suicide-in-the-u-s/.

Federici, Silvia. *Revolution at Point Zero: Housework, Reproduction, and Feminist Struggle*. Oakland: PM Press / Common Notions / Autonomedia, 2012.

Federici, Silvia, and Nicole Cox. "Counterplanning from the Kitchen." In *Revolution at Point Zero: Housework, Reproduction, and Feminist Struggle*, 28–40.

Ferebee, Andrew. *The Dating Playbook For Men: A Proven 7 Step System To Go From Single To The Woman Of Your Dreams*. Andrew Ferebee, 2015.

Ferguson, Ann Arnett. *Bad Boys: Public Schools in the Making of Black Masculinity*. Ann Arbor: University of Michigan Press, 2001.

Fey, Tina. *Bossypants*. New York: Back Bay Books/Little, Brown, 2012.

Fieg, Paul. "Goodbye, Michael." *The Office*. NBC, April 28, 2011.

Fisher, Mark. *Capitalist Realism: Is There No Alternative?* Winchester: Zero Books, 2009.

Flaherty, Colleen. "A Non-Tenure-Track Profession?" *Inside Higher Ed*, October 12, 2018. https://www.insidehighered.com/news/2018/10/12/ about-three-quarters-all-faculty-positions-are-tenure-track-according-new-aaup.

———. "Barely Getting By." *Inside Higher Ed*, April 20, 2020. https://www.insidehighered.com/news/2020/04/20/ new-report-says-many-adjuncts-make-less-3500-course-and-25000-year.

Flury, Annie. "Pedal Power Boosts N Carolina Pupils' Performance." *BBC News*, September 20, 2016, https://www.bbc.com/news/world-us-canada-37420834.

Foote, Stephanie. "No Closure." *Post45*, November 23, 2020. https://post45.org/2020/11/ no-closure/.

Fortunati, Leopoldina. *The Arcane of Reproduction: Housework, Prostitution, Labor and Capital*. Edited by Jim Fleming. Brooklyn: Autonomedia, 1995.

Foucault, Michel. *Madness: The Invention of an Idea*. New York: Harper & Row, 1954.

Fox, Jesse David. "How the Internet and a New Generation of Superfans Helped Create the Second Comedy Boom." *Vulture*, March 30, 2015. https://www.vulture.com/2015/03/ welcome-to-the-second-comedy-boom.html.

———. "Is Netflix Hurting Stand-Up?" *Vulture*, September 18, 2017. https://www.vulture. com/2017/09/netflix-comedy-special-domination.html.

Fraser, Nancy. *Fortunes of Feminism: From State-Managed Capitalism to Neoliberal Crisis*. New York: Verso Books, 2020.

Freud, Sigmund. *The Joke and Its Relation to the Unconscious*. Edited by John Carey. New York: Penguin Books, 2014.

Friend, Tad. "Donald Glover Can't Save You." *The New Yorker*, March 5, 2018. https://www. newyorker.com/magazine/2018/03/05/donald-glover-cant-save-you.

Gandy, Imani. "Also Can Somebody Please Tell Dave Chappelle That There Are Black People Who Are LGBTQ?" *Twitter*, n.d. https://twitter.com/AngryBlackLady/ status/1445787263783215107.

Gaylin, Ann Elizabeth. *Eavesdropping in the Novel from Austen to Proust*. Cambridge: Cambridge University Press, 2002.

Gervais, Ricky. "The Difference Between American and British Humour." *Time*, November 9, 2011, https://time.com/3720218/difference-between-american-british-humour/.

Gervais, Ricky, and Stephen Merchant. "The Merger." *The Office (UK)*. BBC, September 30, 2002.

Gibson, Jasmine. "The Fire This Time?" *Lies II: A Journal of Materialist Feminism*, 2015, 143–56.

Glenn, Evelyn Nakano. *Forced to Care: Coercion and Caregiving in America*. Cambridge: Harvard University Press, 2010.

Goldberg, Whoopi. *Whoopi Goldberg Presents Moms Mabley: The Original Queen of Comedy*. Documentary. HBO, 2013. https://www.hbo.com/documentaries/whoopi-goldberg-presents-moms-mabley-doc.

Gonzalez, Maya, and Cassandra Troyan. "Heart of a Heartless World." *Blind Field: A Journal of Cultural Inquiry*, May 26, 2016, https://blindfieldjournal.com/2016/05/26/3-of-a-heartless-world/.

Gonzalez, Sandra. "Chris Hardwick Returning as Host of 'Talking Dead' Following Investigation." *CNN*, July 25, 2018, https://www.cnn.com/2018/07/25/entertainment/chris-hardwick-talking-dead/index.html.

Goodyear, Dana. "Quiet Depravity." *The New Yorker*, October 17, 2005. https://www.newyorker.com/magazine/2005/10/24/quiet-depravity.

Gordon, Seth. "Double Date." *The Office*. NBC, November 5, 2009.

Gorenstein, Colin. "Amy Schumer: Death Threats Have Made Me Want to 'Use My Voice Even More.'" *Salon*, July 7, 2015, https://www.salon.com/2015/07/07/amy_schumer_death_threats_have_made_me_want_to_use_my_voice_even_more/.

Gournelos, Ted, and Viveca Greene, eds. *A Decade of Dark Humor: How Comedy, Irony, and Satire Shaped Post-9/11 America*. Jackson: University Press of Mississippi, 2011.

Graeber, David. "To Save the World, We're Going to Have to Stop Working." The Anarchist Library. Accessed December 31, 2021. https://theanarchistlibrary.org/library/david-graeber-to-save-the-world-we-re-going-to-have-to-stop-working.

Grattan, Sean Austin. *Hope Isn't Stupid: Utopian Affects in Contemporary American Literature*. Iowa City: University of Iowa Press, 2017.

Gray, Frances. *Women and Laughter*. Charlottesville, Va: University Press of Virginia, 1994.

Gray, Lee-Anne. *Educational Trauma: Examples from Testing to the School-to-Prison Pipeline*. Palgrave Macmillan, 2019.

Gray, Peter. "The Decline of Play and the Rise of Psychopathology." *The American Journal of Play* 3, no. 4 (Spring 2011): 443–64.

Guynes, Sean. "Kimberly Latta Statement." *Twitter*, November 9, 2017. https://twitter.com/saguynes/status/928725320794083328/photo/1.

Hagedorn, Roger. "Technology and Economic Exploitation: The Serial as a Form of Narrative Presentation." *Wide Angle* 10, no. 4 (1988): 4–12.

Harris, Mark. *Mike Nichols: A Director's Life*. New York: Penguin Press, 2021.

The Institute of Politics at Harvard University. "Harvard IOP Spring 2016 Poll." Accessed December 31, 2021. https://iop.harvard.edu/youth-poll/past/harvard-iop-spring-2016-poll.

Hayward, Jennifer. *Consuming Pleasures: Active Audiences and Serial Fictions from Dickens to Soap Opera*. Lexington: University Press of Kentucky, 1997.

Healy, Cheryl. "Discipline and Punishment: How School Suspensions Impact the Likelihood of Juvenile Arrest." *Chicago Policy Review*, March 26, 2014. https://chicagopolicyreview.org/2014/03/26/discipline-and-punishment-how-school-suspensions-impact-the-likelihood-of-juvenile-arrest/.

Healy, Rachael. "'I've Had Men Rub Their Genitals against Me': Female Comedians on Extreme Sexism in Standup." *The Guardian*, August 5, 2020, https://www.theguardian.com/stage/2020/aug/05/creepy-uncomfortable-sexism-harassment-assault-faced-by-female-standups.

Henry, David, and Joe Henry. *Furious Cool: Richard Pryor and the World That Made Him*. Chapel Hill, North Carolina: Algonquin Books of Chapel Hill, 2013.

Hersey, Tricia. "About." *The Nap Ministry*, n.d. https://thenapministry.wordpress.com/.

Hibbs, Thomas S. *Shows about Nothing: Nihilism in Popular Culture*. 2nd rev. and Expanded ed. Waco: Baylor University Press, 2012.

Hitchens, Christopher. "Why Women Aren't Funny." *Vanity Fair*, January 1, 2007. https://www. vanityfair.com/culture/2007/01/hitchens200701.

Hobbes, Thomas. *Leviathan: With Selected Variants from the Latin Edition of 1668*. Indianapolis: Hackett, 1994.

Hochschild, Arlie Russel, and Anne Machung. *The Second Shift*. New York: Avon Books, 1990.

Hogg, Justin. "Between Two Worlds: Race and Authenticity in Cover Songs." *Blind Field: A Journal of Cultural Inquiry*, June 2, 2017, https://blindfieldjournal.com/2017/06/02/ between-two-worlds-race-and-authenticity-in-cover-songs/.

Holden, Stephen. "The Serious Business of Comedy Clubs." *The New York Times*, June 12, 1992, https://www.nytimes.com/1992/06/12/arts/the-serious-business-of-comedy-clubs.html.

Holland, Sharon Patricia. *Raising the Dead: Readings of Death and (Black) Subjectivity*. Durham: Duke University Press, 2000.

Holpuch, Amanda. "Daniel Tosh Apologises for Rape Joke as Fellow Comedians Defend Topic." *The Guardian*, July 11, 2012, https://www.theguardian.com/culture/ us-news-blog/2012/jul/11/daniel-tosh-apologises-rape-joke.

Holt, Brianna. "Now I Understand Why My Parents Were So Strict." *The Atlantic*, June 3, 2020, https://www.theatlantic.com/family/archive/2020/06/ my-black-parents-had-be-strict/612610/.

Hong, Cathy Park. *Minor Feelings: An Asian American Reckoning*. New York: One World, 2020.

hooks, bell. *Writing beyond Race: Living Theory and Practice*. New York: Routledge, 2013.

Horgan, Amelia. *Lost in Work: Escaping Capitalism*. London: Pluto Press, 2021.

Horkheimer, Max, and Adorno, Theodor W. *Dialectic of Enlightenment Philosophical Fragments*. Translated by Edmund Jephcott. Stanford: Stanford University Press, 2002.

Horowitz, Susan. *Queens of Comedy: Lucille Ball, Phyllis Diller, Carol Burnett, Joan Rivers, and the New Generation of Funny Women*. Amsterdam: Gordon and Breach, 1997.

Howe, Elizabeth. *The First English Actresses: Women and Drama, 1660–1700*. Cambridge: Cambridge University Press, 1992.

Hurwitz, Mitchell. "Pilot." *Lady Dynamite*. Netflix, May 20, 2016.

Idenburg, Florian. "The Office Is No More." In *A-Typical Plan: Projects and Essays on Identity, Flexibility, and Atmosphere in the Office Building*, edited by Jeannette Kuo. Zürich: Park Books, 2013.

Isaacson, Johanna. "Hollywood Kills Feminism: The Work of Lizzie Borden," August 14, 2019, https://blindfieldjournal.com/2019/08/14/hollywood-kills-feminism-the-work-of- lizzie-borden/.

Itzkoff, Dave. *Robin*. New York: Henry Holt and Company, 2018.

Jaffe, Sarah. *Work Won't Love You Back: How Devotion to Our Jobs Keeps Us Exploited, Exhausted, and Alone*. New York: Bold Type, 2021.

Jameson, Fredric. "Future City," *New Left Review* 21 (May/June 2003)

———— *The Political Unconscious: Narrative as a Socially Symbolic Act*. Ithaca: Cornell University Press, 1994.

———— *The Seeds of Time*. New York: Columbia University Press, 1994.

————. "Utopia as Method, or the Uses of the Future." In *Utopia/Dystopia: Conditions of Historical Possibility*, edited by Michael D Gordin, Gyan Prakash, and Helen Tilley. Princeton: Princeton University Press, 2010.

Jeselnik, Anthony. "This Daniel Tosh Rape Joke Controversy Really Has Me Second Guessing Some of My Rapes." *Twitter*, July 11, 2012. https://twitter.com/anthonyjeselnik/ status/223172033347981312.

Johnson, Stefanie K., and Juan M. Madera. "Sexual Harassment Is Pervasive in the Restaurant Industry. Here's What Needs to Change." *Harvard Business Review*, January 18, 2018, https://hbr.org/2018/01/sexual-harassment-is-pervasive-in-the-restaurant-industry- heres-what-needs-to-change.

Jones, Charisse, and Kumea Shorter-Gooden. *Shifting: The Double Lives of Black Women in America*. New York: HarperCollins, 2004.

Jones, Claudia. "An End to the Neglect of the Problems of the Negro Woman!" In *Words of Fire: An Anthology of African-American Feminist Thought*, edited by Beverly Guy-Sheftall. New York: New Press, 1995.

Jones, Owen. "Eat the Rich! Why Millennials and Generation Z Have Turned Their Backs on Capitalism." *The Guardian*, September 20, 2021, https://www.theguardian.com/politics/2021/sep/20/eat-the-rich-why-millennials-and-generation-z-have-turned-their-backs-on-capitalism.

Kalb, Luther G., Emma K. Stapp, Elizabeth D. Ballard, Calliope Holingue, Amy Keefer, and Anne Riley. "Trends in Psychiatric Emergency Department Visits Among Youth and Young Adults in the US." *Pediatrics* 143, no. 4 (April 1, 2019), https://doi.org/10.1542/peds.2018-2192.

Karas, Jay. *Ali Wong: Baby Cobra*. Stand-up special. Netflix, 2016.

King, Don Roy. "Kerry Washington." *Saturday Night Live*. NBC, November 2, 2013.

Klauschie, Matthew. "River Butcher: Gender Normativity & An Accidental Catcall." Stand-up. *Comedy Central Stand-Up*. Comedy Central, November 27, 2019.

Knoedelseder, William. *I'm Dying Up Here: Heartbreak and High Times in Stand-Up Comedy's Golden Era*. New York: Hachette, 2009.

Koblin, John, and Nicole Sperling. "Netflix Employees Walk out to Protest Dave Chappelle's Special." *The New York Times*, October 20, 2021, https://www.nytimes.com/2021/10/20/business/media/netflix-protest-dave-chappelle.html.

Kohen, Yael. "'Saturday Night Live': The Girls' Club." *The New Yorker*, October 16, 2012. https://www.newyorker.com/books/page-turner/saturday-night-live-the-girls-club.

———. *We Killed: The Rise of Women in American Comedy*. New York: Farrar, Straus and Giroux, 2012.

Krach, Sören, Frieder Paulus, Maren Bodden, and Tilo Kircher. "The Rewarding Nature of Social Interactions." *Frontiers in Behavioral Neuroscience* 4 (2010): 22. https://doi.org/10.3389/fnbeh.2010.00022.

Kuo, Jeannette. "Introduction." In *A-Typical Plan: Projects and Essays on Identity, Flexibility, and Atmosphere in the Office Building*.

Kwapis, Ken. "Sexual Harassment." *The Office (US)*. NBC, September 27, 2005.

Lacey, Kate, ed. *Listening Publics: The Politics and Experience of Listening in the Media Age*. Cambridge, UK: Polity Press, 2013.

Landy, Marcia. *Monty Python's Flying Circus*. Detroit: Wayne State University Press, 2005.

Lane-McKinley, Madeline. "The Artist in the Age of Meta-Masculinity." *Blind Field: A Journal of Cultural Inquiry*, January 16, 2018, https://blindfieldjournal.com/2018/01/16/the-artist-in-the-age-of-meta-masculinity/.

Lathan, Stan. *Dave Chappelle: The Closer*. Stand-up Special. Netflix, 2021.

Lattanzio, Ryan. "John Cleese Accused of Transphobia After Tweeting 'I Want to Be a Cambodian Police Woman.'" *IndieWire*, November 22, 2020. https://www.indiewire.com/2020/11/john-cleese-defends-jk-rowling-accused-transphobia-twitter-1234600163/.

Le Guin, Ursula K. *Dancing at the Edge of the World: Thoughts on Words, Women, Places*. New York: Grove Press, 1989.

———. *The Wave in the Mind: Talks and Essays on the Writer, the Reader, and the Imagination*. Boston: Shambhala, 2004.

Le Quéré, Corinne, Robert B. Jackson, Matthew W. Jones, Adam J. P. Smith, Sam Abernethy, Robbie M. Andrew, Anthony J. De-Gol, et al. "Temporary Reduction in Daily Global CO_2 Emissions during the COVID-19 Forced Confinement." *Nature Climate Change* 10, no. 7 (July 2020): 647–53. https://doi.org/10.1038/s41558-020-0797-x.

Levin, Sam. "Millionaire Tells Millennials: If You Want a House, Stop Buying Avocado Toast." *The Guardian*, May 15, 2017, https://www.theguardian.com/lifeandstyle/2017/may/15/australian-millionaire-millennials-avocado-toast-house.

Lewinsky, Monica. "Exclusive: Monica Lewinsky on the Culture of Humiliation." *Vanity Fair*, May 28, 2014, https://www.vanityfair.com/style/society/2014/06/monica-lewinsky-humiliation-culture.

Lewis, Sophie. *Full Surrogacy Now: Feminism against Family*. New York: Verso, 2019.

———. "SERF 'n' TERF." *Salvage*, February 6, 2017, https://salvage.zone/in-print/serf-n-terf-notes-on-some-bad-materialisms/.

Lieberman, Hallie. "'It Gets to You': Trans Comedians on Transphobia and Cancel Culture." *The Guardian*, January 23, 2021, https://www.theguardian.com/culture/2021/jan/23/trans-comedians-transphobia-cancel-culture.

Littleton, Darryl. *Black Comedians on Black Comedy: How African-Americans Taught Us to Laugh.* New York: Applause Theatre & Cinema Books, 2006.

Liu, Fangzhou, and Hannah Knowles. "Harassment, Assault Allegations against Moretti Span Three Campuses." *The Stanford Daily*, November 16, 2017, https://stanforddaily.com/2017/11/16/harassment-assault-allegations-against-moretti-span-three-campuses/.

Lockwood, Patricia. "Rape Joke." *The Awl*, July 25, 2013. https://www.theawl.com/2013/07/patricia-lockwood-rape-joke/.

"Long Working Hours Increasing Deaths from Heart Disease and Stroke: WHO, ILO." Accessed December 31, 2021. https://www.who.int/news/item/17-05-2021-long-working-hours-increasing-deaths-from-heart-disease-and-stroke-who-ilo.

Lopate, Carol. "Daytime Television: You'll Never Want to Leave Home." *Feminist Studies* 3, no. 3/4 (1976): 69–82. https://doi.org/10.2307/3177728.

Lorde, Audre. *A Burst of Light: And Other Essays.* Mineola, New York: Ixia Press, 2017.

———. *Sister Outsider: Essays and Speeches.* Berkeley: Crossing Press,1984.

Lotz, Amanda D. "Introduction." In *Beyond Prime Time: Television Programming in the Post-Network Era*, edited by Amanda D. Lotz. New York: Routledge, 2009.

"Louis C.K." *The Daily Show with Jon Stewart.* Comedy Central, July 16, 2012.

Mahler, Jonathan. "A Teacher Made a Hitler Joke in the Classroom. It Tore the School Apart." *The New York Times*, September 5, 2018, https://www.nytimes.com/interactive/2018/09/05/magazine/friends-new-york-quaker-school-ben-frisch-hitler-joke.html.

Malague, Rosemary. *An Actress Prepares: Women and "The Method."* London: Routledge, 2012.

Malkin, Bonnie. "Last Tango in Paris Director Suggests Maria Schneider 'Butter Rape' Scene Not Consensual." *The Guardian*, December 4, 2016, https://www.theguardian.com/film/2016/dec/04/last-tango-in-paris-director-says-maria-schneider-butter-scene-not-consensual.

Mankoff, Robert. "Killing a Frog." *The New Yorker*, March 21, 2012, https://www.newyorker.com/cartoons/bob-mankoff/killing-a-frog.

Marcotte, Amanda. "Gavin McInnes and the Proud Boys: 'Alt-Right without the Racism'?" *Salon*, October 17, 2018, https://www.salon.com/2018/10/17/gavin-mcinnes-and-the-proud-boys-alt-right-without-the-racism/.

Maron, Marc. "Episode 1,278: 'Canceled Comedy' w/ Kliph Nesteroff David Bianculli." *WTF with Marc Maron*, November 11, 2021.

———. "Episode 224: Chris Rock." *WTF with Marc Maron*, November 3, 2021.

———. "Episode 332: Shelley Berman." *WTF with Marc Maron*, November 5, 2012.

———. "Remembering Lynn Shelton, May 16, 2020." *WTF with Marc Maron*, May 18, 2020. http://www.wtfpod.com/podcast/in-memoriam-remembering-lynn-shelton.

Marx, Karl. *Early Writings.* Edited by Rodney Livingstone and Gregor Benton. London: Penguin, 1992.

Marx, Karl, Friedrich Engels. *Karl Marx, Frederick Engels: Collected Works.* New York: International Publishers, 1975.

McClain, Dani. "As a Black Mother, My Parenting Is Always Political." *The Nation*, March 27, 2019. https://www.thenation.com/article/archive/black-motherhood-family-parenting-dani-mcclain/.

McClanahan, Annie. "TV and Tipworkification." *Post45*, January 10, 2019, https://post45.org/2019/01/tv-and-tipworkification/.

Meehan, Eileen R. "A Legacy of Neoliberalism: Patterns in Media Conglomeration." In *Neoliberalism and Global Cinema: Capital, Culture, and Marxist Critique*, edited by Jyotsna Kapur and Keith B Wagner. New York: Routledge, 2011.

"Mental health and psychosocial considerations during COVID-19 outbreak: WHO, ILO" (2020), accessed May 24, 2020, https://www.who.int/docs/default-source/coronaviruse/mental-health-considerations.pdf

Mercado, Kristian. *London Hughes: To Catch a D*ck.* Stand-up special. Netflix, 2020.

Mies, Maria. *Patriarchy and Accumulation on a World Scale: Women in the International Division of Labour.* London: Zed Books, 2001.

Mills, Brett. *The Sitcom.* Edinburgh: Edinburgh University Press, 2009.

Mitchell, Nick. "On Audre Lorde's Legacy and the 'Self' of Self-Care, Part 1 of 3." *low end theory,* accessed January 1, 2022, https://www.lowendtheory.org/post/43457761324/on-audre-lordes-legacy-and-the-self-of.

Mizejewski, Linda. *Pretty / Funny: Women Comedians and Body Politics.* Austin: University of Texas Press, 2015.

Morgan, Danielle Fuentes. "Introduction: Twenty-First-Century African American Satire." *Post45,* June 22, 2021, https://post45.org/2021/06/introduction-twenty-first-century-african-american-satire/.

———. *Laughing to Keep from Dying: African American Satire in the Twenty-First Century.* Urbana: University of Illinois Press, 2020.

Morgan, George, and Pariece Nelligan. *The Creativity Hoax: Precarious Work in the Gig Economy.* London: Anthem Press, 2018.

Munro, Kirstin. "Unproductive Workers and State Repression." *Review of Radical Political Economics* 53, no. 4 (December 1, 2021): 623–30.

———. "Unproductive Workers, 'Life-Making', and State Repression." In *The State Today: Politics, History, Law,* edited by Eva Nanopoulos, Rafael Khachaturian, Rob Hunter, and Umut Özsu. Palgrave Macmillan, 2022.

Nash, Jennifer C. *Black Feminism Reimagined: After Intersectionality.* Durham: Duke University Press, 2019.

Nea, Chingy. "'The Sopranos' Belongs to the Gays Now." *MEL Magazine,* August 13, 2021, https://melmagazine.com/en-us/story/sopranos-queer-culture.

Neimanis, Astrida. *Bodies of Water: Posthuman Feminist Phenomenology.* London: Bloomsbury Academic, 2017.

Nesteroff, Kliph. *The Comedians: Drunks, Thieves, Scoundrels, and the History of American Comedy.* New York: Grove Press, 2015.

Ngai, Sianne. *Our Aesthetic Categories: Zany, Cute, Interesting.* Cambridge: Harvard University Press, 2012.

Norton, Jim. "Some Attention-Seeking Woman Heckled a Comedian, so If Anything, She Owes Him an Apology for Being a Rude Brat." *Twitter,* July 11, 2012. https://twitter.com/JimNorton/status/223119997881434113.

Noys, Benjamin. "He's Just Not That into You: Negging and the Manipulation of Negativity." *Manipuations,* Accessed January 1, 2022. http://www.manipulations.info/hes-just-not-that-into-you-negging-and-the-manipulation-of-the-negativity/.

Owens, Carol. "Not in the Humor: Bulimic Dreams." In *Lacan, Psychoanalysis, and Comedy,* edited by Patricia Gherovici and Manya Steinkoler. New York: Cambridge University Press, 2016.

Pankiw, Ally. "1.5." *Feel Good.* Channel 4 and Netflix, March 18, 2020.

Paradis, Kenneth. *Sex, Paranoia, and Modern Masculinity.* Albany: State University of New York Press, 2007.

Parry, Madeleine. *Hannah Gadsby: Nanette.* Stand-up Special. Netflix, 2018.

Parvulescu, Anca. *Laughter: Notes on a Passion.* Cambridge: MIT Press, 2010.

Pay Us More UCSC. "Rent Burden Calculator," 2020. https://payusmoreucsc.com/rent-burden-calculator/.

Perez, Lexy. "Bill Burr's Controversial 'Saturday Night Live' Monologue Draws Mixed Reactions." *The Hollywood Reporter,* October 11, 2020, https://www.hollywoodreporter.com/tv/tv-news/bill-burrs-controversial-saturday-night-live-monologue-draws-mixed-reactions-4075205/.

Perlin, Ross. *Intern Nation: Earning Nothing and Learning Little in the Brave New Economy.* Revised Edition. New York: Verso, 2012.

Peterson, Cora. "Suicide Rates by Industry and Occupation." *Morbidity and Mortality Weekly Report* 69 (2020), https://doi.org/10.15585/mmwr.mm6903a1.

Popper, Karl R. *The Open Society and Its Enemies,* vol. 1. London: Routledge, 2011.

Porter, Rick. "'The Crown' Sets Single-Week Record in Nielsen Streaming Rankings." *The*

Hollywood Reporter, December 17, 2020, https://www.hollywoodreporter.com/tv/tv-news/the-crown-sets-single-week-record-in-nielsen-streaming-rankings-4106891/.

Power, Robert A, Stacy Steinberg, Gyda Bjornsdottir, Cornelius A Rietveld, Abdel Abdellaoui, Michel M Nivard, Magnus Johannesson, et al. "Polygenic Risk Scores for Schizophrenia and Bipolar Disorder Predict Creativity." *Nature Neuroscience* 18, no. 7 (July 2015): 953–55. https://doi.org/10.1038/nn.4040.

Precarias a la Deriva. "A Very Careful Strike – Four Hypotheses." *Caring Labor: An Archive*, August 14, 2010, https://caringlabor.wordpress.com/2010/08/14/precarias-a-la-deriva-a-very-careful-strike-four-hypotheses/.

Pryor, Richard, and Todd Gold. *Pryor Convictions, and Other Life Sentences*. New York: Pantheon Books, 1995.

Ramstetter, Catherine, and Dale Borman Fink. "Ready for Recess?" American Federation of Teachers, accessed January 1, 2022, https://www.aft.org/ae/winter2018-2019/ramstetter_fink.

Research, Edison. "The Top 50 Most Listened to U.S. Podcasts of 2020." *Edison Research*, February 9, 2021, https://www.edisonresearch.com/the-top-50-most-listened-to-u-s-podcasts-of-2020/.

Richter, Andy. "Maria Bamford." Three Questions with Andy Richter, n.d.

Robinson, Sally. *Marked Men: White Masculinity in Crisis*. New York: Columbia University Press, 2000.

Romano, Aja. "Dave Chappelle vs. Trans People vs. Netflix." *Vox*, October 14, 2021, https://www.vox.com/22722357/dave-chappelle-the-closer-netflix-backlash-controversy-transphobic.

Rose, Alice. "Standup Helped Me Embrace Myself. It's Time to Make Space for Other Trans Comedians to Do the Same." *CBC*, accessed January 1, 2022, https://www.cbc.ca/arts/standup-helped-me-embrace-myself-it-s-time-to-make-space-for-other-trans-comedians-to-do-the-same-1.5699659.

Rose, Jacqueline. *Mothers: An Essay on Love and Cruelty*. New York: Farrar, Straus and Giroux, 2018.

———. *Women in Dark Times*. London: Bloomsbury, 2014.

Sacks, Brianna. "University Awards Student One Of The Largest Rape Settlements Ever." *BuzzFeed News*, January 31, 2017, https://www.buzzfeednews.com/article/briannasacks/uc-santa-cruz-lawsuit-settlement.

Salvato, Nick. *Obstruction*. Durham: Duke University Press, 2016.

Sample, Ian. "New Study Claims to Find Genetic Link between Creativity and Mental Illness." *The Guardian*, June 8, 2015, https://www.theguardian.com/science/2015/jun/08/new-study-claims-to-find-genetic-link-between-creativity-and-mental-illness.

Sandberg, Sheryl. "Foreword." In Nell Scovell, *Just the Funny Parts: And a Few Hard Truths about Sneaking into the Hollywood Boys' Club*. New York: Dey Street, 2018.

———. *Lean in: Women, Work, and the Will to Lead*. New York: Alfred A. Knopf, 2013.

Sargisson, Lucy. *Fool's Gold?: Utopianism in the 21st Century*. New York: Palgrave Macmillan, 2012.

Saul, Scott. *Becoming Richard Pryor*. New York: Harper-Collins, 2014.

Savorelli, Antonio. *Beyond Sitcom: New Directions in American Television Comedy*. Jefferson, NC: McFarland, 2010.

Saxena, Jaya. "For Trans People in the Service Industry, Discrimination Is an Unfortunate Reality of the Job." *Eater*, June 29, 2020, https://www.eater.com/2020/6/29/21304536/trans-workers-struggle-with-discrimination-scotus-ruling.

Schiffer, Zoe. "Netflix Just Fired the Organizer of the Trans Employee Walkout." *The Verge*, October 15, 2021, https://www.theverge.com/2021/10/15/22728337/netflix-fires-organizer-trans-employee-walkout-dave-chappelle.

———. "Netflix Suspends Trans Employee Who Tweeted about Dave Chappelle Special." *The Verge*, October 11, 2021, https://www.theverge.com/2021/10/11/22720724/netflix-suspends-trans-employee-tweeted-dave-chappelle-the-closer.

Schulman, Sarah. *Conflict Is Not Abuse: Overstating Harm, Community Responsibility, and the Duty of Repair*. Vancouver: Arsenal Pulp Press, 2016.

Scott, Sophie. "Why Is Laughter Contagious?" *NPR*, March 4, 2016. https://www.npr.
org/2016/03/04/468877928/why-is-laughter-contagious.

Scovell, Nell. "Letterman and Me." *Vanity Fair*, October 27, 2009. https://www.vanityfair.com/
style/2009/10/david-letterman-200910.

Seresin, Asa. "On Heteropessimism." *The New Inquiry*, October 9, 2019. https://thenewinquiry.
com/on-heteropessimism/.

Seymour, Richard. *The Twittering Machine*. New York: Verso, 2020.

Shales, Tom, and James A Miller. *Live from New York: The Complete, Uncensored History of
"Saturday Night Live" as Told by Its Stars, Writers, and Guests*. New York: Little, Brown,
2015.

Sharf, Zack. "Jerry Seinfeld: Why Louis C.K. Isn't Making His Comeback in the
Right Way." *IndieWire*, October 26, 2018, https://www.indiewire.com/2018/10/
jerry-seinfeld-louis-ck-comeback-interview-1202015667/.

———. "Sarah Silverman Says Louis C.K. Used to Masturbate in Front of Her With
Her Consent." *IndieWire*, October 22, 2018, https://www.indiewire.com/2018/10/
sarah-silverman-says-louis-c-k-masturbate-in-front-of-her-consent-1202014148/.

Sharpe, Christina Elizabeth. *In the Wake: On Blackness and Being*. Durham: Duke University
Press, 2016.

Shonkwiler, Alison, and Leigh Claire La Berge. "A Theory of Capitalist Realism." In *Reading
Capitalist Realism*, edited by Alison Shonkwiler and Leigh Claire La Berge. Iowa City:
University of Iowa Press, 2014.

Silverman, Sarah. "I Will Disappoint You." The Sarah Silverman Podcast, n.d.

Sims, David. "What 'Crashing' Got Right About Stand-Up." *The Atlantic*, April 10, 2017,
https://www.theatlantic.com/entertainment/archive/2017/04/hbo-crashing-season-one-
finale-review/522498/.

Smith, Chris. *Jim & Andy: The Great Beyond*. Mockumentary. Netflix, 2017.

Smith, Kyle. "Louis C.K. Remains Brilliant." *National Review*, April 8, 2020, https://www.
nationalreview.com/2020/04/review-sincerely-louis-c-k-comedian-remains-brilliant/.

Snellin, Luke. "2.6." *Feel Good*. Channel 4 and Netflix, June 4, 2021.

Society of Health and Physical Educators. "2016 Shape of the Nation Full Report." Shape of
the Nation, n.d. https://www.shapeamerica.org/advocacy/son/.

Stahl, Aviva. "Trust in Instinct." *The New Inquiry*, May 9, 2017. https://thenewinquiry.com/
trust-in-instinct/.

Stanton, Lloyd. *Dying Laughing*. Gravitas, 2017. https://catalog.pcpls.org/kanopy/kan1475657.

Strauss, Valerie. "It Looks like the Beginning of the End of America's Obsession with Student
Standardized Tests." *Washington Post*, June 6, 2020, https://www.washingtonpost.com/
education/2020/06/21/it-looks-like-beginning-end-americas-obsession-with-student-
standardized-tests/.

Suárez-Orozco, Carola, and Marcelo M. Suárez-Orozco. *Children of Immigration*. Cambridge:
Harvard University Press, 2002.

Subbaraman, Nidhi. "Some Called It 'Vigilante Justice.' But An Anonymous Campaign
Triggered A Real Investigation Into A UC Santa Cruz Professor." *Buzzfeed
News*, May 22, 2018. https://www.buzzfeednews.com/article/nidhisubbaraman/
gopal-balakrishnan-sexual-harassment-investigation.

———. "UC Santa Cruz Has Fired A Professor After He Violated The University's
Harassment Policy." *BuzzFeed News*, September 24, 2019. https://www.buzzfeednews.
com/article/nidhisubbaraman/gopal-balakrishnan-fired-santa-cruz.

Sundararajan, Arun. *The Sharing Economy: The End of Employment and the Rise of Crowd-Based
Capitalism*. Cambridge: MIT Press, 2016.

Szakolczai, Arpad. *Comedy and the Public Sphere: The Rebirth of Theatre as Comedy and the
Genealogy of the Modern Public Arena*. London: Routledge, 2013.

Tafoya, Eddie. *Icons of African American Comedy*. Santa Barbara: Greenwood, 2011.

Taurino, Giulia. "Crossing Eras: Exploring Nostalgic Reconfigurations in Media Franchises."
In *Netflix Nostalgia: Streaming the Past on Demand*, edited by Kathryn Pallister. Lanham:
Lexington Books, 2019.

Thatcher, Margaret. "Speech to Conservative Women's Conference." Margaret Thatcher Foundation," accessed January 1, 2022, https://www.margaretthatcher.org/document/107248.

"The Economics of Ride-Hailing: Driver Revenue, Expenses and Taxes." Accessed December 31, 2021. https://ceepr.mit.edu/workingpaper/the-economics-of-ride-hailing-driver-revenue-expenses-and-taxes-under-revision/.

"The Tonight Show." NBC, May 8, 1979.

@thenapministry. "Been Seeing This Narrative." *Instagram*, May 3, 2021.

———. "LAY YO ASS DOWN." *Instagram*, February 12, 2021.

———. "We Don't Want a Seat at the Table." *Instagram*, October 12, 2020.

Timberg, Bernard, and Bob Erler. *Television Talk: A History of the TV Talk Show*. Austin, University of Texas Press, 2002.

Tokumitsu, Miya. *Do What You Love: And Other Lies about Success and Happiness*. New York: Regan Arts, 2015.

"Top 15 Podcast Advertisers - September 2020." Accessed January 1, 2022. https://www.magellan.ai/pages/archive/2020/top-15-podcast-advertisers-september-2020.

Statista. "Topic: Podcasting Industry." Accessed January 1, 2022. https://www.statista.com/topics/3170/podcasting/.

Vaneigem, Raoul. *The Revolution of Everyday Life*. Translated by Donald Nicholson-Smith. Oakland: PM Press, 2012.

Volkow, Nora D. "Collision of the COVID-19 and Addiction Epidemics." *Annals of Internal Medicine* (2020) 173(1): 61–2. doi: 10.7326/M20-1212.

Walsh, Fintan. *Male Trouble: Masculinity and the Performance of Crisis*. New York: Palgrave Macmillan, 2010.

Wang, Jackie. "Oceanic Feeling and Communist Affect of Contemporary Art." RIGA International Biennial. Accessed January 1, 2022. https://www.rigabiennial.com/en/riboca-2/programme/event-dreams-jackie-wang.

Weber, Harold. *The Restoration Rake-Hero: Transformations in Sexual Understanding in Seventeenth-Century England*. Madison: University of Wisconsin Press, 1986.

Weeks, Kathi. *The Problem with Work: Feminism, Marxism, Antiwork Politics, and Postwork Imaginaries*. Durham: Duke University Press, 2011.

West, Natalie. "Introduction." In *We Too: Essays on Sex Work and Survival*, edited by Tina Horn, Selena, and Natalie West. New York: Feminist Press, 2021.

Willett, Cynthia. *Irony in the Age of Empire: Comic Perspectives on Democracy and Freedom*. Bloomington: Indiana University Press, 2008.

Willett, Cynthia, and Julie A. Willett. *Uproarious: How Feminists and Other Subversive Comics Speak Truth*. Minneapolis: University of Minnesota Press, 2019.

Williams, Janice. "Richard Pryor's 1977 Speech about Capitalism Leading to Racism Is Striking a Chord Decades Later." *Newsweek*, July 24, 2020, https://www.newsweek.com/richard-pryors-1977-speech-about-capitalism-leading-racism-striking-chord-decades-later-1520293.

Willis, Jay. "Trevor Noah: Here's Why Donald Trump Is Like a Stand-Up Comic—or a Penis-Shaped Asteroid." *GQ*, September 7, 2017, https://www.gq.com/story/trevor-noah-donald-trump-stand-up-comic.

Wilstein, Matt. "Tig Notaro: Louis C.K. Needs to 'Handle' His Sexual-Misconduct Rumors." *The Daily Beast*, August 23, 2017, https://www.thedailybeast.com/tig-notaro-louis-ck-needs-to-handle-his-sexual-misconduct-rumors.

Wingfield, Adia Harvey, and Renee Skeete. "Maintaining Hierarchies in Predominantly White Organizations: A Theory of Racial Tasks as Invisible Labor." In *Invisible Labor: Hidden Work in the Contemporary World*, edited by Winifred Poster, Marion G. Crain, and Miriam A. Cherry. Oakland: University of California Press, 2016.

Winn, Ross. "2021 Podcast Stats & Facts (New Research From Apr 2021)." *Podcast Insights*, December 28, 2021, https://www.podcastinsights.com/podcast-statistics/.

Witchel, Alex. " 'Update' Anchor: The Brains Behind Herself." *The New York Times*, November 25, 2001, https://www.nytimes.com/2001/11/25/style/counterintelligence-update-anchor-the-brains-behind-herself.html.

Wolov, Julia. "Counterpoint: I Didn't Consent to Louis C.K. Masturbating in Front of Me." *The Canadian Jewish News*, November 12, 2019, https://thecjn.ca/perspectives/opinions/counterpoint-i-didnt-consent-to-louis-c-k-masturbating-in-front-of-me/.

Woodrough, Elizabeth, ed. *Women in European Theatre*. Oxford: Intellect Books, 1995.

Woolf, Nicky. "'Negging': The Anatomy of a Dating Trend." *New Statesman*, May 25, 2012, https://www.newstatesman.com/politics/2012/05/negging-latest-dating-trend.

Woolf, Virginia. *A Room of One's Own and Three Guineas*. New York: Oxford University Press, 2015.

"Workplace Suicides Reach Historic High in 2018." U.S. Bureau of Labor Statistics," accessed January 1, 2022, https://www.bls.gov/opub/ted/2020/workplace-suicides-reach-historic-high-in-2018.htm.

Yu, Jessica. *Maria Bamford: Old Baby*. Stand-up special. Netflix, 2017.

Zamata, Sasheer. "Racist Radio," May 23, 2014. https://ucbcomedy.com/media/1187.

Zeavin, Hannah. *The Distance Cure: A History of Teletherapy*. Cambridge: MIT Press, 2021.

Zeisler, Andi. "Laugh Riot: Feminism and the Problem of Women's Comedy." In *Bitchfest: Ten Years of Cultural Criticism from the Pages of Bitch Magazine*, edited by Lisa Miya-Jervis and Andi Zeisler. New York: Farrar, Straus and Giroux, 2006.

Zenovich, Marina. *Richard Pryor: Omit the Logic*. Documentary. Showtime, 2013. https://www.sho.com/titles/3361052/richard-pryor-omit-the-logic.

———. *Robin Williams: Come Inside My Mind*. HBO, 2018. https://www.hbo.com/documentaries/robin-williams-come-inside-my-mind.

Zer0 Books. "Chappelle's Latest Special Is Legitimately Moving. People Who Are Angry at Him about Transphobia Clearly HAVE NOT Watched the Show." *Twitter*, https://twitter.com/Zer0Books/status/1446596174148890625.

Zinoman, Jason. "Comedy Is Booming. I Can't Wait for the Bust." *The New York Times*, November 22, 2017, https://www.nytimes.com/2017/11/22/arts/television/comedy-is-booming-i-cant-wait-for-the-bust.html.

Zmuda, Bob, and Lynne Elaine Margulies. *Andy Kaufman: The Truth, Finally*. Dallas: BenBella Books, 2014.

Zoglin, Richard. "The First Comedy Strike." *Time*, February 4, 2008, http://content.time.com/time/arts/article/0,8599,1709866,00.html.

Zou, Carol. "9 Theses on Pandemic and Reproductive Labor." *A Blade of Grass*, accessed January 1, 2022, https://www.abladeofgrass.org/articles/9-theses-on-pandemic-and-reproductive-labor/.

ABOUT THE AUTHOR

Madeline Lane-McKinley is a writer, professor, and Marxist-feminist with a PhD in Literature from the University of California, Santa Cruz. She is a founding member of *Blind Field: A Journal of Cultural Inquiry*. Her writing has appeared in publications such as *Los Angeles Review of Books*, *Boston Review*, *The New Inquiry*, *Entropy*, *GUTS*, and *Cultural Politics*. She is also the author of the chapbook *Dear Z* and a contributor to *The Museum of Capitalism*.

ABOUT COMMON NOTIONS

Common Notions is a publishing house and programming platform that fosters new formulations of living autonomy. We aim to circulate timely reflections, clear critiques, and inspiring strategies that amplify movements for social justice.

Our publications trace a constellation of critical and visionary meditations on the organization of freedom. By any media necessary, we seek to nourish the imagination and generalize common notions about the creation of other worlds beyond state and capital. Inspired by various traditions of autonomism and liberation—in the US and internationally, historical and emerging from contemporary movements—our publications provide resources for a collective reading of struggles past, present, and to come.

Common Notions regularly collaborates with political collectives, militant authors, radical presses, and maverick designers around the world. Our political and aesthetic pursuits are dreamed and realized with Antumbra Designs.

www.commonnotions.org
info@commonnotions.org

BECOME A MONTHLY SUSTAINER

These are decisive times, ripe with challenges and possibility, heartache and beautiful inspiration. More than ever, we need timely reflections, clear critiques, and inspiring strategies that can help movements for social justice grow and transform society.

Help us amplify those necessary words, deeds, and dreams that our liberation movements and our worlds so urgently need.

Movements are sustained by people like you, whose fugitive words, deeds, and dreams bend against the world of domination and exploitation.

For collective imagination, dedicated practices of love and study, and organized acts of freedom.

By any media necessary.
With your love and support.

Monthly sustainers start at $12 and $25.

Join us at commonnotions.org/sustain.

MORE FROM COMMON NOTIONS

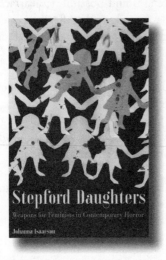

Stepford Daughters: Weapons for Feminists in Contemporary Horror

By Johanna Isaacson

978-1-942173-69-4
$20
208 pages

Capitalism and patriarchy create monsters—but inside the darkness there lurks a strange utopia. In *Stepford Daughters*, Johanna Isaacson explores an emerging wave of horror films that get why class horror and gender horror must be understood together. In doing so, Isaacson makes the case that this often-maligned genre is in fact a place where oppressed people can understand, navigate and confront an increasingly ugly and horrifying world.

What happens when your smile is no longer yours? Films like *Hereditary* and *The Babadook* show women coming apart at the seams as the promises of both the family and waged work fail them. In *Get Out*, we see how poor women and women of color perform the invisible labor that makes society run while experiencing domestic work as a kind of possession. In "coming of rage" films such as *Assassination Nation* and *Teeth*, we see the ways social reproduction leads to a futureless horizon. Robbed of their dreams but not their power to resist, these heroines emerge as the monsters and avengers we need.